History and September 11th

In the series

Critical Perspectives on the Past

edited by Susan Porter Benson, Stephen Brier, and Roy Rosenzweig

Overleaf: A group prays at the wall outside the Family Assistance Center at the Lexington Avenue armory, where families and colleagues had posted images of those they feared lost in the September 11, 2001, attack on the World Trade Center. (Photograph by Bronston Jones; courtesy of Bronston Jones.)

History and September 11th

EDITED BY

Joanne Meyerowitz

for *The Journal of American History*

Temple University Press

PHILADELPHIA

Temple University Press, Philadelphia 19122
Published 2003
Printed in the United States of America

⊗ The paper used in this publication meets the requirements of
the American National Standard for Information Sciences—Permanence
of Paper for Printed Library Materials, ANSI Z39.48-1984

Library of Congress Cataloging-in-Publication Data

History and September 11th / edited by Joanne Meyerowitz.
      p.   cm. — (Critical perspectives on the past)
      "The [main] articles in this collection first appeared in the *Journal of American History*'s
September 2002 special issue, 'History and September 11'"—Acknowledgments
   Includes bibliographical references and index.
      ISBN 1-59213-202-2 (cloth : alk. paper) — ISBN 1-59213-203-0 (pbk. : alk. paper)
      1. September 11 Terrorist Attacks, 2001. 2. World politics—1995–2005. 3. War
on Terrorism, 2001– . 4. History, Modern—20th century. I. Meyerowitz, Joanne J.
(Joanne Jay). II. Series.

HV6432.7.H57 2003
973.931—dc21
                                                                        2003044047

2 4 6 8 9 7 5 3 1

Contents

Acknowledgments

Except for the final essay by Marilyn Blatt Young and the primary source documents, the articles in this collection first appeared in the *Journal of American History*'s September 2002 special issue, "History and September 11." Thanks are due to the editorial board members who shaped that issue by recommending themes and contributors and by commenting on various essays and also to the authors of the essays who took time from their busy schedules to write and revise for the *JAH*. I owe a special debt to the *Journal*'s associate editor Steven M. Stowe, my co-conspirator in editing, who read and commented on all the essays and on the volume's introduction. As always, Susan Armeny and Mary Jane Gormley used their extraordinary copy editing skills to shape the essays and clean the prose. Lori A. Creed took on the extra task of seeking permissions for illustrations for this book as well as for the *Journal*, and Donald W. Maxwell and Deborah A. Kraus went beyond the call of duty in selecting and editing the primary source documents. Nancy J. Croker compiled the manuscript in multiple electronic forms, and Scott M. Stephan wrote the abstracts of the articles that appeared initially in the *JAH*. In sum, this book is a collaborative project, involving all the usual pleasures (and only a few of the frustrations) of collective endeavors. It would not have been possible without the peerless staff of the *JAH*. Thanks also to Janet Francendese at Temple University Press for her enthusiasm for this book and for her sound advice on editing it, and to Lee Formwalt and Annette Windhorn at the Organization of American Historians, who worked from early on to market the special issue and transform it into a book.

Joanne Meyerowitz
Editor, *Journal of American History*
December 2002

History and September 11th

Introduction

Joanne Meyerowitz

On September 12, 2001, a *New York Times* editorial described the horrific attacks of the previous day as "one of those moments in which history splits, and we define the world as 'before' and 'after.'"[1] Yet as all of us know, history never rips in two. "Before" and "after" are never entirely severed, even in the moments of greatest historical rupture. The discontinuities of the past always remain within the whole cloth of the *longue durée*. In fact, historians devote entire careers to placing the seemingly new in historical contexts.

In the aftermath of September 11, the editors of the *Journal of American History* heard from colleagues and friends who longed for such historical perspective. Some wanted to teach about September 11 in their history classrooms; others hoped that historians would have a voice in shaping the public discourse on war, terrorism, and national ideals. In response, we decided to invite a handful of scholars to write short essays for the *Journal*. At first, we proposed a forum on the concept of terrorism and its history. But as we discussed the possibilities with our editorial board and other colleagues, we discovered demand for a broader range of investigation. In the end, we chose scholars with noted expertise on issues pertaining to terrorism, anti-Americanism, the Middle East, fundamentalist religious movements, and foreign relations, and we asked them for deliberative essays, scholarly pieces with deeper research and greater intellectual engagement than typically found in newspapers and magazines. The resulting essays first appeared in the September 2002 issue of the *Journal*.

The *Journal of American History* is read primarily by professional historians, but the events of September 11 are clearly of concern to a broader audience, including teachers and students. So we decided to reprint the essays as a book that could be used in a variety of history courses. For this volume, we included the original essays in the *Journal*'s special issue, and we added a new essay by Marilyn Blatt Young that addresses more recent developments in U.S. foreign policy. We also included a set of primary source documents, which supplement the essays with reports, speeches, and commentaries that illustrate the larger points that our historian essayists make.[2]

The essays in this book draw on several scholarly traditions—international relations, cultural studies, and religious studies, as well as history—and the authors approach their topics from different points on the political map. Nonetheless, a few themes appear throughout the essays. Our authors comment on the dangers of forging or analyzing policy without keen awareness of history, and they tell cautionary tales involving critical moments in the past. They reject the sweeping panoramas that portray an age-old "clash of civilizations" between Islam and the West. They ask us to look instead at particular times and places and to remember the specific histories of American nationalist ideals, anti-American sentiments, U.S. involvement in Afghanistan, the war on terrorism, Islamic fundamentalism, and U.S. foreign policy. The histories they relate are neither symbols nor rallying cries; they are instead nuanced accounts that involve contestation, ambiguities, and unintended consequences.

When the essays turn inward to the United States, they bring renewed attention to American national identity, to the stories Americans have told themselves and others about the meaning and power of this nation. After September 11, the legitimate anger and sense of injury led to stories in the popular press and elsewhere about "American" values and promoted fantasies of revenge and rescue in the name of a powerful nation done wrong. In his essay in this collection, Michael H. Hunt finds a "long-lived but perhaps hollow American nationalism" that obscures the history of U.S. interventions abroad and the complexities of local politics in other regions of the world. This nationalism has reduced complicated and multifaceted interactions to a temptingly simple struggle of "us" against "them" or good versus evil, and it has also promised more than it can deliver. Hunt calls for careful attention to the complicated history of U.S. foreign policy in the Middle East and asks us to replace caricatures of fanatic Islamic fundamentalists with serious analyses of Islamic politics.

Other authors in this volume also place nationalist ideals within a longer history of American culture and U.S. foreign policy. Some of the nationalist stories told today rework older stories about America as the paternalist protector of the weak, the iconic beacon of freedom, or the benevolent vanguard of modernity. Emily S. Rosenberg, for example, examines older nationalist narratives about America as a patriarchal nation that rescues women and children. After the events of September 11, she finds, the Bush administration expressed a new interest in rescuing the women of Afghanistan from the oppressive dictates of the Taliban regime. The stories about rescuing women and children echoed older tales of America as a "civilized" nation that protects the weak from alleged foreign barbarity and as a manly nation that safeguards dependent women from violation by other men. She contrasts that tradition of humanitarian rescue and masculine strength with a competing tradition of transnational women's networks that work to end the subordination of women. The Bush administration, it seems, drew, at least temporarily, on both of these traditions. Nick Cullather focuses on the stories of "modernization" that have justified U.S. interventions in other parts of the world. In these stories, the United States appears at the forefront of modernity, destined to bring technology and progress to allegedly backward nations. In both their older and newer guises, these narratives of the nation tend to hide the *realpolitik* of self-interest, as well as the practical blunders, that often accompanied the language of morality, liberty, and progress, and in so doing they tend to reinforce long-standing myths of America as an exceptional and superior nation.

But if we learned anything from the events of September 11, we should have learned, once again, that we cannot understand American history by dwelling solely on the United States. The attacks of September 11 force us to turn outward and to see the United States not in isolation, but in and of a world in which other peoples have sometimes embraced, sometimes reframed, and sometimes repudiated the mythic promise of America. Ussama Makdisi, for example, provides us with an interpretive overview of two hundred years of Arab-American relations. In the early twentieth century, he finds, many Arabs admired the United States and contrasted it with the invasive imperial powers of Europe. After World War II, though, specific U.S. foreign policies inspired the anti-American sentiments that still exist today. As the U.S. government attempted to win the Cold War and to protect American oil interests, its responses to Arab and Iranian nationalism and its support for Israel contributed to the deterioration of American standing in much of the region. Anti-Americanism, then, is not ageless, but has a specific and recent history.

In this volume, as in many recountings of twentieth-century world history, the Cold War plays a significant part. Our authors refer to the legacies of Cold War patriotism, the policies and programs used to assert and maintain U.S. power in the face of the perceived Soviet threat, and the limited wars, covert operations, and peculiar alignments of allies and enemies that followed. The anti-American sentiments that resulted swept across the nations of the Third World and help answer the question, Why do they hate us?, asked so often today. In a case study of Turkey, Nur Bilge Criss reminds us that 1960s anti-Americanism involved secular protesters more than it involved religious fundamentalists. Leftist radicals opposed the U.S. government's violations of other nations' sovereignty, violations that were strikingly routine during the Cold War era and perhaps still routine today. In Turkey, the Cold War–era protests led to internal battles that raged through the 1970s between leftist factions, on the one side, and right-wing ultranationalists and Islamic fundamentalists, on the other.

Our authors also demonstrate how Cold War visions led the United States to enter Afghanistan from the late 1940s on. Nick Cullather looks at the failed American attempts to reform Afghanistan—and ally it with the United States—in the 1950s and 1960s. The centerpiece of the nation-building effort was an ambitious project to construct dams and canals and irrigate desert for agricultural use. The attempt to impose American technological know-how on the different terrain and culture of Afghanistan resulted in sustained environmental damage, undermined the local pastoral economy, and elicited resistance from both the nomads and the farmers who inhabited the region. John Prados investigates a subsequent phase in this history, the 1980s anti-Soviet forays of the Central Intelligence Agency (CIA) in Afghanistan. In order to fight the Soviet Union, the CIA engaged in a secret war to support the Muslim fundamentalists who opposed Communist rule, and thus the U.S. government ended up promoting the very forces that supported the September 11 attacks. In sum, the recent war in Afghanistan has a Cold War history, replete with earlier U.S. attempts to reconstruct a nation and to woo allies among the warring peoples of Afghanistan.

The events of September 11 also direct us to other lines of international fracture. Most notably, they underscore the significance of the Middle East as a key zone of conflict in the late twentieth century. The Iranian revolution of 1979 now appears as a neglected turning point or perhaps a harbinger of post–Cold War American and world history. The hostage crisis that ensued demonstrated the depth of anti-Americanism in the Muslim world, promoted the decline of the Cold War mentality among American foreign policy makers, and brought international terrorism into American public culture in unprecedented ways. The Iranian revolution also made manifest a new stage in the politicization of Islam. In this volume, R. Scott Appleby and Bruce B. Lawrence examine the history of the new Islamic fundamentalism, which was not an ancient tradition, but a modern adaptation. Fundamentalists—Christian, Jewish, and Muslim—have a particular vision of the past, Appleby argues, characterized by a story of declension, in which the faithful endure persecution, suffering, and humiliation, all as a prelude to a dramatic, apocalyptic reversal that will usher in a godly future. Modern Islamic fundamentalists emerged in the 1920s and formed an influential organization, the Muslim Brotherhood, in Egypt in 1928. Their intellectual leaders wrote a history of modern moral and religious decline that accompanied their call for Islamic law and Islamic government. That version of history helped inspire Islamic extremism in the Iranian revolution, in the Taliban regime in Afghanistan, and in Osama bin Laden's Al-Qaeda terrorist network, to name just a few of the most obvious cases. Bruce B. Lawrence emphasizes the economic roots of modern Islamic extremism. He looks to the history of poverty and shifts our attention away from religious fundamentalism and toward global inequities.

If nationalist ideals, anti-Americanism, U.S. interventions in Afghanistan, and politicized Islam have their own (sometimes overlapping) histories, then so too does the U.S. war on terrorism. Melani McAlister tells us that "the war without end" had its beginnings well before September 11, 2001. In the 1970s the American mass media presented sympathetic stories on Israel's war on terrorism, and in the 1980s the Reagan administration explicitly formulated anti-terrorist policies. In the 1970s, in the wake of the Vietnam War, journalists, commentators, policy makers, and politicians engaged in serious debates about how to define terrorism and whether military power could win a war against it. By the 1980s, after Iranian revolutionaries had held fifty-two Americans for 444 days, the war against terrorism provided a rationale for military buildup and intervention in the Middle East. Meanwhile, the mass media, especially Hollywood movies, told and retold stories about combating terrorists, stories that had recognizable subplots concerning assertions of U.S. strength and the rescue of hostages. After September 11, McAlister points out, the "new" war seemed to draw on the Hollywood version of the war on terrorism and also seemed to erase the earlier moment of serious discussion and open debate.

The war on terrorism also pushes us to rethink the history of U.S. foreign policy. In this volume, Bruce R. Kuniholm looks to the shifting geopolitical contexts in which U.S. presidents since World War II have set forth doctrines or rationales to guide their foreign policy practices in the Middle East and Southwest Asia. In a primer on foreign policy, Kuniholm reviews those doctrines, from President Harry S. Truman's commitment to contain communism to President Bill Clinton's determination to contain the hegemonic aspirations of Iran and Iraq. What should a "Bush doctrine" look like? Kuniholm calls on President George W. Bush to elaborate on his vision of containing both terrorists and the regimes that sponsor them. He offers his own suggestions for a new presidential doctrine, which include a greater recognition of the need for international cooperation and more positive plans to alleviate the hardships of individuals in the region. A few months after Kuniholm wrote his essay, the Bush administration provided just the kind of fleshed-out doctrine that Kuniholm had requested. In a postscript to his essay, Kuniholm applauds this more recent foreign policy pronouncement.

In her afterword essay, written in the fall of 2002, Marilyn Blatt Young also addresses the more recent changes in U.S. foreign policy, but her assessment differs sharply from Kuniholm's. Young offers a forceful critique of the saber-rattling, war-making policies of the Bush administration. She remembers the restraint involved in the Cold War policies of containment and deterrence and the years of international cooperation in forging rules of acceptable conduct. Young sees ominous signs in the threats of unilateral and preemptive action, and she worries that the Bush administration is moving toward an unabashed imperialism in which the U.S. government strong-arms other nations to embrace its vision of a U.S.-led world order.

Although we can outline the historical developments that shaped the attacks of September 11 and the U.S. responses to it, we can only begin to write the history of September 11 itself. What happened on that day, and how did it transform the lives of the thousands of people directly affected by it? One way to approach that history is through oral history interviews. In this collection, Mary Marshall Clark describes an oral history project, sponsored by Columbia University, which has already interviewed close to four hundred people. The interviews give us a ground-level social history of confusion, terror, and trauma, and they show us how people construct events as memories and eventually as histories. They also demonstrate that the study of history includes more than the analysis of nations, nationalisms, wars, religions, and policies. A more comprehensive history also addresses the individual lives and everyday voices of ordinary people.

History is always political; that is, it always involves the political assumptions and standpoints of those who write it as well as those who make it. But the history of recent events is often more overtly politicized than the history of the more distant past. Some of the authors in this book comment directly on current events and broadcast their political views. We expect that readers of this book will have their own assessments of current events and their own political views. But all of us, we hope, can agree that we cannot make sense of the present or imagine the future unless we study the past.

Notes

1. *New York Times*, Sept. 12, 2001, p. A26.

2. In the chapter endnotes and in the primary source section, we have provided a number of relevant Web site addresses, all of which were active in 2002. We apologize if some of the Web addresses no longer work.

In the Wake of September 11

The Clash of What?

Michael H. Hunt

Michael H. Hunt questions the historical analyses that undergird the "war on terrorism" that was sparked by the horrors of September 11. He warns against justifications for U.S. policy that rest on simple and self-congratulatory binaries—the battle of modernity and tradition or the defense of civilization against barbarism. Americans bring to the crisis a nationalism that is universalist, ahistorical, and inclined to simplify other cultures. An alternative, he suggests, is to recognize the hostility created by a half century of U.S. intervention in the Middle East and the yearning for domestic renovation that fuels Islamic politics.

Acute problems attend the interpretive framing of an unfolding foreign policy crisis. Just when perspective is most valuable, it is also hardest for policy makers and commentators alike to find because of the pressure to act and the value of quick and simple ways of understanding.[1] Historians have something important to say at such a moment. Understanding of the past is a useful, perhaps even essential, way of providing orientation in the midst of the press of confusing events. Historical perspective will not make any easier the resolution of the difficulties now facing the United States in the Middle East. On the other hand, it would be reckless to engage ever more deeply and especially militarily in the region without first considering the possible pitfalls that a historical perspective might reveal.

The argument advanced here is that the nature of the conflict sparked by the horrors of September 11 and represented by the "war on terrorism" has been ill defined historically by those who have declared that war. Their justifications rest on simple binaries, usually couched in terms of defense of civilization and the march of the modern. We need instead a framework that eschews superiority and inevitability and prompts both some degree of self-consciousness among Americans with a voice in the policy debate and a modicum of awareness about those supposedly arrayed against us and ostensibly teetering on the brink of barbarism or trapped in tradition. The pairing proposed here is a bit less neat and a bit less symmetrical. On the one side is a seemingly potent and long-lived but perhaps hollow American nationalism quick to see evil, ready to combat barbarism, devoted to the advance of its way of life, and forgetful of a long record of U.S. intervention in the Middle East. On the other side is something considerably more complex—a multivalent politics in an Islamic key with decades of history behind it and with a striking range of articulations among Muslims in far-flung places. "Fundamentalism" does not begin to do justice to its diversity, and positing some blind hostility to "the West" and "the modern world" misses the genuine, specific grievances varying from country to country and inspiring both intellectual ferment and political action.

Let us begin by considering the two most popular ways of interpretively framing the crisis of September 11. One reading with perhaps the widest currency derives from Samuel P. Huntington. In 1993 he advanced the view that the United States as the leader of the West was caught in a clash of civilizations. The main challenge, as he saw it, came from Confucian Asia (primarily China) and the Islamic world (Iran seemed at the time of writing the embodiment of militant regional resistance).[2] Huntington's interpretation, with its stark and value-laden delineation of regions in conflict, commanded considerable attention when it appeared and has won fresh converts in the wake of September 11.

This "clash" interpretation has flaws that are troubling but also familiar in American foreign policy thinking. Huntington's notion of civilization is monolithic, static, and essentialist—much like the Cold War–era view of the Communist enemy. Reacting against the revived interest in Huntington's argument after September 11, Edward Said warned of the dangers of making "'civilizations' and 'identities' into what they are not: shut-down, sealed-off entities that have been purged of the myriad currents and countercurrents that animate human history, and that over centuries have made it possible for that history not only to contain wars of religion and imperial conquest but also to be one of exchange, cross-fertilization and sharing."[3] Seen in even longer-term perspective, Huntington is heir to one of the most ethnocentric and aggressive notions in American history. Like nineteenth-century advocates of Manifest Destiny faced by the perceived barbarism of Native Americans, Latin Americans, the Spanish, and the Chinese, he posits U.S.

civilizational superiority and on that basis calls for a kind of moral re-armament to promote and defend Western values. In his construction, countries determined to find their own way are not part of a culturally diverse world, but wrong-headed rebels against a preponderant and en-lightened West.

The clash of modernity is an alternative, more intellectually refined formulation. But it too is ethnocentric, and it too has a dubious pedi-gree. The social science modernizers of the 1950s and early 1960s cham-pioned the notion that old values and institutions (deemed "traditional") holding back the Third World were to give way to new ones (deemed "modern").[4] In the new rendition of modernization as in the old, moder-nity takes at least implicitly American form (for example, in Paul Kennedy's formulation "laissez-faire economics, cultural pluralism and political democracy"), and tradition is embodied by countries cursed with seemingly static and rigid cultures that block development and breed popular dissatisfaction. In its most recent incarnation, modern-ization appears as part of the popular view of impersonal forces of glob-alization sweeping around the world and inexorably creating social and cultural as well as economic uniformity—and leaving behind backwaters of failure where tradition either refuses to surrender its hold or collapses into anarchy. The Middle East has figured as one of those backwaters, a natural breeding ground for crazed fanatics given to psychotic behav-ior. This view has been most widely disseminated in the snappy, enthu-siastic writing about the new laissez-faire world by Thomas Friedman, the *New York Times* reporter turned columnist, and by Robert D. Kaplan, a journalist who has painted a dark picture of parts of the world frag-menting under mounting social, demographic, and environmental pres-sures.[5]

The proponents of the modernization perspective conjure up a tradition-bound world in images of exotic dress and rituals, bizarre theo-cratic rule, a fanatic faith, inexplicable group identities, and women locked in the harem.[6] While Huntington calls for manning the walls against barbarians at the gate, the modernizers offer the comforting no-tion that "progress" will inevitably bring most countries into the fold of the modern world, leaving only a few lagging farther and farther be-hind. In this view, the duty of the United States is to align itself with the forces of history, pushing the reluctant ahead, calling to heel those stray-ing from the designated path, and washing its hands of "failed states" hopelessly trapped in the difficult transition from the traditional to the modern. Relentlessly teleological and culturally tone-deaf, modernizers now as earlier have difficulty imagining more complicated historical processes by which societies change in idiosyncratic ways involving borrowing, indigenization, localization—all terms meant to suggest a dynamic of cultural amalgamation and accommodation. It is as if China, Japan, India, Iran, and Turkey—all striking examples of indigenous values and institutions interacting with outside social, political, and economic forces to create new forms—did not exist.

The shortcomings of these two influential American interpretations of the Middle East suggest the need for some self-reflection, especially on the nationalist impulses that animate both of them. The events of September 11 jolted U.S. officials and most of the public into an impressive outpouring of nationalist feeling. The heavy, horrifying loss of civilian life was part of the reason. Another was the violation of American soil. Finally, the existence of an easily recognizable "evil other" (the Muslim fanatic retailed widely in public pronouncements and popular culture the last several decades) provided a clear and ready villain. The president went before Congress on September 20, 2001, and in a televised speech that was widely praised vowed to fight back. Liberally sprinkled through the text were the keywords from a century and more of public foreign policy discourse: national mission, the fate of human freedom, world leadership, strength and courage in the face of a dark threat.

> As long as the United States of America is determined and strong, this will not be an age of terror; this will be an age of liberty, here and across the world. (Applause.) . . . [I]n our grief and anger we have found our mission and our moment. Freedom and fear are at war. The advance of human freedom—the great achievement of our time, and the great hope of every time—now depends on us. Our nation—this generation—will lift a dark threat of violence from our people and our future. We will rally the world to this cause by our efforts, by our courage. We will not tire, we will not falter, and we will not fail. (Applause.)[7]

Reading these lines calls at once to mind passages from such classic early Cold War statements as the Truman Doctrine and NSC-68. Once more policy makers proclaim a time of national testing with the fate of the globe hanging in the balance.

The new patriotic consensus expressed itself in a wide variety of ways familiar from previous national trials. The consensus was rapidly evident in proliferating flags on cars, storefronts, and office doors and in heated language on radio talk shows and in official pronouncements. In the name of "civilization" the innocuously named American Council of Trustees and Alumni decried too-free speech, moral relativism, and national self-loathing supposedly evident in critical academic reactions to the "war on terrorism." Muslims around the country came under close official and popular scrutiny and prudently self-censored. Public debate sputtered and died; dissenters fell to the margins of political respectability. The media at once got in step and deferentially made government press conferences, speeches, and press releases the staple of its reporting.[8] The war on terrorism became a compelling story told in familiar nationalist terms of a country rallying and readying to strike back. A corps of instant experts appeared to satisfy the public hunger for information about those big, confusing, overlapping entities—the Middle East, the Arabs, and Islam—suddenly thrust into popular consciousness.

The most remarkable feature of this nationalist upsurge, for a historian at least, has been the ability of policy makers and most pundits to maintain a sense of injured innocence through an audacious repression of a half century of U.S. intervention in the Middle East. That deep entanglement began with the Cold War and the related campaign to promote stable, secular, pro-U.S. regimes that would shore up the anticommunist containment line in the region and assure the flow of oil. A variety of critics—from Arab nationalists to economic nationalists to Marxists to neutralists—challenged the American vision of the Middle East tied politically and economically to the interests of the United States and its European allies. U.S. policy makers soldiered on and in the process made two critical decisions with legacies still playing out today: first, to support Israel, and, second, to overthrow a neutralist, economically nationalist government in Iran in 1953 and replace it with a regime tightly tied to U.S. interests (that of Mohammed Reza Shah Pahlavi).[9]

Since the 1970s, the Middle East has emerged for U.S. policy as the chief zone of conflict, a dubious distinction that East Asia had surrendered after a quarter century of crises and war. Over the last three decades we have remained an active player in the political, military, economic, and cultural life of the region. We have been on both the receiving and giving end of suspicion, misunderstanding, retaliation, and violence. Troubles began with an oil embargo in 1973 and continued with the overthrow of an unpopular, U.S.-backed shah and the taking of American hostages in Iran in 1979, support for Iraq in its long, bloody war with Iran in the 1980s, Ronald Reagan's bombing of Libya, the involvement of marines in fighting in Lebanon in 1983 following the Israeli invasion, the Gulf War of 1990–1991, the residual American military presence in the Persian Gulf, continued containment of Iran, a policy of economic and military pressure against Iraq, and the ongoing diplomatic cover and military and financial support for a territorially expansionist Israel.

Well after September 11, most Americans still do not have the foggiest notion of this pattern of U.S. entanglement. The relevant past has been instead the grand narrative of American confrontation with heterodox ideologies from fascism to totalitarianism to fundamentalism. Or the past simply disappears in timeless contests between good and evil or civilization and barbarism. But this U.S. entanglement is widely understood and resented in the Middle East. Americans too need to understand it if we are to imagine how our role might, at least among some, generate a resentment that would inspire deadly and indiscriminate retaliation. It has been easy for critics in the region—secular as well as religious—to denounce the official U.S. presence as an obstacle to economic development, social justice, cultural integrity, and democracy. It has also been easy to label as neocolonial the order promoted by Washington, in effect linking U.S. policy to the earlier British and French imperial enterprises. Like Britain, the United States has established bases, shored up governments headed by amenable elites (notably in Israel, Jordan, Egypt over the last several decades, and Saudi Arabia), and opposed both openly and covertly governments not responsive to U.S. goals (such as Egypt under Gamal Abdel Nasser, Syria, Iraq, and Iran). By working closely with our British allies in carrying out these policies, we have provided a constant reminder of the link between the British era of dominance and the more recent American one.

The post–September 11 nationalist upsurge in the United States with its impressive capacity to blank out an inconvenient past has sturdy antecedents. Its immediate antecedents include the popular patriotism of World War I and the early Cold War, the nationalist revitalization project undertaken by neoconservatives in the aftermath of the Vietnam War and the seeming loss of moral fortitude in the Nixon years, Reagan's appeal for the country to stand tall in the world, and the celebration following a Gulf War victory banishing the specter of national decline. Perhaps the predictions of global theorists are wrong—the state is not in steep decline but, to the contrary, remains a potent symbol of popular loyalty and a formidable mobilizing force. Nationalism *seems* still a vital force in American life.

But how seriously should we take this recent explosion of nationalist sentiment? Is it a mile wide and an inch deep? Two general studies of the relation of nationalism to U.S. foreign policy—my own in 1987 and Anders Stephanson's in 1995—diverge on whether this ideology was becoming attenuated at the end of the twentieth century.[10] The emotional nationwide outpouring immediately after September 11, almost seamlessly tied to the Bush administration response, tends to support my own claim for durability and persistence. But, once beyond shock and grief over the loss of American life, the national response had the feel not of a great crisis or cause whose course would define the life of a generation, but of a sporting event at which the home team sweeps the outclassed opposition from the field or (perhaps more commonly) a quickly satisfied hunger for revenge and a quiet longing for security from future attacks. Every bit as much as the Gulf War, this anti-terrorist war evoked tough talk and soaring aspirations while following a cautious military strategy designed to hold down U.S. losses. Meanwhile, the president called reassuringly for business as usual on the home front, and consumers complied. Stephanson's skeptical appraisal increasingly seems closer to the mark.

This strange disconnect between the epochal issues ostensibly at stake and the minimal sacrifices asked of Americans carries forward a pattern familiar to historians. The public seems as ambivalent today about the direct involvement of Americans in combat as it was during the war in Vietnam or earlier in Korea or even earlier after World War I or earlier still in the course of fighting in the Philippines or still earlier in the war with Mexico. Vietnam and Korea offer especially dramatic illustrations of the public's allergy to protracted or open-ended commitments that result in the heavy loss of American life.[11] Consumer values and the closely related notion of individualism made it difficult for policy makers to elicit significant, sustained popular sacrifice. That public allergy has persisted, confirming its influence following loss of American soldiers serving in Beirut and Somalia and the hesitation over intervention in Bosnia and Kosovo.

The generation of military leaders who had served in Vietnam as junior officers shared the public's aversion and helped to formulate prudential rules to guide decisions on committing U.S. forces to combat. The classic statement by Secretary of Defense Caspar Weinberger, issued in November 1984, included the following almost paralyzing set of preconditions for the use of force: Act only in defense of vital national interests, devise clear political and military objectives, commit to win, use the appropriate size and type of force, be sure of the support of the American people and Congress, and seek first nonmilitary solutions to the problem. Secretary of State Colin Powell, himself a Vietnam veteran, called during his tenure as chair of the Joint Chiefs of Staff for a seemingly more flexible if nonetheless cautious rule of thumb: "The use of force should be restricted to occasions where it can do some good and where the good will outweigh the loss of lives and other costs that will surely ensue. Wars kill people."[12] Powell did not make clear how policy makers without the gift of clairvoyance were to tot up the overall costs and benefits of military action.

Even while military leadership passes from one generation to another, the caution remains. The evidence is to be found in the expeditionary model that the armed forces adopted during the 1980s and 1990s. From Beirut to Libya to the Persian Gulf to Somalia to Haiti, American forces undertook variously to punish, order, and feed—but always at a low cost in American lives and with the maximum use of air power. These police and social welfare actions maximized the use of U.S. high-tech weaponry and minimized the exposure of U.S. soldiers to danger. The intervention in Afghanistan neatly fits into this pattern. U.S. bombs clear the way for ground forces, preferably allies alongside or in front of U.S. troops. So far it has worked.

But the Bush administration finds itself by virtue of its commitment to a war on terrorism in a familiar—and dangerous—situation. The war's geographical range and vague goals raise the risks; the U.S. public and Congress seem permissive; and so the president may by choice or inadvertence place (or find) his military in a situation that would prove more costly or intractable than anticipated. Then patriotism would receive its true test. Americans would then have to face the serious challenge that lurks behind this foreign policy crisis: whether a country with pretensions to lead and change the world is too self-absorbed even to grasp the dimensions of those gargantuan ambitions or to pay the price in treasure and lives when the bill inevitably comes due. The United States thus hangs suspended between the dominant nationalism that by its very nature constantly risks overreaching and an alternative national identity that is more modest in its goals but less able to supply an emotionally satisfying sense of collective identity and power.

If American nationalism is one side of a new binary, what should we place on the other side? Seen through the prism of that nationalism, "Islamic fundamentalism" (also referred to as "militant Islam") would seem the obvious answer. Here is the most often cited source of evil, darkness, and terror coming out of the Middle East. Buried in that phrase are appealing if vague explanations for such brutal acts as September 11 and for the troubled advance of modern life that makes fanaticism and irrational anger fester in the region. Like all broadly appealing ideological gestures, this one dispenses with considerable complexity. It offers a marvelous economy of explanation at the price of conflating a wide variety of religiously inspired political movements and ignoring the wide variety of ways that religious ideas have assumed a prominence among the countries that are the home of well over a billion Muslims on the planet. In a sweep of territory running from northern Africa to Southeast Asia, there are at least as many public, political expressions of Islam as there are countries, each with its own linguistic, ethnic, and historical profile. The challenge is to understand Islam as among other things a source of political ideas that have taken quite distinct national forms, that are also transnational in their reach, and that thus resist easy categorization or generalization.

Islamic politics, a more useful, complex binary to set against U.S. nationalism, needs to be understood primarily in local terms—as an expression of sharpening disillusionment with secular regimes over the last quarter century.[13] Opposition—sometimes electoral, sometimes violent—appeared in places as widespread and culturally diverse as Iran, Algeria, Egypt, Turkey, Syria, and Iraq. All were states that had sought to build a "modern" society on the basis of socialism, nationalism, capitalism, or liberalism. Those wanting to anchor national life instead in religious values not only attacked the moral bankruptcy of a secular path but also condemned the U.S. government for propping up hated secular leaders divorced from their own people, for guaranteeing the survival of the no less hated state of Israel, and for promoting a soulless materialism. For those critical of the status quo, the American presence has become deeply entangled with national as well as regional problems, and thus solutions to those problems seem to involve unavoidably a confrontation of some sort with the U.S. government. Those wielding the weapon of terror may not elicit much open support in the Middle East or elsewhere in the Islamic world, but their radical critique of present conditions, their potent amalgam of religion and politics, and their determination to act even against the odds enjoy strong popular appeal.[14]

Following this line of argument, the regional past to set September 11 against is not the one favored by critics of the Bush administration—the anti-Soviet war in Afghanistan and the "blowback" from that covert effort that Americans are now experiencing. To be sure, covert U.S. support for the resistance in Afghanistan had unintended, damaging consequences (as virtually all such interventions do). But the blowback thesis flirts with the same ethnocentric notions of U.S. power entertained by the Bush administration. They share a tendency, as Francis Fitz-Gerald has phrased it, "to relate the fall of sparrows in distant lands to some fault or virtue of American policy."[15] Just as some policy critics make the United States the main source of evil in the world, so do leading policy makers assume a boundless national capacity to combat evil.

Rather than focusing on Afghanistan and the blowback thesis, we might more fruitfully look to the Iranian revolution of 1978–1979 as a more pertinent past. That revolution was a defining, watershed moment when Islam assumed formidable political proportions with reverberations not only in Iran but also throughout the region.[16] It demonstrated the power of religious ideas and leaders to mobilize the public and effect change. Islamists across the region hailed Ayatollah Ruhollah Khomeini's triumph as a harbinger of cultural and political resurgence that would turn back the inroads of the West and Israel and overthrow secular elites. The revolution's powerful impact on its neighbors helped almost at once to destabilize the region. Afghanistan was the first domino to fall when Soviet forces invaded in 1979 to head off what the Kremlin feared would be the spread of Islamic unrest in Central Asia.[17] By throwing its protection over the Shi'a majority in Iraq, the Iranian revolutionary regime also helped provoke the Iran-Iraq war of 1980–1988. That war in turn prepared the way for Iraq's invasion of Kuwait in 1990 and the Gulf War of 1991. The war with Iran had drained Saddam Hussein's treasury, created good relations with Washington, and fed his ambitions. Kuwait was tempting and seemingly easy pickings. This string of conflicts ignited by Iran's newfound political faith would set the stage for the current crisis: devastation and civil war within Afghanistan, resentment over the American military presence in Saudi Arabia, and the U.S. dual containment policy directed against Iran and Iraq.[18]

Finally, the Iranian revolution deserves special attention because it throws into sharp relief the very problems that policy makers face today. The run-up to the revolution found the Carter administration unable to grasp the appeal of an Islamic political movement. That administration was also unaware of Iranian resentment over the role of the CIA (Central Intelligence Agency) in overthrowing the government of Mohammed Mossadeq in 1953 and over U.S. support for the shah and his program of secularization, militarization, and ties to Israel over the following decades. Anti-Americanism seemed in 1979, as much as it seems now, an irrational, incomprehensible outburst by wild-eyed radicals. The legacy of anger and incomprehension has made it easier for U.S. policy makers, including the current Bush administration, to fixate on Tehran as a sponsor of terror and to ignore a lively political and social experiment that experienced observers invest with considerable promise and that Muslims everywhere watch with great interest.[19]

If the clash unfolding before us involves some sort of fundamentalism, it is tempting to say that it is as much ours as theirs—that there are strong strains of fundamentalism on both sides. Americans bring to the September 11 crisis a deeply rooted nationalist faith that is universal in its application, ahistorical in its thinking, and reductive in its view of other cultures. The talk from the White House, the Justice Department, and the Pentagon draws from a familiar nationalist repertoire that reduces complex situations to easily grasped terms familiar from other times of tension and fear. The result is the ethnocentric invocation of a great conspiracy, an axis of evil, a monolith of terror. This is the language of the crusader. Posed against this official American position with broad popular appeal is something more amorphous but demonstrably powerful—a set of values that has come to the fore in Muslim countries, that is preoccupied above all with domestic renovation, and that is in the main opposed to the United States for what it does politically and militarily to sustain a bankrupt old order and obstruct efforts to create something better.

There may be dangers lurking as Americans make their way deeper into the affairs of the region. Taking guidance from convenient simplifications is not likely to prove in practice any wiser today than it has in the past. It may well be now in the Middle East, as earlier in East Asia, that historical perspective will find little if any place in policy decisions and public debate. Ignoring history or embracing a simple, comforting version of it is always an attractive option. U.S. policy makers are likely to plunge heedlessly ahead. A fundamental reconsideration of policy may then have to wait until they encounter resistance that imposes costs higher than the public is willing to pay and that finally creates a kind of education through violence. This is a grim prospect with much uncertainty and much human suffering likely to attend it.

Notes

Acknowledgments: I am deeply in the debt of Curtis F. Jones, a student of the Middle East for half a century. Jones helped keep track of the voluminous public commentary and reporting since September 11 and then joined Christopher Endy, Peter Filene, Matthew Jacobs, Alan McPherson, Joanne Meyerowitz, Nancy Mitchell, and Sarah Shields in offering thoughtful comments on a draft version of these reflections. I would also like to thank those in Chapel Hill who invited my views in the aftermath of September 11, notably the UNC General Alumni Association (forum of September 13, 2001), the North Carolina Association of Former Members of Foreign Affairs Agencies (a lively luncheon exchange on October 26, 2001), and the UNC Program in the Humanities (a thoughtful panel discussion on February 2, 2002).

1. For reflections on these and other features of a time of acute international tension, see Michael H. Hunt, *Crises in U.S. Foreign Policy: An International History Reader* (New Haven, 1996), chap. 8.

2. Samuel P. Huntington, "The Clash of Civilizations?" *Foreign Affairs,* 72 (Summer 1993), 22–49.

3. Edward W. Said, "The Clash of Ignorance," *Nation,* Oct. 22, 2001, p. 12. See also Fred Halliday, *Islam and the Myth of Confrontation: Religion and Politics in the Middle East* (London, 1996); and the impassioned and sharply critical essay, Arundhati Roy, "The Algebra of Infinite Justice," *Guardian,* Sept. 29, 2001 <http://www.guardian.co.uk/Archive/Article/0,4273,4266289,00.html> (Feb. 11, 2002).

4. On the Cold War version of the modernization faith, see Michael E. Latham, *Modernization as Ideology: American Social Science and "Nation Building" in the Kennedy Era* (Chapel Hill, 2000).

5. Paul Kennedy, review of *What Went Wrong* by Bernard Lewis, *New York Times Book Review,* Jan. 27, 2002, p. 9. Kennedy endorses Lewis's most recent articulation of his favorite theme: the Muslim world's self-hatred and search for demons as it falls ever farther behind in the march toward modernity and especially in the creation of free societies. For slippage into the tradition-modernity dichotomy in an otherwise perceptive article, see Michael Howard, "What's in a Name? How to Fight Terrorism," *Foreign Affairs,* 81 (Jan.–Feb. 2002), 12–13. Thomas Friedman, *The Lexus and the Olive Tree* (New York, 2000); Robert D. Kaplan, *The Ends of the Earth: A Journey at the Dawn of the Twenty-first Century* (New York, 1996).

6. To highlight the cartoon quality of one facet of these perceptions, see Leila Ahmed, *Women and Gender in Islam: Historical Roots of a Modern Debate* (New Haven, 1992). Ahmed traces changing gender discourses over millennia and finds no "true tradition" of subordinating women. For an engaging set of vignettes that reveals the diversity of contemporary women's lives and the surprising turns negotiations over gender norms are taking, see Geraldine Brooks, *Nine Parts of Desire: The Hidden World of Islamic Women* (New York, 1996).

7. George W. Bush, "Address to a Joint Session of Congress and the American People" (Sept. 20, 2001), in *The White House* <http://www.whitehouse.gov/news/releases/2001/09/20010920-8.html> (Nov. 21, 2001).

8. A telling treatment of this pattern of media passivity in the early stages of crisis can be found in David C. Hallin, *The "Uncensored War": The Media and Vietnam* (Berkeley, 1989).

9. A good place to start on the evolution of U.S. regional policy is H. W. Brands, *Into the Labyrinth: The United States and the Middle East, 1945–1993* (New York, 1994). On U.S. reactions to developments in the Middle East, see Fawaz A. Gerges, *America and Political Islam: A Clash of Cultures or Clash of Interests?* (Cambridge, Eng., 1999); and Melani McAlister, *Epic Encounters: Culture, Media, and U.S. Interests in the Middle East* (Berkeley, 2001).

10. Michael H. Hunt, *Ideology and U.S. Foreign Policy* (New Haven, 1987), chap. 6; Anders Stephanson, *Manifest Destiny: American Expansion and the Empire of Right* (New York, 1995), 127–29.

11. The erosion of public support for these two limited wars is traced in John E. Mueller, *War, Presidents, and Public Opinion* (New York, 1973).

12. Caspar W. Weinberger, remarks at the National Press Club, Washington, D.C., Nov. 28, 1984, in *Intervention: The Use of American Military Force in the Post–Cold War World*, by Richard N. Haass (Washington, 1999), 197–205; Colin L. Powell, "U.S. Forces: Challenges Ahead" (1992), *ibid.*, 220.

13. On the current political-intellectual ferment within the Islamic world, see Gilles Kepel, "Islamists versus the State in Egypt and Algeria," *Daedalus*, 124 (Summer 1995), 109–27; Emmanuel Sivan, "Arab Nationalism in the Age of the Islamic Resurgence," in *Rethinking Nationalism in the Arab Middle East*, ed. James Jankowski and Israel Gershoni (New York, 1997), 207–8; Dale F. Eickelman, "Inside the Islamic Revolution," *Wilson Quarterly* (Winter 1998) <http://wwics.si.edu/OUTREACH/WQ/WQSELECT/ISLAM.HTM> (Dec. 11, 2001); Quintan Wiktorowicz, "The New Global Threat: Transnational Salafis and Jihad," *Middle East Policy*, 8 (Dec. 2001), 18–38; Ray Takeyh, "The Lineaments of Islamic Democracy," *World Policy Journal*, 18 (Winter 2001–2002), 59–67; and Michael Scott Doran, "Somebody Else's Civil War," *Foreign Affairs*, 81 (Jan.–Feb. 2002), 22–42.

14. For fascinating polling conducted in Egypt, Turkey, Pakistan, and Uzbekistan by the Pew Global Attitudes Project, see <http://people-press.org/reports/display.php3?ReportID=145> (June 20, 2002). Among opinion leaders around the world, those surveyed in those four countries were most inclined to see a conflict looming between the West and Islam (41%), to think that the United States was too supportive of Israel (95%) and overreacting in its war on terror (62%), and to believe that ordinary people in their country had a negative view of the

United States (49%) and attributed the terrorist attack to U.S. policy (81%). Recent, more broadly based polls confirm the elite impressions of marked popular antagonism toward current U.S. policy; see <http://people-press.org/commentary/display.php3?AnalysisID=46> (June 20, 2002).

15. Francis FitzGerald, *Way Out There in the Blue: Reagan, Star Wars, and the End of the Cold War* (New York, 2000), 474.

16. The argument that follows builds on the treatment of the Iranian revolution in Hunt, *Crises in U.S. Foreign Policy*, chap. 7. It also builds on a literature so rich that it makes all the more puzzling the neglect of that revolution's significance to current developments. On the revolution itself, the place to begin is Shaul Bakhash, *The Reign of the Ayatollahs: Iran and the Islamic Revolution* (New York, 1990). For critical political and social developments from the late nineteenth century to the revolution of 1979, see Ervand Abrahamian, *Iran between Two Revolutions* (Princeton, 1982). An indispensable treatment of a powerful body of political thought can be found in Ervand Abrahamian, *Khomeinism: Essays on the Islamic Republic* (Berkeley, 1993). Anyone interested in a direct encounter with the views of Iran's leading revolutionary should consult Hamid Algar, ed. and trans., *Islam and Revolution: Writings and Declarations of Imam Khomeini* (Berkeley, 1981). For an artful introduction to the physical and intellectual world of the clerics, see Roy P. Mottahedeh, *The Mantle of the Prophet: Religion and Politics in Iran* (New York, 1985). First-rate overviews of the interplay between U.S. Cold War policy and Iranian politics from the 1940s onward are available in James A. Bill, *The Eagle and the Lion: The Tragedy of American-Iranian Relations* (New Haven, 1988); and Richard W. Cottam, *Iran and the United States: A Cold War Case Study* (Pittsburgh, 1988).

17. For a revealing reconstruction from Soviet materials, see Odd Arne Westad, "The Road to Kabul: Soviet Policy on Afghanistan, 1978–1979," in *The Fall of Détente: Soviet-American Relations during the Carter Years*, ed. Odd Arne Westad (Oslo, 1997), 118–48.

18. This argument about the consequences of the Iranian revolution is taken even farther in David W. Lesch, *1979: The Year That Shaped the Modern Middle East* (Boulder, 2001).

19. On Iran as an experiment still in progress, see Brooks, *Nine Parts of Desire*, esp. chap. 5; Robin Wright, "Iran's New Revolution," *Foreign Affairs*, 79 (Jan.–Feb. 2000), 133–45; and Daniel Brumberg, *Reinventing Khomeini: The Struggle for Reform in Iran* (Chicago, 2001), esp. chap. 8 and the conclusion.

Damming Afghanistan

Modernization in a Buffer State

Nick Cullather

President George W. Bush has pledged to "help Afghanistan develop an economy that can feed its people" so that it will never again
threaten the United States. Wait, writes Nick Cullather, we did that
once before. Strewn across the battlefield of Operation Enduring
Freedom are the ruins of American development schemes undertaken during the 1950s and 1960s—airports, suburbs, schools, hospitals, and a massive dam project modeled on the Tennessee Valley
Authority. The United States practiced nation building for thirty
years in Afghanistan, but the nation was crumbling even before the
Soviet tanks rolled in. Cullather probes the resilient American faith
in modernization—and the concomitant blindness to failure—that
the Afghan episode reveals.

In May 1960, the historian Arnold J. Toynbee left Kandahar and
drove ninety miles on freshly paved roads to Lashkar Gah, a modern
planned city known locally as the New York of Afghanistan. At the con-
fluence of the Helmand and Arghandab rivers, close against the ancient
ruins of Qala Bist, Lashkar Gah's eight thousand residents lived in sub-
urban-style tract homes surrounded by broad lawns. The city boasted
an alabaster mosque, one of the country's best hospitals, Afghanistan's
only coeducational high school, and the headquarters of the Helmand
Valley Authority, a multipurpose dam project funded by the United
States. This unexpected proliferation of modernity led Toynbee to reflect on the warning of Sophocles: "The craft of his engines surpasseth·
his dreams." In the area around Kandahar, traditional Afghanistan had
vanished. "The domain of the Helmand Valley Authority," he reported,
"has become a piece of America inserted into the Afghan landscape. . . .
The new world they are conjuring up out of the desert at the Helmand
River's expense is to be an America-in-Asia."[1]

Toynbee's image sits uneasily with the visuals of the recent war. In the
granite battlescapes captured by the cameras of the Al-Jazeera network

in the days after September 11, 2001, Afghanistan appeared as perhaps the one spot on earth unmarked by the influence of American culture. When correspondents referred to Afghanistan's history it was to the Soviet invasion of the 1980s or the earlier "great game" that ended with the British Empire's departure from South Asia in 1947. There was a silence about the three decades in between. During that time, Afghanistan was aptly called an "economic Korea," divided between the Soviet Union in the north and the United States in the south.[2] In the 1950s and 1960s, the United States made southern Afghanistan a showcase of nation building with a dazzling project to "reclaim" and modernize a swath of territory comprising roughly half the country. The Helmand venture is worth remembering today as a precedent for renewed efforts to rebuild Afghanistan, but it was also part of a larger project—alternately called development, nation building, or modernization—that deployed science and expertise to reconstruct the entire postcolonial world.

When President Harry S. Truman announced Point IV, a "bold new program . . . for the improvement . . . of underdeveloped areas," in January 1949, the global response was startling. Truman "hit the jackpot of the world's political emotions," *Fortune* noted. National delegations lined up to receive assistance that a few years earlier would have been seen as a colonial intrusion. Development inserted into international relations a new problematic and a new concept of time, asserting that all nations followed a common historical path and that those in the lead had a moral duty to those who followed. "We must frankly recognize," a State Department official observed in 1953, "that the hands of the clock of history are set at different hours in different parts of the world." Leaders of newly independent states, such as Mohammad Zahir Shah of Afghanistan and Jawaharlal Nehru of India, accepted these terms, merging their own governmental mandates into the stream of nations moving toward modernity. Development was not simply the best but the only course. "There is only one-way traffic in Time," Nehru observed.[3]

Aided by social science theory, development came into its own by the mid-1950s both as a policy ideology in the United States and as a global discourse for assigning obligations and entitlements among rich and poor nations.[4] Nationalism and modernization held equal place in the postcolonial creed. As Edward Shils observed in 1960, nearly every state pressed for policies "that will bring them well within the circle of modernity." But nation-building schemes, even successful ones, rarely unfolded quietly. The struggles, often subtle and indirect, over dam projects, land

Pan American Airlines technician Richard Frisius instructs Afghan pilot candi-
dates in 1960. U.S. development aid through the Helmand Authority helped
establish the national airline, Ariana, and build a modern airport at Kandahar.
The airport is today the U.S. Army's forward base in Afghanistan. (Reprinted
from U.S. Operations Mission to Afghanistan, *Afghanistan Builds on an Ancient Civilization*, 1960.)

reforms, and planned cities generally concerned the *meaning* of development, the persons, authorities, and ideals that would be associated
with the spectacle of progress. To modernize was to lay claim to the future and the past, to define identities and values that would survive to
guide the nation on its journey forward. It was this double sense of time,
according to Clifford Geertz, that gave "new-state nationalism its peculiar air of being at once hell-bent toward modernity and morally outraged by its manifestations."[5]

Vulnerable to shifts in policy, funding, or theoretical fashion, Cold
War–era development schemes suffered from deficiencies reasonably
attributed to their piecemeal approach and shortages of commitment,
resources, or time. Such failures, James Ferguson has observed, only reinforced the paradigm, as modernization theory supplied the necessary
explanations while new policy furnished solutions.[6] The Helmand
scheme had no such excuse. It came under American supervision in 1946
and continued until the departure of the last reclamation expert in 1979,

outlasting all the theories and rationales on which it was based. It was lavishly funded by U.S. foreign aid, multilateral loans, and the Afghan government, and it was the opposite of piecemeal. It was an "integrated" development scheme, with education, industry, agriculture, medicine, and marketing under a single controlling authority. Nation building did not fail in Afghanistan for want of money, time, or imagination. In the Helmand Valley, the engines and dreams of modernization ran their full course, spooling out across the desert until they hit limits of physics, culture, and history.

Planners presented the Helmand project as applied science, as a rationalization of nature and social order, but they also trafficked in dreams. Because of its scale and longevity, the Helmand venture assumed roles in a succession of modernizing myths. Modernization, Michael Latham notes, demanded a "projection of American identity."[7] Exporting an American model of progress required continual redefinition of the sources of American greatness and renewed efforts to plant its unique characteristics in foreign landscapes. The New Deal, the New Look, and the New Frontier each revised the stakes and symbolism of development, and each had to interlace these filaments of meaning with the webs of significance Afghans wove around the project. Within Afghanistan's government, the impulse to modernize went back to the early twentieth century when tribal and ethnic loyalties were reformed as a national identity. Planting a modern city next to the colossal ruins of Qala Bist was a calculated gesture asserting an imagined line of succession from the eleventh- and twelfth-century Ghaznavid dynasty to the royal family presiding in Kabul. The Helmand project symbolized the transformation of the nation, representing the legitimacy of the monarchy, the expansion of state power, and the destiny of the Pashtun race. Every development scheme involves representations of this kind, and a complex project can accommodate overlapping sets of symbolic meanings that justify and sustain it, even in failure.

The Accidental Nation

Afghanistan, at its origin, was an empty space on the map that was not Persian, not Russian, not British, "a purely accidental geographic unit," according to Lord George N. Curzon, who put the finishing touches on its silhouette. Both the monarchy and the nation emerged from strategies Britain used to pacify the Pashtun peoples along India's northwest frontier in the last half of the nineteenth century. Consisting of nomadic,

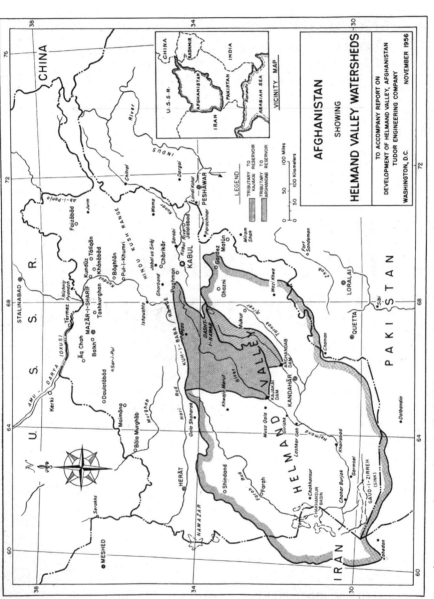

Stretching across the southern half of Afghanistan, the Helmand Valley development was designed by the U.S. government to act as an economic buffer, shielding the U.S. "northern tier" allies Pakistan and Iran from Soviet influence. (Reprinted from *Report on Development of Helmand Valley, Afghanistan,* 1956.)

seminomadic, and settled communities with no common language or ancestry, Pashtuns (Pathans in Hindustani) made up for colonial officials a single racial grouping.[8] They occupied a strategically vital region stretching from the southern slopes of the Hindu Kush range through the northern Indus Valley into Kashmir.

To prevent tribal feuds from inviting Russian influence, colonial officials devised a double-pronged strategy to bring the Pashtun belt under British control. First, they split it in half by surveying the Durand Line, the 1,200-mile boundary that today separates Afghanistan and Pakistan. Plotted in 1893, the "scientific frontier" followed a topographic ridgeline that could be held at strongpoints blocking key mountain passes.[9] By bisecting tribal homelands and the seasonal migration routes of three million pastoralists who followed herds of Persian fat-tailed sheep between lowland and upland grazing areas, the Durand Line restricted Pashtun autonomy and facilitated new forms of indirect influence over peoples on both sides of it.[10]

Rather than demarcating the spatial limit of British sovereignty, the Durand Line marked a division between types of imperial control. On the India side, a smaller Pashtun population, the "assured clans," could be co-opted and deployed as a proxy army against Pashtuns on the Afghan side, precluding the emergence of a regime in Kabul hostile to British interests. The Mohammadzai—the clan of Zahir Shah, ruler of Afghanistan from 1933 to 1973—was such a subaltern force, benefiting from British power without being fully constrained by it.[11] Straddling the Khyber Pass, they used subsidies and arms to overwhelm their rivals on the Afghan side. This variety of indirect rule, known as the Forward Policy, kept Afghanistan firmly under British influence for the first half of the twentieth century.[12]

The Durand Line complemented a cultural strategy of pacification known as the Pathan (Pashtun) Renaissance, through which colonial agents aligned their own interests with those of their tribal allies. Cultivating a Pashtun identity as a unitary "pure" race in contrast to the "mixed" Tajiks, Baluchis, Hazaras, and others with whom they were mingled, colonial officials invented the reputation of the Pashtuns as a warrior caste. They were "our chaps," natural rulers, the equals of the British. "You're white people, sons of Alexander, and not like common, black Mohammedans," the title character of Rudyard Kipling's *The Man Who Would Be King* (1891) explained to the Afghans. Pashtuns were entitled to subsidies, to rank in the Indian army, and to a direct relationship to the Crown. Schooling internalized the racial taxonomy, supplanting allegiances to village, family, and clan while linking Pashtun identity with modernization. Edwardes and Islamia colleges, founded in Peshawar in the early twentieth century, inculcated a consciousness of Pashtun nationhood and suggested "the place which the Pathan might fill in the development of a subcontinent." An awareness of race distinguished the literate few from the vast majority of uneducated Afghans, who were unable to discriminate between ethnographic types.[13]

As it was meant to, the sublimation of the Pashtuns reconfigured politics on both sides of the frontier. When Nadir Shah crossed the Durand Line and seized Kabul from the Tajiks in 1929, he established a monarchy based on Pashtun nationalism with overtones of scientific racism. Comprising less than half the Afghan population, Pashtuns claimed an entitlement based on their status as an advanced race, the bearers of modernity and progress.[14] Punitive expeditions against Tajiks in the north and Hazaras in the south and west, in which German-made aircraft supported mounted troops, broke the autonomous power of these regions, opening them to Pashtun settlement. Nadir Shah built a professional army—new in Afghan tradition—of forty thousand troops, linked by kinship and personal loyalty to the monarchy and trained by French and German advisers.[15] A system of secularized schools and a change of the national language from Dari, a Persian dialect, to Pashto demonstrated the new regime's determination to bring Afghanistan's ungovernable tribes under the control of a rationalized, central state.

For Nadir Shah and his son Zahir, who assumed the throne after his father's assassination in 1933, political survival depended on enlarging and deepening the authority of the state. To its new rulers, Afghanistan was an unknown and dangerous country. It had few roads, only six miles of rail (all of it in Kabul), and few internal telegraph or phone lines. For most of the ten or twelve million Afghans (Afghanistan has never completed a census), encounters of any kind with the central government were rare and unpleasant. Laws were made and enforced in accordance with local custom and without reference to the state; internal taxes existed only on paper. Evidence of royal authority—easily visible on Kabul streets patrolled by Prussian-helmeted palace guards—disappeared as rapidly as the pavement beneath a traveler leaving the city in any direction. There were no cadastral maps, city plans, or housing registries, an absence that made Afghanistan less *legible*, and therefore less governable, than countries that had been formally colonized.[16] Modern states are able to govern through manipulation of abstractions—unemployment, public opinion, literacy rates, etc.—but in Afghanistan interventions of any kind, and the reactions to them, were brutally concrete. The prime minister, the king's uncle, on his infrequent inspection tours of the countryside, traveled under heavy guard.[17]

Zahir Shah sought help from Japanese, Italian, and German advisers, who laid plans for a modern network of communications and roads. In 1937 a German-built radio tower in Kabul allowed instant links to remote villages and the outside world for the first time. Through a national bank and state cartels, the government supervised a cautious and tightly controlled economic modernization. German engineers built textile mills, power plants, and carpet and furniture factories to be run by monopolies under royal license.[18] Tax codes and state trading firms began to bring lawless sectors, such as stock raising and trading, within reach of accountants and assessors in Kabul. These efforts met with sporadic—and occasionally bloody—resistance, but the regime persisted in slowly, firmly, laying "the barren politics of abstraction and principle" over "the warm, cruel politics of the heart."[19]

During World War II the United States replaced Germany as the external partner in the young king's plans. The Holocaust and submarine warfare caused Afghanistan's external trade to undergo a sudden and advantageous reorientation. One of the country's chief exports was karakul, the pelt of the Persian fat-tailed sheep converted in the hands of skilled furriers into the glossy black fur known as astrakhan, karakul, or Persian lamb. The former centers of fur making, Leipzig, London, and Paris, closed down during the war years, and the industry moved in its entirety to New York. From 1942 through the 1970s, New York furriers consumed nearly the entire Afghan export, two and a half million skins a year, which resold as lustrous black coats and hats ranging in price from $400 to $3,500. A tiny fraction of the retail revenue went back to Afghanistan, but the fractions added up. The government employed exchange rate manipulations to exact an effective tax rate of over 50 percent on karakul, making it the country's most lucrative source of exchange as well as revenue. Afghanistan ended World War II with $100 million in reserves, and, in the midst of the postwar "dollar gap" crisis in international liquidity, Afghanistan was favored with a small but steady source of dollar earnings.[20]

The collapse of the British Empire created a chance for Pashtun reunification and lent new significance to the modernization project. From the vantage of Kabul, the partition of India in 1947 ended whatever justification the Durand Line had once had. A Pashtun separatist movement emerged in Peshawar and Kashmir, and, with the encouragement of India, Zahir Shah proposed the creation of an ethnic state—Pushtunistan—consisting of most of northern Pakistan, which would give the assured clans an option to merge with Kabul at some future date. It was a hopeless proposal—the frontier was internationally recognized—but the king stuck to it rather than allow Pakistan to inherit the decisive instruments and influence of the Forward Policy. The assured clans represented a continuing threat to the Afghan state. After 1947, members of the royal family spoke of building in Afghanistan a secure, prosperous base for the recovery of Pashtun lands.[21]

Over the next two decades the Pushtunistan controversy drew Afghanistan into the Cold War. U.S. diplomats dismissed it as fantasy, but to the Afghan monarchy Pushtunistan was as solid as France. A visitor in 1954 found government offices in Kabul hung with maps on which the "narrow, wriggly object" plainly appeared, "wedged in between Afghanistan on one flank, and the remains of West Pakistan on the other." The dispute periodically turned hot, with reciprocal sacking of embassies and border incidents that gradually converted the Durand Line into the kind of politico-geographic feature that typified the Cold War, an impassable boundary. The movement of goods across the frontier was tightly restricted, and in 1962 Pakistan closed the passes to migration, terminating the seasonal movement of the herds.[22] From the mid-1950s until the end of the Soviet occupation, Afghan exports and imports moved almost exclusively through the Soviet Union, which discounted freight rates to encourage the dependency.[23]

In the immediate aftermath of World War II, however, the Soviet Union was preoccupied with internal reconstruction, and Afghanistan looked to the United States for help in consolidating a centralized state that could assume responsibility for the public welfare.[24] Through its development programs, the monarchy assumed a relationship of trusteeship over the nation, presenting the king as retaining custody of the state during a dangerous transitional period but ready to relinquish power once modernity was achieved. Official terminology coupled underdevelopment and Afghan identity. "Afghanistan is a backward country," insisted Mohammed Daoud, the king's brother-in-law, cousin, and prime minister. "We must do something about it or die as a nation."[25] Large-scale development projects, visible signs of national energy, would stake a claim to the future for the Pashtuns and to the present for the royal

family. One such scheme particularly appealed to the king; he wanted
to build a dam.

A TVA for the Hindu Kush

Nothing becomes antiquated faster than symbols of the future, and it is
difficult, at only fifty years remove, to envision the hold concrete dams
once had on the global imagination. In the mid-twentieth century, the
austere lines of the Hoover Dam and its radiating spans of high-tension
wire inscribed federal power on the American landscape. Vladimir Lenin
famously remarked that communism was Soviet power plus electrifica-
tion, an equation captured by the David Lean film *Dr. Zhivago* (1965)
in the image of water surging, as a kind of redemption, from the spill-
way of an immense Soviet dam. In 1954, standing at the Bhakra-Nangal
canal, Nehru described dams as the temples of modern India. "Which
place can be greater than this," he declared, "this Bhakra-Nangal, where
thousands of men have worked, have shed their blood and sweat, and laid
down their lives as well? . . . When we see big works, our stature grows
with them, and our minds open out a little."[26] For Nehru, for Zahir
Shah, for China today, the great blank wall of a dam was a screen on
which they would project the future.

Dams also symbolized the sacrifice of the individual to the greater
good of the state. A dam project allows, even requires, a state to appropriate and redistribute land, plan factories and economies, tell people
what to make and grow, design and build new housing, roads, schools,
and centers of commerce. Tour guides are fond of telling about the
worker (or workers) accidentally entombed in dams, and construction
of these vast works customarily requires huge, unnamed sacrifices. To
displace thousands from ancestral homes and farms, bulldoze graveyards
and mosques, and erase all trace of memory and history from the land
is a process familiar to us today as ethnic cleansing. But when done in
conjunction with dam construction, it is called land reclamation and can
be justified even in democratic systems by the calculus of development.
India's interior minister, Morarji Desai, told a public gathering at the unfinished Pong Dam in 1961 that "we will request you to move from your
houses after the dam comes up. If you move, it will be good. Otherwise
we shall release the waters and drown you all."[27]

A dam-building project would vastly expand and intensify the authority that could be exercised by the central government at Kabul. Remaking and regulating the physical environment of an entire region

Morrison Knudsen engineers surveyed and built the Helmand Valley project's major works between 1946 and 1960. The Soviet press described the company as "a kind of training centre where young Afghans are moulded to [an] American pattern." (Reprinted from *Collier's*, Aug. 2, 1952.)

would, for the first time, translate Afghanistan into the legible inventories of material and human resources in the manner of modern states. In 1946, using its karakul revenue, the Afghan government hired the largest American heavy engineering firm, Morrison Knudsen, Inc., of Boise, Idaho, to build a dam. Morrison Knudsen, builder of the Hoover Dam, the San Francisco Bay Bridge, and later the launch complex at Cape Canaveral, specialized in symbols of the future. The firm operated all over the world, boring tunnels through the Andes in Peru, laying airfields in Turkey. Its engineers, who called themselves Emkayans, would be drawing up specifications for a complex of dams in the gorges of the Yangtze River in 1949 when Mao Zedong's People's Liberation Army drove them out.[28] The firm set up shop in an old Moghul palace outside Kandahar and began surveying the Helmand Valley.

The Helmand and Arghandab rivers constitute Afghanistan's largest river system, draining a watershed covering half the country. Originating in the Hindu Kush a few miles from Kabul, the Helmand travels through upland dells thick with orchards and vineyards before merging with the Arghandab twenty-five miles from Kandahar, turning west across the arid plain of Registan and emptying into the Sistan marshes of Iran. The valley was reputedly the site of a vast irrigation works destroyed by Genghis Khan in the thirteenth century. The entire area is dry, catching two to three inches of rain a year. Consequently, river flows fluctuate unpredictably within a wide range, varying from 2,000 to 60,000 cubic feet per second.[29] Before beginning, Morrison Knudsen had to create an infrastructure of roads and bridges to allow the movement of equipment. Typically, they would also conduct extensive studies on soils and drainage, but the company and the Afghan government convinced themselves that in this case it was not necessary, that "even a 20 percent margin of error . . . could not detract from the project's intrinsic value."[30]

The promise of dams is that they are a renewable resource, furnishing power and water indefinitely and with little effort once the project is complete, but dam projects are subject to ecological constraints that are often more severe outside of the temperate zone. Siltation, which now threatens many New Deal–era dams, advances more quickly in arid and tropical climates. Canal irrigation involves a special set of hazards. Arundhati Roy, the voice of India's antidam movement, explains that "perennial irrigation does to soil roughly what anabolic steroids do to the human body," stimulating ordinary earth to produce multiple crops in the first years while slowly rendering the soil infertile.[31] Large reservoirs raise the water table in the surrounding area, a problem worsened by extensive irrigation. Waterlogging itself can destroy harvests, but it produces more permanent damage, too. In waterlogged soils, capillary action pulls soluble salts and alkalies to the surface, leading to desertification. Early reports warned that the Helmand Valley was vulnerable, that it had gravelly subsoils and salt deposits. The Emkayans knew Middle Eastern rivers were often unsuited to extensive irrigation schemes. But these apprehensions' "impact was minimized by one or both parties."[32] From the start, the Helmand project was primarily about national prestige and only secondarily about the social benefits of increasing agricultural productivity.

Signs of trouble appeared almost immediately. Even when only half completed, the first dam, a small diversion dam at the mouth of the Boghra canal, raised the water table to within a few inches of the surface of the ground. A snowy crust of salt could be seen in areas around the reservoir. In 1949, the engineers and the government faced a decision. Tearing down the dam would have resulted in a loss of face for the monarchy and Morrison Knudsen, but from an engineering standpoint the project could no longer be justified. The necessary reconsideration never took place, however, because it was at this moment that the unlucky Boghra works was enfolded into the global project of development.

Truman's Point IV address reconfigured the relationship between the United States and newly independent nations. The confrontation between colonizer and colonized, rich and poor, was with a rhetorical gesture replaced by a world order in which all nations were either developed or developing. The president explicitly linked development to American strategic and economic objectives. Poverty was a threat not just to the poor but to their richer neighbors, he argued, and alleviating misery would assure a general prosperity, lessening the chances of war.[33] But the "triumphant action" of development superseded the merely ideological conflict of the Cold War: Communism and capitalism were competing carriers bound for the same destination. Development justified interventions on a grand scale and made obedience to foreign technicians the duty of every responsible government. Afghanistan—solvent, untouched by the recent war, and able to hire technicians when it needed them—suddenly became "underdeveloped" and, owing to its position bordering the Soviet Union, the likely recipient of substantial assistance. Point IV's technical aid could take many forms—clinics, schools, new livestock breeds, assays for minerals and petroleum—but the uncompleted Boghra works was an invitation to something grander, a reproduction of an American developmental triumph.

When Truman thought of aid, he thought of dams, specifically of the Tennessee Valley Authority (TVA), the complex of dams on the Tennessee River that transformed the economy of the upper South. "A TVA in the Yangtze Valley and the Danube," he proposed to the TVA's director, David Lilienthal; "These things can be done and don't let anybody tell you different. When they happen, when millions and millions of people are no longer hungry and pushed and harassed, then the causes of war will be less by that much." Truman's internationalization of the TVA repositioned the New Deal for a McCarthyite age. Dams were the American alternative to Communist land reform, Arthur M. Schlesinger argued in *The Vital Center*. Instead of a "crude redistribution" of land, American engineers could create "wonderlands of vegetation and power" from the desert. The TVA was "a weapon which, if properly employed, might outbid all the social ruthlessness of the Communists for the support of the peoples of Asia."[34]

The TVA had totemic significance for American liberals, but in the diplomatic setting it had the additional function of redefining political conflict as a technical problem. Britain's solution to Afghanistan's tribal wars had been to script feuds of blood, honor, and faith within the linear logic of boundary commissions, containing conflict within two-dimensional space. The United States set aside the maps and replotted tribal enmities on hydrologic charts. Resolution became a matter of apportioning cubic yards of water and kilowatt-hours of energy. Assurances of inevitable progress further displaced conflict into the future; if all sides could be convinced that resource flows would increase, problems would vanish, in bureaucratic parlance, downstream. Over the next two decades the United States would propose river authority schemes as solutions to the most intractable international conflicts: Palestine ("Water for Peace") and the Kashmir dispute. In 1965, Lyndon B. Johnson famously suggested a Mekong River Authority as an alternative to the Vietnam War.[35]

Afghanistan applied for and received a $12 million Export-Import Bank loan for the Helmand Valley in 1950, the first of over $80 million over the next fifteen years. Afghanistan's loan request contained a line for soil surveys, but the bank refused it as an unnecessary expense. Point IV supplied technical support.[36] In 1952, the national government created the Helmand Valley Authority—later the Helmand and Arghandab Valley Authority (HAVA)—removing 1,800 square miles of river valley from local control and placing it under the jurisdiction of expert commissions in Kabul. The monarchy poured money into the project; a fifth of the central government's total expenditures went into HAVA in the 1950s and early 1960s. From 1946 on, the salaries of Morrison Knudsen's advisers and technicians absorbed an amount equivalent to Afghanistan's total exports. Without adequate mechanisms for tax collection, the royal treasury passed costs on to agricultural producers

The Arghandab Dam, 200 feet high and a third of a mile long, was heralded at its completion in 1952 as a majestic symbol of technological prowess. Later, U.S. diplomats complained that the American reputation hung on "a strip of concrete." (Reprinted from U.S. Operations Mission to Afghanistan, *Afghanistan Builds on an Ancient Civilization*, 1960.)

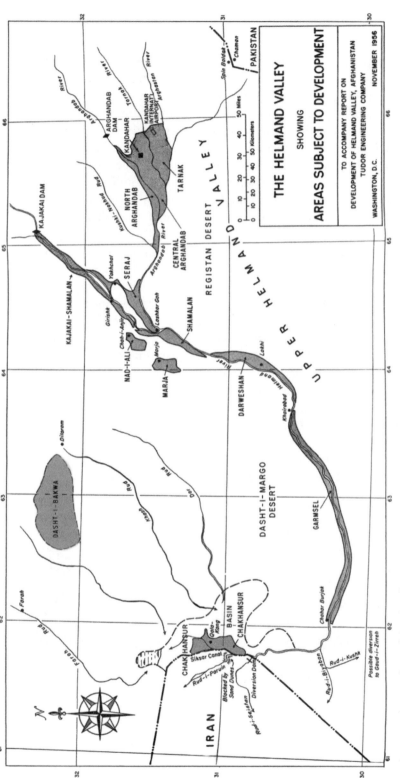

This map depicts the Helmand Valley as envisioned in 1956. The Zahir Shah Canal would cut across the Arghandab watershed to irrigate regions around Kandahar. The Darweshan and Shamalan canals paralleled the river, watering riparian areas, while other canals traversed the desert to feed islands of reclaimed land at Marja and Nad-i-Ali. Works on the lower river, below Khairobad, were never completed. (Reprinted from *Report on Development of Helmand Valley, Afghanistan*, 1956.)

through inflation and the diversion of export revenue, offsetting any gains irrigation produced.[37] Although it pulled in millions in international funding, HAVA soaked up the small reserves of individual farmers and may well have reduced the total national investment in agriculture.

HAVA supplemented the initial dam with a vast complex of dams. Two large dams—the 200-foot-high Arghandab Dam and the 320-foot-high Kajakai Dam—for storage and hydropower were supplemented by diversion dams, drainage works, and irrigation canals. Reaching out from the reservoirs were three hundred miles of concrete-lined canals. Three of the longer canals, the Tarnak, Darweshan, and Shamalan, fed riparian lands already intensively cultivated and irrigated by an elaborate system of tunnels, flumes, and canals known as juis. The new, wider canals furnished an ampler and purportedly more reliable water source. The Zahir Shah Canal supplied Kandahar with water from the Arghandab reservoir, and two canals stretched out into the desert to polders of reclaimed desert: Marja and Nad-i-Ali. Each extension of the project required more land acquisition and displaced more people. To remain flexible, the royal government and Morrison Knudsen kept the question of who actually owned the land in abeyance. No system of titles was instituted, and the bulk of the reclaimed land was farmed by tenants of Morrison Knudsen, the government, or contractors hired by the government.[38]

The new systems magnified the problems encountered at the Boghra works and added new ones. Waterlogging created a persistent weed problem. The storage dams removed silt that once rejuvenated fields downstream. Deposits of salt or gypsum would erupt into long-distance canals and be carried off to deaden the soil of distant fields. The Emkayans had to contend with unpredictable flows triggered by snowmelt in the Hindu Kush. In 1957, floods nearly breached dams in two places, and water tables rose, salinating soils throughout the region. The reservoirs and large canals also lowered the water temperature, making plots that once held vineyards and orchards suitable only for growing grain.[39] After a decade of work, HAVA could not set a schedule or a plan for completion. As its engineering failures mounted, HAVA's symbolic weight in the Cold War and in Afghanistan's ethnic politics steadily grew.

Like the TVA, HAVA was a multipurpose river authority. U.S. officials described it as "a major social engineering project," responsible for river development but also for education, housing, health care, roads, communications, agricultural research and extension, and industrial development in the valley. The U.S. ambassador in Kabul in 1962 noted that, if successful, HAVA would boost Afghanistan's "earnings of foreign exchange and, if properly devised, could foster the growth of a strata of small holders which would give the country more stability." This billiard-ball alignment of capital accumulation, class formation, and political evolution was a core proposition of the social science approach to modernization that was just making the leap from university think tanks to centers of policy making. An uneasiness about the massive, barely understood forces impelling two-thirds of the world in simultaneous and irreversible social movement—surging population growth, urbanization, the collapse of traditional authority—overshadowed policy toward "underdeveloped" areas. Modernization theory offered reassurance that the techniques of Point IV could discipline these processes and turn them to the advantage of the United States. Development, the economists Walt W. Rostow and Max Millikan of the Massachusetts Institute of Technology assured the CIA (Central Intelligence Agency) in 1954, could create "an environment in which societies which directly or indirectly menace ours will not evolve."[40]

A Strange Kind of Cold War

Following behavioral explanations of development, U.S. aid officials sought to ally themselves with tutelary elites possessing the transitional personalities that could generate nonviolent, nonrevolutionary change. At first glance, the king and his retinue appeared almost ideally suited. Educated in Europe and the United States, royal government officials spoke in familiar terms of ways to engineer progress. Mohammed Daoud presided as supreme technocrat. Educated (like the king) in France and at English schools in Kabul, he became prime minister in 1953. "We members of the royal family," he told the anthropologist Louis Dupree, "were all trained in the West and have adopted Western ideas as our own."[41] Since coming to power in 1953, Daoud had accelerated the tempo of economic development, believing that without rapid growth Afghanistan would dissolve into factionalism and be divided among its neighbors. He was sure that U.S. and Soviet generosity sprang from temporary conditions and that his government had only a short time in which to take all it could. To American officials, Afghan modernizers appeared too eager, too ready to jump ahead without the necessary planning and information-gathering steps, and too ready to take aid from any source. Daoud's receptiveness to Soviet and Chinese aid was particularly troubling. As Dupree put it, "A nation does not accept technology without ideology. A machine or a dam is a product of a culture."[42]

Daoud's regime made no effort to disguise its chauvinism. Controlling positions in government, the army, the police, and the educational system were held by Pashtuns to such a degree that the appellation Afghan commonly referred only to Pashtuns and not to the minorities who collectively constituted the majority. A U.S. diplomat described the kingdom as a Soviet-style "police state, where there is no free press, no political parties, and where ruthless suppression of minorities is the established pattern."[43] But despite their favored status, Pashtuns revolted against the Mohammadzai eight times between 1930 and 1960. Open violence between minorities was less common than conflict that pitted clan autonomy against central authority. In 1956, Daoud welcomed Soviet military aid and advisers. His security forces kept order with a heavy hand, and, when mullahs in Kandahar again led a movement against the government in 1959, the army used tanks and MiGs to crush the rebellion.[44] Daoud had brought the Cold War to Afghanistan.

To the Eisenhower administration, Morrison Knudsen's outpost in Kandahar was the scientific frontier of American power in Central Asia, guarding the high passes between risk and credibility. The company was "one of the chief influences which maintain Afghan connections with the West," Secretary of State John Foster Dulles believed. "Its departure would create a vacuum which the Soviets would be anxious to fill." He wanted to preserve Afghanistan's buffer role, but the perennial provocations along the Durand Line conjured scenarios in Dulles's mind in which a Soviet-backed Afghan army attacked U.S.-allied Pakistan— another Korea, this time beyond the reach of U.S. air and naval power. Daoud's Pashtun extremism led his government to welcome Soviet arms while instigating mob attacks on Pakistani consulates and border posts. In 1955, Dulles dissuaded Pakistan from a plan to overthrow the royal family, while his brother, Allen, head of the CIA, suggested using against Daoud the same methods that had recently worked to depose Mohammed Mossadeq in Iran.[45] The United States wanted to separate the dual ambitions of Pashtun nationalism, preserving Daoud's modernization drive while disposing of the Pushtunistan issue.

The Helmand project offered a way to counter Soviet influence by giving Daoud what he wanted, a Pashtun homeland. As originally envisioned, HAVA would irrigate enough new fertile land to settle eighteen to twenty thousand families on fifteen-acre farms. Working with Afghan officials, U.S. advisers launched a program to immobilize the nomadic Pashtuns, whose migrations were a source of friction with Pakistan.[46] To American and royal government officials, this floating population and its disregard for laws, taxes, and borders symbolized the country's backwardness. Settling Pashtun nomads in a belt from Kabul to Kandahar would create a secure political base for the government and bring them within reach of modernization programs. Diminishing the transborder flows would reduce smuggling and the periodic incidents that inflamed the Pushtunistan issue. A complementary dam development project in the Indus Valley, also funded by the United States, settled Pashtun nomads on the other side of the Durand Line.[47]

HAVA's mandate included the social reconstruction of the region. Those seeking land, as well as families already occupying ancestral plots, were required to apply to HAVA for housing, water, and implements. In the late 1950s, HAVA began constructing whole communities for transplanted pastoralists in the Shamalan, Marja, and Nad-i-Ali districts, while simultaneously trying to break the authority of nomadic clan leaders known as maliks. Maliks would lead their people, "Moses-like, to the promised land," according to a U.S. report. HAVA "always informed the new settlers that they could choose new village leaders, to be called *wakil*, if they so desired. None did."[48] Resettled families would receive a pair of oxen, a grant of two thousand Afghanis, and enough seed for the first year. To replace the need for winter pastures, the United Nations brought in Swiss experts to teach nomads to use long-handled scythes to cut forage for sheep from high plateaus. But even with the closing of the border and the attraction of subsidies and well-watered homesteads, it proved difficult to entice Ghilzai Pashtun to become ordinary farmers. Freer and wealthier than the peasants whose lands they crossed, the nomads regarded their new Tajik and Hazara neighbors with contempt. This may have served Kabul's purposes, too. The government, according to Hafizullah Emadi, planned to "use these new settlers as a death squad to crush the uprisings of the non-Pashtun people of the west, southwest, and central part of the country."[49]

The Helmand project symbolized Pashtun power, and the royal government resisted efforts to attach alternate meanings to it. U.S. advisers made several attempts to imitate the "grass roots" inclusivity of the TVA. Aiming to dispel tribal feuds and foster a common professional identity among farmers, they established local co-ops and 4-H clubs, but Daoud's security forces broke them up. Courting the Muslim clergy was also forbidden. Agricultural experts found the mullahs to be a progressive force, "constantly look[ing] for things to improve their communities, better seed, new plants, improved livestock."[50] Regarding religion as an inoculation against communism, policy makers wanted to associate the Helmand project with Islam. In 1956, the U.S. Information Agency produced "a 45-minute full color motion picture, which featured economic development, particularly the Helmand Valley Project, and the religious heritage of Afghanistan." Daoud, however, regarding the mullahs as a subversive element, discouraged their contact with foreign advisers, and resented, according to U.S. intelligence, "any reference made in his presence to Islam as a bulwark against communism or as a unifying force."[51]

In 1955, Afghanistan became the first target of Premier Nikita Khrushchev's "economic offensive," the Soviet Union's first venture in foreign aid. Over $100 million in credits to Afghanistan financed a fleet of taxis and buses and paid Soviet engineers to construct airports, a cement factory, a mechanized bakery, a five-lane highway from the Soviet border to Kabul, and, of course, dams. The Soviets constructed the Jalalabad dam and canal and organized a river development scheme for the Amu Darya River. By the 1960s, Afghanistan had Soviet, Chinese, and West German dam projects underway. It was receiving one of the highest levels of development aid per capita of any nation in the world. *U.S. News and World Report* described it as a "strange kind of cold war," fought with money and technicians instead of spies and bombs. The *Atlantic* called it a "show window for competitive coexistence."[52] Publicly, U.S. officials said this was the kind of Cold War they wanted, just a chance to show what the different systems could do in a neutral contest.

Afghanistan had become a new kind of buffer, a neutral arena for a tournament of modernization. James A. Michener toured Afghanistan in 1955 and assessed the price and the stakes of the developmental contest. The turbulent Helmand "symbolize[d] the wild freedom of Afghanistan," and he regretted "that such a river must be brought under control."[53] Historians have observed that novels, films, and Broadway musicals validated modernization by associating it with mythic conventions in which an American overcomes Asian hostility by a display of competence.[54] In *Caravans*, his 1963 novel of Afghanistan, Michener invites readers to choose between futures imagined by two characters: Nur Mohammed, religious, proud, and suspicious of change, and Nazrullah, a foreign-educated expert, impatient, outspoken, and eager for help from the Americans if possible, the Soviets if necessary. Nazrullah was an engineer, damming the Helmand with boulders blasted from a nearby mountain. "Each day we must throw similar rocks into the human river of Afghanistan," he tells the American narrator. "Here a school, there a road, down in the gorge a dam. So far, our human river isn't aware that it's been touched. But we shall never halt until we've modified it completely."[55]

Competition altered the significance, but not the fortunes, of the Helmand project in the 1960s. Launching the "Development Decade," John F. Kennedy determined not only to surpass Soviet initiatives but to demonstrate the superiority of American methods of development. Since the superpowers were offering similar kinds of aid, distinctions were not easily made, but catastrophic crop failures in the Soviet Union and China in 1959 and 1960 clarified the difference. "Wherever communism goes, hunger follows," Secretary of State Dean Rusk declared in 1962. Famine in China and North Vietnam proved that the "humane and pragmatic methods of free men are not merely the right way, morally, to develop an underdeveloped country; they are technically the efficient way." Kennedy characteristically linked the new policy to the rejuvenation of the United States and the world, calling for a "scientific revolution" in agriculture that would engage the energies of "a new generation of young people." Diplomats and aid officials carried the message that free men ate better. The presidential emissary Averell Harriman, sent to Kabul in 1965, complimented Afghan officials on the new Soviet factories but observed that the real measure of modernity was the ability to grow food. The Soviets could not, he explained, "due to character of farm work which requires hardworking individuals with personal stake in operation, rather than hourly paid factory hands paced by machine."[56]

Evidence for the efficiency of American techniques was scarce in the Helmand Valley. The burden of American loans for the project and the absence of tangible returns was creating, according to the *New York Times*, "a dangerous strain on both the Afghan economy and the nation's morale" which "may have unwittingly and indirectly contributed to driving Afghanistan into Russian arms."[57] Waterlogging had advanced in the Shamalan area to the point that structural foundations were giving way; mosques and houses were crumbling into the growing bog. In the artificial oases, the problem was worse. An impermeable crust of conglomerate underlay the Marja and Nad-i-Ali tracts, intensifying both waterlogging and salinization. The remedy—a system of discharge channels leading to deep-bore drains—would remove 10 percent of the re-claimed land from cultivation. A 1965 study revealed that crop yields per acre had actually dropped since the dams were built, sharply in areas already cultivated but evident even in areas reclaimed from the desert. Withdrawing support from HAVA was impossible. "With this project," the U.S. ambassador noted, "the American reputation in Afghanistan is completely linked."[58] For reasons of credibility alone the United States kept pouring money in, even though by 1965 it was clear the project was failing. Diplomats complained that the reputation of the United States hung on "a strip of concrete," but there was no going back. Afghanistan was an economic Korea, but Helmand was an economic Vietnam, a quagmire that consumed money and resources without the possibility of success, all to avoid making failure obvious.

Revisions in modernization theory reinforced the new emphasis on agriculture and the urgency of changing strategy in the Helmand. Dual economy theory, positing a division of each economy into a self-propelling modern industrial sector and a retrograde but vitally important agricultural sector, gained the attention of policy makers in the early 1960s. "Agricultural development is vastly more important in modernizing a society than we used to think," Rostow noted. Agriculture was "a system" like industry, and modernizing it required "that the skills of organization developed in the modern urban sectors of the society be brought systematically into play around the life of a farmer." Development was still fundamentally a problem of scarcity, but, while the Emkayans had filled voids with water and power, the U.S. Agency for International Development (USAID) sought to build reservoirs of organization, talent, and mentality. Rejuvenating Afghan agriculture, aid officials believed, would require "a revolution in mental concepts."[59]

The Kennedy and Johnson administrations renewed the U.S. commitment to HAVA with a fresh infusion of funds and initiatives, raising the annual aid disbursement from $16 million to $40 million annually. The "green revolution" approach pioneered by the Rockefeller Foundation would bring a new organizational system into play around the farmer. In 1967, USAID and the royal government imported 170 tons of the experimental dwarf wheat developed by Norman Borlaug in Mexico. The high-yield seed, together with chemical fertilizers and tightly controlled irrigation, was expected to produce grain surpluses that would be distributed through new marketing and credit arrangements. Resettlement subsidies had paid off by the mid-1960s, and the Helmand Val-

Modernization meant creating orderly landscapes such as the one pictured in the foreground, over which authority could be exercised. Yet Afghanistan's cultivated expanses produced less wealth than its uncharted mountainous highlands, seen here in the distance, where nomadic shepherds fiercely guarded their autonomy. (Reprinted from U.S. Operations Mission to Afghanistan, *Afghanistan Builds on an Ancient Civilization,* 1960.)

ley was beginning to have a lived-in look. The large corporate and state farms had vanished, and nearly all of the land that could successfully be farmed was privately held, much of it by smallholders. Legal titles were still clouded by HAVA's inattention to land surveys, but the settlers had nonetheless sculpted wide tracts of empty land into irregular fifteen-acre parcels divided by meandering juis, the tree-lined canals that served as boundary, water source, and orchard for each farm.[60]

Unfortunately, the juis system proved incompatible with the new plans. The small, hilly, picturesquely misshapen fields contributed to runoff and drainage problems and prevented the regular, measured applications of water, chemicals, and machine cultivation necessary for modern agriculture. A green revolution would require, in effect, a land reform in reverse: merging small holdings into large level fields divided at regular intervals by laterals running from control gates on the main canals. As the wheat improvement program got underway, a team of

U.S. Department of Agriculture advisers proposed that HAVA remove all of the resettled families, "level the whole area with bulldozers," and then redistribute property "in large, uniform, smooth land plots."[61] HAVA adopted the land preparation scheme, but implementation proved difficult. Farmers objected to the removal of trees, which had economic value and prevented wind erosion, but they objected chiefly to the vagueness of HAVA's assurances. HAVA itself acknowledged, as bulldozing proceeded, that questions of what to do with the population while the land was being prepared, how to redistribute the land after completion, and whether to charge landowners for improvements were "yet to be worked out." When farmers "met the bulldozers with rifles," according to a USAID report, it presented a "very real constraint" that "consumed most of the time of the American and Afghan staffs in the Valley throughout the 1960s."[62]

The valley's unrest coincided with Afghanistan's brief experiment with political liberalization. Daoud stepped down in 1963, and the monarchy issued a constitution permitting an independent legislature and government ministries. The economy remained under central guidance. Political parties were banned, and the king continued to control the army and maintain a paternal supervision over government, but high ministerial posts went for the first time to persons outside the royal family. Laws requiring women to wear the burka were lifted (although custom maintained the practice in much of the country), and restrictions on speech and assembly were eased. In Kabul, an energetic student and café politics emerged, with daily street demonstrations by socialist, Maoist, and liberal factions, while outside of the capital dissent coalesced around Islamic mullahs who articulated, according to U.S. embassy officials, "latent dissatisfaction with the low level of economic development and progress in the Afghan hinterland." In the partyless parliament, ethnic politics took precedence as minority representatives attacked Pashtun privileges while the majority defended them.[63] Legislative deadlock, the stalling modernization drive, and the growing burden of external debt fed perceptions of official ineptitude. The government of Prime Minister Mohammad Maiwandwal, which initiated the wheat improvement effort, needed modernization to produce tangible results.

By 1969, the new grains had spread to a modest 300,000 acres, leading to expectations of an approaching "yield takeoff," but the 1971 El Niño drought destroyed much of the crop. Monsoon rains failed through 1973, reducing the Helmand to a rivulet. In 1971, the Arghandab reservoir dried up completely, a possibility not foreseen by planners. With the coming of détente in 1970, levels of aid from both the United States and the Soviet Union dropped sharply. The vision of prosperous, irrigation-fed farms luring nomads into their green embrace proved beyond HAVA's grasp. Wheat yields were among the lowest in the world, four bushels an acre (Iowa farms produced 180); farm incomes in the valley were below average for Afghanistan and declining. State Department officials found it difficult to measure the magnitude of the economic crisis "in Afghanistan where there are no statistics," but student strikes and the suspension of parliament pointed to a "creeping crisis" in mid-1972. "The food crisis," the embassy reported, "seems to have been the real clincher for which neither the King nor his government were prepared."[64] In July 1973, military units loyal to Mohammed Daoud deposed the king, who was vacationing in Europe, and terminated both the monarchy and the constitution. U.S. involvement in HAVA was scheduled to end in July 1974, and USAID officials strenuously opposed suggestions that it be renewed. Nonetheless, when Henry Kissinger visited Kabul in February, Daoud described the Helmand Valley as an "unfinished symphony" and urged the United States not to abandon it.[65] Kissinger relented. Land reclamation officers remained with the project, while making little progress against its persistent problems, until the pro-Soviet Khalq party seized power in 1978.

Soviet economic development also failed to create a stable, modernizing social class. The Khalq was not broadly enough based to hold onto authority unaided. Against the threat of takeover by an Islamic party, the Soviet Union launched the invasion of 1979. During the Soviet war, both sides found ways to make use of the Helmand Valley's infrastructure. In early 1980, according to M. Hassan Kakar, "about a hundred prisoners" of the Khalq "were thrown out of airplanes into the Arghandab reservoir." The project's concrete water channels provided cover for the anti-Soviet Mujaheddin fighters, and its broken terrain was the site of intense fighting between the resistance and Soviet forces and among ethnic factions after the Soviets withdrew in 1988. The warriors felled trees, smashed irrigation canals, and planted mines throughout the fields and orchards, driving the population into refugee camps in Pakistan.[66] The Taliban movement began here in 1994 as an alliance of Pashtun clans supported with arms and money from across the Durand Line. Even after the capture of Kabul in 1996, Kandahar remained the Taliban capital. The Helmand Valley provided the new regime's chief source of revenue. The opium poppy grows well in dry climates and in alkaline and saline soils. In 2000, according to the United Nations Drug Control Programme, the Helmand Valley produced 39 percent of the world's heroin.[67] During its five years in power, the Taliban government invested in the dams and finished one project begun but not completed by the Americans: linking the Kajakai Dam's hydroelectric plant to the city of Kandahar. Work was finished in early 2001, just a few months before American bombers destroyed the plant.[68]

Official and unofficial postmortems identified misperceptions at the root of the project's failures. Lloyd Baron, an economist given access to the U.S. aid mission's records in the 1970s, noted a "development myopia" that identified water scarcity as the sole obstacle to agricultural abundance. Planners subordinated complex social and political problems within the more manageable engineering problem of overcoming the water constraint. An official USAID review in 1983 concluded that the project suffered from a commitment/leverage paradox. The perception that HAVA was a "donor project" relieved the Afghan government of ultimate responsibility and left the United States without influence to demand corrective steps.[69]

The ongoing critique of modernization theory furnishes a broader context for these conceptual flaws. James C. Scott explains that the "high modernist" experiments of the mid-twentieth century were founded on a schematic view of the human and natural world that failed to account for the full range of variation—in motivations, climate, effects ("*even a 20 percent margin of error*"), and human ingenuity—actually encountered. The project's human subjects were rendered as productive units, "abstract citizens" whose motives conformed to the goals of the planner. "Any anthropologist could have predicted with confidence," Arnold Fletcher observed in 1965, "that the happy notion of settling Afghan nomads on the reclaimed lands would not work out."[70] Nonetheless, that prediction was not made or, if made, not listened to, just as two years later HAVA failed to anticipate settlers' unsurprising objection to being turned off the land so their homes could be bulldozed.

The goals and effects of the project were never viewed outside the distorting mirror of modernization theory. Pastoralists produced the country's primary export and most of its foreign exchange revenue, and yet HAVA's plan to convert them into wheat farmers was never seriously questioned. The outcomes that were hoped for—tax earnings, political stability, creation of a middle class, resolution of the Pushtunistan issue, credibility, and legitimacy—were seen as concomitants of eventual developmental success rather than as goals to be pursued directly. Precautionary moves were easily brushed aside by the same assurance that time and effort would bring improvement. Belief in development imposes, according to Gilbert Rist, a "social constraint" on the expression of shared doubts.[71]

If illusions doomed the project, they also created and sustained it. HAVA's evolutionary advantage was an ability to take on the protective coloration of a succession of modernizing myths. The disastrous effects of dam building were visible in 1949 and only became more obvious as the project grew. But, camouflaged by dreams of Pashtun ascendancy and American influence, HAVA was as resilient as modernization theory itself, able to survive repeated debunkings while shedding the blame and the memory of failure. Proponents of a fresh nation-building venture in Afghanistan, unaware of the results of the last one, have resurrected its imaginings. Supporters justify development aid to the new Pashtun-led government in Kabul as a form of international social control. It will provide a buffer against terrorism and "prevent future Osama bin Ladens from arising."[72] The centerpiece of the modernization effort, a writer for the *New York Times* suggests, should be "dams to provide water for irrigation."[73]

Notes

Acknowledgments: This essay was researched and written between the beginning of the bombing campaign in late September and the mopping up of Taliban resistance around Tora Bora in early December 2001. Like many colleagues, I found myself called upon, without benefit of expertise, to place the war in a historical context. The lecture that became this essay was based on materials found in the Indiana University Library and online and in a few archival documents sent by friends. This is a preliminary study that I hope will inspire additional research on the history of the United States in Afghanistan. I am grateful to Lou Malcomb and the staff of the Government Publications Department of the Indiana University Library, Melvyn Leffler, Andrew Rotter, and Michael Latham for helpful comments; to David Ekbladh for his contribution of documents; and to Alison Lefkovitz for research assistance.

1. Mildred Caudill, *Helmand-Arghandab Valley, Yesterday, Today, Tomorrow* (Lashkar Gah, 1969), 55–59; Hafizullah Emadi, *State, Revolution, and Superpowers in Afghanistan* (New York, 1990), 41. Sophocles quoted in Arnold J. Toynbee, *Between Oxus and Jumna* (New York, 1961), 12; *ibid.*, 67–68.

2. Louis Dupree, "Afghanistan, the Canny Neutral," *Nation*, Sept. 21, 1964, p. 135.

3. Harry S. Truman, inaugural address, Jan. 20, 1949, in *Public Papers of the Presidents, Harry S. Truman, 1949: Containing the Public Messages, Speeches, and Statements of the President, January 1 to December 31, 1949* (Washington, 1964), 114–15. "Point IV," *Fortune* (Feb. 1950), 88. Henry A. Byroade, "The World's Colonies and Ex-Colonies: A Challenge to America," *Department of State Bulletin*, Nov. 16, 1953, p. 655. Jawaharlal Nehru, *The Discovery of India* (New York, 1960), 393.

4. On the history of development ideas, see H. W. Arndt, *Economic Development: The History of an Idea* (Chicago, 1987); Gerald M. Meier and Dudley Seers, eds., *Pioneers in Development* (New York, 1984); M. P. Cowen and R. W. Shenton, *Doctrines of Development* (New York, 1996); Nick Cullather, "Development Doctrine and Modernization Theory," in *Encyclopedia of American Foreign Policy*, ed. Alexander DeConde, Richard Dean Burns, and Fredrik Logevall (3 vols., New York, 2002), I, 477–91. On development as discourse, see Arturo Escobar, *Encountering Development: The Making and Unmaking of the Third World* (Princeton, 1995); and Tim Mitchell, "America's Egypt: Discourse of the Development Industry," *Middle East Report*, 169 (March–April 1991), 18–34. On the social sciences and modernization theory, see Robert A. Packenham, *Liberal America and the Third World: Political Development Ideas in Foreign Aid and Social Science* (Princeton, 1973); Nils Gilman, "Paving the World with Good Intentions: The Genesis of Modernization Theory, 1945–1965" (Ph.D. diss., University of California, Berkeley, 2001); Frederick Cooper and Randall Packard, eds., *International Development and the Social Sciences: Essays on the History and Politics of Knowledge* (Berkeley, 1997); and Christopher Simpson, ed., *Universities and Empire: Money, Politics, and the Social Sciences during the Cold War* (New York, 1998).

5. Edward Shils, "Political Development in the New States," *Comparative Studies in Society and History*, 2 (April 1960), 265. Clifford Geertz, *The Interpretation of Cultures* (New York, 1973), 243.

6. James Ferguson, *The Anti-Politics Machine: Development, Depoliticization, and Bureaucratic Power in the Third World* (New York, 1990), 254–56; see also Michael E. Latham, *Modernization as Ideology: American Social Science and "Nation Building" in the Kennedy Era* (Chapel Hill, 2000), 181.

7. Michael Latham, "Introduction: Modernization Theory, International History, and the Global Cold War," in *Staging Growth*, ed. David Engerman et al. (Boston, forthcoming, 2002); Akhil Gupta, *Postcolonial Developments: Agriculture in the Making of Modern India* (Durham, 1998), 40–42.

8. Lord George N. Curzon quoted in Cuthbert Collin Davies, *The Problem of the North-West Frontier, 1890–1908* (Cambridge, 1932), 153. Defining the Pashtun threat in the absence of reliable linguistic or pigmentary markers was a vital strategic and scientific undertaking. A summary of the early ethnographic work is contained in John Cowles Prichard, *Researches into the Physical History of Mankind* (4 vols., London, 1844), IV, 81–91; see also H. G. Raverty, "The Independent Afghan or Patan Tribes," *Imperial and Asiatic Quarterly Review and Oriental and Colonial Review*, 7 (1894), 312–26; R. C. Temple, "Remarks on the Afghans Found along the Route of the Tal Chotiali Field Force in the Spring of 1879," *Journal of the Asiatic Society of Bengal*, 49 (no. 1, 1880), 91–106; and H. W. Bellew, *The Races of Afghanistan: Being a Brief Account of the Principal Nations Inhabiting That Country*

(Calcutta, 1880). See also Conrad Schetter, "The Chimera of Ethnicity in Afghanistan," *Neue Zürcher Zeitung*, Oct. 31, 2001 <http://www.nzz.ch/english/background/2001/10/31_afghanistan.html> (Nov. 9, 2001). On the importance of ethnology to the colonial mission, see Gyan Prakash, *Another Reason: Science and the Imagination of Modern India* (Princeton, 1999), 26–30.

9. George McMunn, *Afghanistan from Darius to Amanullah* (London, 1929), 225–28; Sultana Afroz, "Afghanistan in U.S.-Pakistan Relations, 1947–1960," *Central Asian Survey*, 8 (no. 2, 1989), 133.

10. Davies, *Problem of the North-West Frontier*, 162–63; C. L. Sulzberger, "Nomads Swarming over Khyber Pass," *New York Times*, April 24, 1950, p. 6. On the British construction of "Afghanistan," see Nigel J. R. Allan, "Defining Place and People in Afghanistan," *Post-Soviet Geography and Economics*, 41 (no. 8, 2001), 545–60.

11. W. K. Fraser-Tytler, *Afghanistan: A Study of Political Developments in Central and Southern Asia* (London, 1953), 332. British officials located the Mohammadzai's homeland in Hastnagar, now in Pakistan: India Army, General Staff, *A Dictionary of the Pathan Tribes* (Calcutta, 1910), 34.

12. J. G. Elliott, *The Frontier, 1839–1947* (London, 1968), 53. Afghan nationalists believed Britain had secretly annexed Afghanistan by supporting the Mohammadzai, leading the constitutionalist Young Afghan movement to assassinate both the king, Nadir Shah, and his brother, Mohammad Aziz, who was ambassador to Germany. In 1933 an attempt was also made on the British embassy. Hasan Kakar, "Trends in Modern Afghan History," in *Afghanistan in the 1970s*, ed. Louis Dupree and Linette Albert (New York, 1974), 31; McMunn, *Afghanistan from Darius to Amanullah*, 228.

13. Akbar S. Ahmend, "An Aspect of the Colonial Encounter in the North-West Frontier Province," *Asian Affairs*, 9 (Oct. 1978), 319–27. Rudyard Kipling, *The Man Who Would Be King* (1891), in *The One Volume Kipling* (New York, 1932), 735. Olaf Caroe, *The Pathans, 550 B.C.–A.D. 1957* (Karachi, 1958), 429–30. In 1962, the anthropologist Louis Dupree tried a free association experiment on students at Kabul University using the terms "Afghanistan," "United States," etc. Students identified Afghanistan and the United States as "white" countries, Pakistan and India as "black-skinned." Louis Dupree, "Landlocked Images: Snap Responses to an Informal Questionnaire," *American Universities Field Staff Reports, South Asia Series*, 6 (June 1962), 51–73.

14. Arnold Fletcher, *Afghanistan: Highway of Conquest* (Ithaca, 1965), 245. Alfred Janata, "Afghanistan: The Ethnic Dimension," in *The Cultural Basis of Afghan Nationalism*, ed. Ewan W. Anderson and Nancy Hatch Dupree (New York, 1990), 62.

15. The campaign against the Kuhestani Tajiks north of Kabul was particularly severe. Prisoners were executed by being blown from the mouths of cannon. "Eleven Afghans Blown from Guns at Kabul," *New York Times*, April 6, 1930, p. 8; "Afghan Revolt Reported," *ibid.*, Nov. 21, 1932, p. 7; Vladimir Cervin, "Problems in the Integration of the Afghan Nation," *Middle East Journal*, 6 (Autumn 1952), 407; Bhalwant Bhaneja, *Afghanistan: Political Modernization of a Mountain Kingdom* (New Delhi, 1973), 20.

16. Louis Dupree, "A Note on Afghanistan," *American Universities Field Staff Reports, South Asia Series*, 4 (Aug. 1960), 13. Afghanistan was the type of "illegible" state described by James C. Scott, *Seeing like a State* (New Haven, 1998), 77–78.

17. Rosita Forbes, "Afghan Dictator," *Literary Digest*, Oct. 16, 1937, p. 29.

18. Donald N. Wilber, ed., *Afghanistan* (New Haven, 1956), 238–43.

19. Lawrence Durrell, *Prospero's Cell* (New York, 1996), 72.

20. "Karakul Sheep," *Life*, July 16, 1945, pp. 65–68; Peter G. Franck, "Problems of Economic Development in Afghanistan," *Middle East Journal*, 3 (July 1949), 302. Abdul Haj Kayoumy, "Monopoly Pricing of Afghan Karakul in International Markets," *Journal of Political Economy*, 77 (March–April 1969), 219–37; Ali Mohammed, "Karakul as the Most Important Article of Afghan Trade," *Afghanistan* (Kabul), 4 (Dec. 1949), 48–53. The "dollar gap" was a global shortage of dollar reserves and dollar earnings that threatened to stifle economic recovery and international trade. See William S. Borden, *The Pacific Alliance: United States Foreign Economic Policy and Japanese Trade Recovery, 1947–1955* (Madison, 1984).

21. Najibullah Khan, "Speech Delivered over the Radio," *Afghanistan* (Kabul), 3 (April–June 1948), 13.

22. Ian Stephens, *Horned Moon* (Bloomington, 1955), 263. See the series of reports by Louis Dupree, "'Pushtunistan': The Problem and Its Larger Implications," *American Universities Field Staff Reports, South Asia Series*, 5 (Nov.–Dec. 1961), 19–51.

23. S. M. M. Quereshi, "Pakhtunistan: The Frontier Dispute between Afghanistan and Pakistan," *Pacific Affairs*, 39 (Spring–Summer 1966), 99–144; on the U.S. position, see Dennis Kux, *The United States and Pakistan, 1947–2000* (Baltimore, 2000), 42–43, 78; and Afroz, "Afghanistan in U.S.-Pakistan Relations," 138–40.

24. Paul Overby, *Holy Blood: An Inside View of the Afghan War* (Westport, 1993), 30.

25. Louis Dupree, "An Informal Talk with Prime Minister Daoud," Sept. 13, 1959, *American Universities Field Staff Reports, South Asia Series*, 3 (Sept. 1959), 18.

26. Jawaharlal Nehru, "Speech at the Opening of the Nangal Canal," July 8, 1954, in *Jawaharlal Nehru's Speeches* (4 vols., Delhi, 1958), III, 353.

27. On the political uses to which dams have been put, see Ann Danaiya Usher, *Dams as Aid: A Political Anatomy of Nordic Development Thinking* (New York, 1997). Morarji Desai quoted in Arundhati Roy, *The Cost of Living* (New York, 1999), 13.

28. Robert De Roos, "He Changes the Face of the Earth," *Collier's*, Aug. 2, 1952, pp. 28–30.

29. A. H. H. Abidi, "Irano-Afghan Dispute over the Helmand Waters," *International Studies* (New Delhi), 16 (July 1977), 358–59; Fraser-Tytler, *Afghanistan*, 8.

30. Aloys Arthur Michel, *The Kabul, Kunduz, and Helmand Valleys and the National Economy of Afghanistan: A Study of Regional Resources and the Comparative Advantages of Development* (Washington, 1959), 153.

31. Scientists believe the ecological effects of large dams may include global climate change, seismic disturbances, and a quickening of the earth's rotation; for an inventory of environmental effects, see Egil Skofteland, *Freshwater Resources: Environmental Education Module* (Paris, 1995); France Bequette, "Large Dams," UNESCO *Courier*, 50 (March 1997), 44–46; Robert S. Divine, "The Trouble with Dams," *Atlantic Monthly* (Aug. 1995), 64–74; and Peter Coles, "Large Dams—The End of an Era," UNESCO *Courier*, 53 (April 2000), 10–11. Roy, *Cost of Living*, 68.

32. Vandana Shiva, *The Violence of the Green Revolution* (London, 1997), 121–39. Michel, *Kabul, Kunduz, and Helmand Valleys and the National Economy of Afghanistan*, 152–53.

33. Gilbert Rist, *The History of Development: From Western Origins to Global Faith*, trans. Patrick Camiller (New York, 1997), 70–75. Harry S. Truman, "Remarks to the American Society of Civil Engineers," Nov. 2, 1949, *Public Papers of the Presidents, Harry S. Truman, 1949*, 547.

34. Truman quoted in Alonzo L. Hamby, *Liberalism and Its Challengers: FDR to Reagan* (New York, 1985), 72–73. Arthur M. Schlesinger, *The Vital Center: The Politics of Freedom* (London, 1970), 233.

35. On the Jordan Valley project, see "Press Conference: Statement by the Secretary," *Department of State Bulletin*, Nov. 30, 1953, p. 750; and "Eric Johnston Leaves on Mission to Near East," *ibid.*, Oct. 26, 1953, p. 553. David Ekbladh, "A Workshop for the World: Modernization as a Tool in U.S. Foreign Relations in Asia, 1914–1974" (Ph.D. diss., Columbia University, 2002); Lloyd C. Gardner, *Pay Any Price: Lyndon Johnson and the Wars for Vietnam* (Chicago, 1995), 191.

36. C. L. Sulzberger, "Afghan Shah Asks World Bank Loan," *New York Times*, April 20, 1950, p. 15; Cynthia Clapp-Wincek and Emily Baldwin, *The Helmand Valley Project in Afghanistan* (Washington, 1983). On the soil survey refusal, see Lloyd Baron, "Sector Analysis—Helmand Arghandab Valley Region: An Analysis," typescript, Feb. 1973, p. 15 (Library of Congress, Washington, D.C.). On Point IV, see Department of State, International Cooperation Administration, *Fact Sheet: Mutual Security in Action, Afghanistan* (Washington, 1959).

37. Wilber, ed., *Afghanistan*, 169. Emadi, *State, Revolution, and Superpowers in Afghanistan*, 53. Nake M. Kamreny, *Peaceful Competition in Afghanistan: American and Soviet Models for Economic Aid* (Washington, 1969), 29.

38. Senate, U.S. Congress, Special Committee to Study the Foreign Aid Program, *South Asia: Report on U.S. Foreign Assistance Programs*, 85 Cong., 1 sess., March 1957, p. 23. Baron, "Sector Analysis," 17, 31.

39. Ira Moore Stevens and K. Tarzi, *Economics of Agricultural Production in Helmand Valley, Afghanistan* (Denver, 1965), 30, 38.

40. Department of State, "Elements of U.S. Policy toward Afghanistan," March 27, 1962, p. 17, *Declassified Documents Reference System* (microfiche, Carrollton Press, 1978), fiche 65B; see also Clapp-Wincek and Baldwin, *Helmand Valley Project*, 5. Department of State, "Elements of U.S. Policy toward Afghanistan," 17. Max Millikan and Walt W. Rostow, "Notes on Foreign Economic Policy," May 21, 1954, in *Universities and Empire*, ed. Simpson, 41.

41. On the importance of psychology in modernization thinking, see Ellen Herman, *The Romance of American Psychology* (Berkeley, 1995), 136–48. Dupree, "Informal Talk with Prime Minister Daoud," 19.

42. Dupree, "Afghanistan, the Canny Neutral," 134–37. Dupree, "Informal Talk with Prime Minister Daoud," 4; State Department, Bureau of Intelligence and Research, "Biographic Report: Visit of Afghanistan's Prime Minister Sardar Mohammad Daoud," June 13, 1958, *Declassified Documents Reference System* (microfiche, Carrollton Press, 1996), fiche 11. National Security Council, "Progress Report on South Asia," July 24, 1957, *Foreign Relations of the United States, 1955–1957* (25 vols., Washington, 1985–1990), XIII, 49.

43. Leon Poullada described it as "a government of, by, and for Pashtun": Leon Poullada, "The Search for National Unity," in *Afghanistan in the 1970s*, ed. Dupree

and Albert, 40. Leon B. Poullada, *The Pushtun Role in the Afghan Political System* (New York, 1970), 22. Angus C. Ward to Department of State, Dec. 14, 1955, *Foreign Relations of the United States, 1955–1957*, VIII, 204.

44. Wilber, ed., *Afghanistan*, 103. Poullada, "Search for National Unity," 44.

45. John Foster Dulles to U.S. Embassy in Pakistan, July 12, 1955, *Foreign Relations of the United States, 1955–1957*, VIII, 189. Editorial note, *ibid.*, VIII, 202.

46. For proposed settlement figures, see Franck, "Problems of Economic Development in Afghanistan," 425. Clapp-Wincek and Baldwin, *Helmand Valley Project*, 8; "Export-Import Bank Loan to Afghanistan," *Department of State Bulletin*, May 31, 1954, p. 836; Tudor Engineering Company, *Report on Development of Helmand Valley Afghanistan* (Washington, 1956), 16, 90; Richard Tapper, "Nomadism in Modern Afghanistan," in *Afghanistan in the 1970s*, ed. Dupree and Albert, 126–43; Cervin, "Problems in the Integration of the Afghan Nation," 400–416.

47. James W. Spain, *The Way of the Pathans* (Karachi, 1962), 126.

48. Baron, "Sector Analysis," 18.

49. Ritchie Calder, "Hope of Millions," *Nation*, Aug. 1, 1953, pp. 87–89; Wilber, ed., *Afghanistan*, 222. Emadi, *State, Revolution, and Superpowers in Afghanistan*, 41.

50. Dana Reynolds, "Utilizing Religious Principles and Leadership in Rural Improvement," [1962], box 125, John H. Ohly Papers (Harry S. Truman Library, Independence, Mo.).

51. National Security Council, "Progress Report on NSC 5409," Nov. 28, 1956, *Foreign Relations of the United States, 1955–1957*, VIII, 15. State Department, Bureau of Intelligence and Research, "Biographic Report . . . Daoud."

52. Robert J. McMahon, "The Illusion of Vulnerability: American Reassessments of the Soviet Threat, 1955–56," *International History Review*, 18 (Aug. 1996), 591–619. "Soviet-Afghan Communique," *Pravda*, April 30, 1965, in *Current Digest of the Soviet Press*, May 19, 1965, p. 26. Many of the other projects were as poorly conceived as the Helmand scheme. In the early 1970s, West Germany built a hydroelectric dam at Mahipar that, because of low rainfall, held water only four months a year. A 1973 study concluded that it "may never be productive." Marvin Brandt, "Recent Economic Development," in *Afghanistan in the 1970s*, ed. Dupree and Albert, 103. *Ibid.*, 99. "Strange Kind of Cold War," *U.S. News and World Report*, Nov. 15, 1957, p. 160; "Atlantic Report: Afghanistan," *Atlantic* (Oct. 1962), 26.

53. James A. Michener, *Caravans* (New York, 1963), 161; see also James A. Michener, "Afghanistan: Domain of the Fierce and the Free," *Reader's Digest* (Nov. 1955), 161–72.

54. Richard Slotkin, *Gunfighter Nation: The Myth of the Frontier in Twentieth Century America* (New York, 1992), 449; James T. Fisher, *Dr. America: The Lives of Thomas A. Dooley, 1927–1961* (Amherst, 1997); Christina Klein, "Musicals and Modernization: Rodgers and Hammerstein's *The King and I*," in *Staging Growth*, ed. Engerman et al.; and Jonathan Nashel, "The Road to Vietnam: Modernization Theory in Fact and Fiction," in *Cold War Constructions*, ed. Christian Appy (Amherst, 2000), 132–54.

55. Michener, *Caravans*, 161.

56. On John F. Kennedy's foreign aid programs, see W. W. Rostow, *Eisenhower, Kennedy, and Foreign Aid* (Austin, 1985); and Stephen G. Rabe, "Controlling Revolutions: Latin America, the Alliance for Progress, and Cold War Anti-Communism,"

in *Kennedy's Quest for Victory*, ed. Thomas G. Paterson (New York, 1989), 105–22. Dean Rusk, "The Tragedy of Cuba," *Vital Speeches of the Day*, Feb. 15, 1962, p. 259. J. F. Kennedy, "Statement at the Opening Ceremony of the World Food Congress," June 4, 1963, in *President John F. Kennedy's Office Files, 1961–1963*, ed. Paul Kesaris and Robert E. Lester (microfilm, 103 reels, University Publications of America, 1989), Part 1, reel 11, frame 1018. Embassy Afghanistan to Department of State, March 3, 1965, *Foreign Relations of the United States, 1964–1968* (34 vols., Washington, 1992–2001), XXV, 1051.

57. Peggy Streit and Pierre Streit, "Lesson in Foreign Aid Policy," *New York Times Magazine*, March 18, 1956, p. 56. The loan repayment problem was worsening by the 1960s; see Fletcher, *Afghanistan*, 268.

58. Baron, "Sector Analysis," 55. Stevens and Tarzi, *Economics of Agricultural Production in Helmand Valley*, 29. Department of State, "Elements of U.S. Policy toward Afghanistan."

59. Gustav Ranis, "A Theory of Economic Development," *American Economic Review*, 51 (Sept. 1961), 533–65; Dale W. Jorgensen, "The Development of a Dual Economy," *Economic Journal*, 66 (June 1961), 309–34. W. W. Rostow, "Some Lessons of Economic Development since the War," *Department of State Bulletin*, Nov. 9, 1964, pp. 664–65; see also W. W. Rostow, *View from the Seventh Floor* (New York, 1964), 124–31. Morrison Knudsen left in 1960, turning its operations over to USAID; Baron, "Sector Analysis," 52.

60. "Tangible Tokens," *Time*, April 7, 1967, p. 18. Lester R. Brown, *Seeds of Change: The Green Revolution and Development in the 1970s* (New York, 1970), 19. Public Administration Service, *A Final Report on the Land Inventory Project of Afghanistan, January 1972* (Chicago, 1972), 9; Baron, "Sector Analysis," 44.

61. Proposals quoted in Clapp-Wincek and Baldwin, *Helmand Valley Project*, 5; and Baron, "Sector Analysis," 50. See also Shafie Rahel, ed., *The Kabul Times Annual, 1970* (Kabul, 1970), 359.

62. Baron, "Sector Analysis," 53. USAID report quoted in Clapp-Wincek and Baldwin, *Helmand Valley Project*, 5.

63. Louis Dupree, "The Decade of Daoud Ends," *American Universities Field Staff Reports, South Asia Series*, 7 (May 1963), 7. U.S. Embassy Kabul to Department of State, "Afghanistan's Clerical Unrest: A Tentative Assessment," June 24, 1970, in *National Security Archive Electronic Briefing Book No. 59*, ed. William Burr, Oct. 26, 2001 <http://www.gwu.edu/~nsarchiv/NSAEBB/NSAEBB59> (Nov. 8, 2001). Janata, "Afghanistan: The Ethnic Dimension," 62.

64. Baron, "Sector Analysis," 50; Mike Davis, *Late Victorian Holocausts: El Nino Famines and the Making of the Third World* (London, 2001), 244. Kamreny, *Peaceful Competition in Afghanistan*, 36; Clapp-Wincek and Baldwin, *Helmand Valley Project*, 4. Embassy quoted in Robert A. Flaten, "Afghan Politics, the Creeping Crisis," May 31, 1972, in *National Security Archive Electronic Briefing Book No. 59*, ed. Burr.

65. Clapp-Wincek and Baldwin, *Helmand Valley Project*, 6.

66. The misfortunes of the Khalq are analyzed in M. Hassan Kakar, *Afghanistan: The Soviet Invasion and the Afghan Response, 1979–1982* (Berkeley, 1995). *Ibid.*, 203. Ahmed Rashid, *Taliban: Militant Islam, Oil, and Fundamentalism in Central Asia* (New Haven, 2000), 20.

67. Tim Weiner, "With Taliban Gone, Opium Farmers Return to Their Only Cash Crop," *New York Times*, Nov. 26, 2001, p. B1; Christopher Grey-Wilson, *Poppies: A Guide to the Poppy Family in the Wild and in Cultivation* (Portland, 2000), 24; United Nations Drug Control Programme, Afghanistan Programme, *Afghanistan: Annual Opium Poppy Survey 2000* (Islamabad, 2000). Afghanistan produces the bulk of the world's opium, largely as a result of poverty and war. Production has grown steadily since the Soviet invasion, peaking in 1999, when 90,000 hectares were under cultivation. In 2000, the Taliban, seeking international aid and to sell existing stocks at an elevated price, imposed an opium ban, which eliminated cultivation in the Helmand and the principal producing areas in the 2001 growing season. Production resumed in the fall of 2001. United Nations Economic and Social Council, *World Situation with Regard to Illicit Drug Trafficking and Reports of Subsidiary Bodies of the Commission on Narcotic Drugs* (Vienna, 2001).

68. Richard Lloyd Parry, "Campaign against Terrorism: Warning—UN Fears 'Disaster' over Strikes near Huge Dam," *Independent* (London), Nov. 8, 2001, p. 4.

69. Lloyd Baron, "The Water-Supply Constraint: An Evaluation of Irrigation Projects and the Role in the Development of Afghanistan" (Ph.D. diss., McGill University, 1975), 2; Clapp-Wincek and Baldwin, *Helmand Valley Project*.

70. Scott, *Seeing like a State*, 347–49. On humans as productive units, see also C. Douglas Lummis, *Radical Democracy* (Ithaca, 1996), 64. Fletcher, *Afghanistan*, 268.

71. Rist, *History of Development*, 239.

72. Nicholas D. Kristof, "Give the Afghans a Hand," *New York Times*, Dec. 13, 2001, p. A31.

73. M. Ishaq Nadiri, "Rebuilding a Ravaged Land," *ibid.*, Nov. 26, 2001, p. A17.

A Short History of Anti-Americanism and Terrorism

The Turkish Case

Nur Bilge Criss

What causes anti-Americanism and the terrorism sometimes associated with it? How can they be minimized? Nur Bilge Criss finds the history of U.S.-Turkish relations since the 1950s instructive. The two countries have long been allies in the North Atlantic Treaty Organization (NATO), and Turkey has a secular, democratic government. But U.S. affronts to Turkish sovereignty led military and civilian officials as well as leftist radicals to resist American influence. As Turkish politics polarized, some opponents turned to terrorism. To manage the gift and burden of power well and to enhance U.S. and global security, Criss argues, the United States should rein in the urge to unilateralism.

Throughout the past century, anti-Americanism crescendoed and then subsided in rough proportion to the global power projected by the United States. In Turkey, anti-American protests reached a new level of intensity in the late 1960s when U.S. actions challenged Turkey's sovereignty. While subtle acts of resistance came from the military and other government officials, most protests came from ideologically motivated leftists who clashed with equally dogmatic ultranationalists and Islamists. The ensuing battles resulted in the most prolonged era of terrorist violence in modern Turkish history. Thus, anti-Americanism in Turkey can serve as an instructive case study. In this essay I conclude that anti-Americanism stemmed from Turkish efforts to preserve sovereignty as well as from the ideological commitments of the Turkish Left.

Terrorism, the political use of violence to provoke fear, was a different matter. It was reactionary and ethnocentric, concerned with internal conflicts and policies as well as transnational ones. In view of its deep roots and its lethality, some observers suggest that terrorism's causes are irrelevant: Political violence need only be dealt with through punitive legal action. In contrast, in this essay I argue that U.S.-Turkish relations formed part of the context in which terrorism arose and that the history of those relations thus provides cautionary lessons on the sources of anti-Americanism and the terrorism with which it is sometimes associated.

Anti-Westernism in Turkey has differed from that elsewhere in the Middle East. The Turkish republic, as an heir to the Ottoman Empire, has a long tradition of statehood. Although it fought repeated wars against European imperialism from 1911 to 1922, its heartland was never colonized. While Mustafa Kemal Atatürk, the founder of the Turkish republic, was in power (1919–1938), he insisted on independence and sovereignty, but he did not hesitate to seek the "assistance of the Western powers for the peaceful development of Turkey. . . . Modern Turks present an unusual phenomenon—an oriental nation looking to the occident for help in the regeneration of their country."[1] For once, an "oriental" country had the freedom to do so, guided by its age-old foreign policy orientation toward the West. Extremely jealous of its sovereignty, the young republic was careful in not allowing ties to any foreign power to monopolize its foreign policy until the 1950s. Then dependence on the North Atlantic Treaty Organization (NATO) in general and the United States in particular began to cause repercussions within Turkish society.

Sovereignty and Anti-Americanism

When Turkey became a member of NATO in 1952, the end of its military and diplomatic isolation brought new issues of sovereignty to the fore. Turkey regarded NATO as an extension of the United States and put few restraints on American action: "The American way was to be exalted as the model . . . little need was felt to insert stringent qualifications on the scope of U.S. activity in Turkey."[2] In turn, the Americans used their freedom of action in Turkey for purposes other than simply containing communism, such as gathering intelligence from within the Soviet Union.

Throughout the 1960s, friction between the Turkish and American militaries increased. In 1960, when the Soviets forcibly grounded a U-2 aircraft that had taken off from Incirlik Air Force Base, a major diplomatic scandal ensued, involving Turkish compliance in violating Soviet airspace. The Turkish press reported the matter as if Turkey had not been involved, and the Turkish government agreed. On May 8, 1960, the Turkish Foreign Ministry announced that the government had never given permission for a U.S. airplane to make reconnaissance flights from its soil and that Turkey bore no responsibility for flights outside its airspace, other than those by its own aircraft. The implication was that the Turkish government had no knowledge of such reconnaissance flights, though the top echelons of the Turkish general staff probably knew. But on May 13, 1960, the Soviets delivered a diplomatic note to Turkey protesting the use of Turkish territory by a third party for intelligence gathering in the Soviet Union.[3]

The issue of sovereignty arose again in 1965 when an American RB-57 reconnaissance aircraft crashed into the Black Sea. Soviet naval authorities informed Turkey of the crash, but the U.S. military mission insisted on investigating the accident unilaterally. The Turkish intelligence and navy claimed that such an investigation was Turkey's affair. The Americans then tried to force their way to the Black Sea through the Dardanelles. A U.S. destroyer did not acknowledge Turkish warnings and made its way from the Aegean Sea to Ahirkapi, Istanbul, but was stopped there by Turkish naval ships. The Turkish navy recovered the black box of the aircraft, and Turkish military intelligence eventually concluded that the American pilot, while flying in a westerly direction over the Soviet border, had exceeded the safe altitude level, and that the airplane had collapsed.[4]

Later that year the government of Prime Minister Süleyman Demirel banned reconnaissance flights from Turkish territory. But the ban did not prevent another incident in 1967. Maj. Gen. Benjamin "Pony" Evans, chief of the Joint United States Military Mission for Aid to Turkey, his American pilot, and his Turkish interpreter were grounded by the Soviets when their airplane entered Soviet airspace while flying over Turkey's eastern border. The American general claimed that they had been on a cultural reconnaissance trip to observe ancient Armenian ruins. Both the Soviets and the Turks eventually accepted this account, but the general's tenure in Turkey was short-lived.[5]

As a result of these incidents, Turkey began to exercise more control over U.S. installations on Turkish territory. Twice Turkey had occasion to remind the United States that bases on Turkish territory could not be used as military staging areas for activities outside the NATO area as defined in Article 6 of the organization's treaty without the permission of the Turkish government. The first occasion was the 1967 Six-Day War between the Arabs and Israelis, and the other was the Lebanon crisis of 1969. At the time of the Six-Day War, "Prime Minister Süleyman Demirel felt it necessary to announce that interference in the 'internal affairs' of another country was not one of the purposes of the joint U.S.-Turkey bases."[6]

Despite the growing sensitivity to issues of sovereignty, the Turkish government continued to court U.S. involvement. In 1959 Turkey had signed a bilateral agreement with the United States whereby it agreed to deploy intermediate range ballistic missiles, Jupiter (SM-78) missiles that could carry nuclear warheads, on Turkish territory under the Agreement Relating to the Introduction of Modern Weapons into NATO Defense Forces in Turkey. That decision brought Turkey dangerously close to nuclear war. During the Cuban missile crisis of 1962, Turkey became the subject of secret diplomacy and of bargaining between President John F. Kennedy and Soviet premier Nikita Khrushchev. In return for the U.S. promise to remove the Jupiter missiles from Turkey, the Soviets would withdraw their missiles from Cuba. Within ten years of joining NATO, then, Turkish decision makers had inadvertently made their country into a bargaining chip in other powers' negotiations, a position dreaded since the nineteenth century.[7] There was no compelling reason for Turkey to want strategic nuclear missiles on its territory; the risks definitely outweighed the benefits. But Turkish decision makers apparently hoped to increase U.S. strategic dependence on Turkey. Increased aid from the United States might follow at a time when poor harvests and a Europe reluctant to underwrite Turkish public industrial investment programs threatened the ruling Democratic party. Promoting mutual dependence also seemed a way to insure against a possible East-West rapprochement.

Before and after the 1960 military coup, Turkish governments justified the placement of the Jupiters as a NATO issue and distinguished the agreement from bilateral relations between Turkey and the United States. That face-saving discourse, however, did not alter the risk associated with such dangerous liaisons during the Cold War. By 1964 the Soviet embassy in Ankara had leaked information about the U.S.-Soviet bargain. Although the Turkish and American governments denied it, leftists in Turkey believed it wholeheartedly. By the time scholars could verify such a bargain (twenty-five years later), the issue had made its way into a Hollywood movie, *Thirteen Days*.[8] The crisis was over, but the "rumor" of a bargain contributed to the polarization of the Turkish Right and Left over the American presence.

Turkey's relations with the United States continued to deteriorate. During the 1963 Christmas season, Greek Cypriot militants massacred Turkish Cypriots in attempts to scare their compatriots into emigrating from the island. The Turkish government tried to orchestrate pressure by Turkey, Great Britain, and Greece in their legal role as guarantor states of the republic of Cyprus. To put pressure on the parties and as a last resort, Prime Minister Ismet Inönü suggested that Turkey might intervene unilaterally, after which President Lyndon B. Johnson sent him a letter. The Johnson letter cautioned Inönü: If unilateral Turkish action on the island invited a Soviet attack, then NATO was not obligated to defend Turkey. The letter was leaked to the Turkish press. Clearly intended for domestic consumption, it served to put the blame for Turkish inaction in Cyprus elsewhere. Turkey had few means to carry out such action as the Turkish military had no landing vessels. The letter saved Turkey from a probable failure in an action that Inönü had not wanted to engage in.[9] However, its wording brought home the fact that the national security interests of Turkey and of its allies were not necessarily confluent. The Johnson letter was a turning point in the Turkish shift toward a multidimensional foreign policy.

Meanwhile, a social problem in the United States that was totally unrelated to defense issues, increased drug addiction and drug-related crime, gave rise to a political problem between the allies. American diplomats were not able to convince the elected governments, as of 1965, that Turkey should ban cultivation of the opium poppy in the west-central Anatolian plains. Ninety thousand Anatolian families were engaged in opium farming. The Turkish government, which feared both losing votes and appearing unconditionally pro-American, did not respond to American requests. By 1971 reports to the U.S. House and Senate indicated that 80 percent of the illicit drugs in the U.S. were smuggled from Turkey. The U.S. government hoped to stop the problem at the source. After the 1971 Turkish coup, Prime Minister Nihat Erim of the new nonpartisan technocratic government agreed to ban opium cultivation "for humanitarian reasons." The farmers were financially compensated, but they saw the change as economic suicide. In 1974, when Bülent Ecevit was elected prime minister, he decreed that the cultivation of poppies for opium would be permitted in seven provinces. The United States threatened to cut off aid to Turkey, and editorials in the U.S. press suggested bombing the poppy fields in

Turkey. By then drug traffic from the Golden Triangle region (in South-east Asia) to the United States outweighed the illicit trade from Turkey, but the latter seemed a closer and an easier target. Turkey cooperated with the United Nations (UN) and the U.S. Drug Enforcement Administration to develop a control plan that limited cultivation areas. The poppy straw harvesting technique, which eliminated production of the opium gum used in manufacturing heroin, proved effective. Soon after, opium became a nonissue in Turkish-American relations. But for the political Left in Turkey and for many ordinary citizens, this was just another example of harsh U.S. treatment of Turkey as a client state, not an ally.[10]

In 1974 another Cyprus crisis further deteriorated pro-American sentiments. After a coup on the island, the new leader, Nikos Sampson, whom an American scholar has described as an "international terrorist," hoped to rid the island of Turkish Cypriots and to annex Cyprus to Greece. Turkey, Great Britain, and Greece were by treaty the guarantors of the republic of Cyprus. Greece, then ruled by a military junta, supported Sampson. After exhaustive diplomatic efforts to mount a two-power British-Turkish intervention failed, Turkey undertook military operations. In 1975 the U.S. Congress placed an embargo on transferring military equipment to Turkey on the premise that U.S. military equipment was not to be used for non-NATO purposes. Ankara retaliated by suspending all U.S. base operations on Turkish territory. The bases and a reduced number of American personnel remained, but their activities were curtailed. The embargo was lifted in 1978, but the disputes had fed the political Left's anti-American "anti-imperialism." Anti-Americanism, coupled with the mismanagement of dissent by successive Turkish governments, resulted in prolonged domestic terrorism until the 1980 military coup.[11]

Ideologically Motivated Anti-Americanism

In the 1960s the Turkish political system was dominated by two parties: the secularist Republican People's party (RPP), created by Atatürk at the founding of the republic, and the Justice party (JP), a probusiness and anticommunist party dating from the 1950s. The military generally left politics to elected civilians, although there had been a coup in 1960 (to be followed by coups in 1971 and 1980). From 1961 to 1965, Turkey was ruled by coalition governments headed by the RPP leader, Ismet Inönü. In the 1965 and 1969 general elections, the JP won the majority of the popular vote.

In Turkey as elsewhere, the 1960s saw an upsurge in political interest and activity among liberal intellectuals and leftists, including many university students. They called for social justice, land reform, a more equitable distribution of income, and nonalignment, and anti-American and anti–Vietnam War sentiments helped fuel their radicalism. Leftist intellectuals had established the Turkish Labor party (TLP) in 1961, but it never garnered more than 3 percent of the popular vote. The party program advocated socialism through parliamentary democracy. The mere existence of the party, however, aroused the latent fear of communism. In 1963 a member of the right-of-center JP founded the Turkish Association to Combat Communism.[12]

When in 1963 the leader of TLP made public the contents of secret bilateral agreements between Turkey and the United States, the government was obliged to renegotiate them because some clauses were incompatible with Turkish sovereignty. But radicals demanded that Turkey withdraw from NATO altogether. The NATO issue came to a head on April 19, 1966, when the U.S. secretary of state, Dean Rusk, arrived in Turkey to attend the Central Treaty Organization (CENTO) meetings. The debate club of Ankara University's political science faculty held a protest meeting, denouncing NATO and CENTO as opposed to the principles of Turkish independence. When the leftist Türk-Is trade union organized a protest demonstration on behalf of Turkish workers employed on U.S. bases, students and workers for the first time shouted anti-American slogans on Turkish city streets.[13]

Leftist students viewed the JP government of Süleyman Demirel as supporting the "monopolist bourgeoisie," which collaborated with "U.S. imperialism" and subordinated the Turkish economy to it. When the rightists staged demonstrations in 1966 and 1968 to "condemn communism," leftists reacted with demonstrations to "condemn the United States," and they were immediately physically attacked by rightist militants. When the U.S. Sixth Fleet visited Istanbul in 1968, university students protested. Some American sailors were thrown into the Bosporus. And during the ensuing riots, one student was killed by Turkish security forces.[14] This was a defining moment for the Turkish Left and proponents of Third Worldism in Turkey. By 1969, terrorist acts had begun. Leftist militants began sincerely to believe that Turkey was ripe for

Turks protest against the visit of the U.S. Sixth Fleet in Istanbul, July 1968. (Courtesy of Fahri Aral, Istanbul Bilgi University Press.)

A poster depicts the burning of U.S. ambassador Robert Komer's car at the Middle East Technical University in Ankara, 1969. The figure next to Uncle Sam represents members of the Turkish government whom socialists saw as collaborating with the United States. *Bir daha bir daha* (once again) calls for a renewed fight for national independence. (Courtesy of Fahri Aral, Istanbul Bilgi University Press.)

a socialist revolution. Rightist commandos mobilized to fight them. The government could no longer rely on its undermanned security forces, which were also ideologically divided.

The government introduced the religious element into the struggle in an attempt to combat communism. Both leftists and rightists were militantly active on university campuses. Schools training imams (Muslim religious officials), which before 1965 used to be vocational schools, were elevated to the status of secondary schools and by 1973 were made coeducational, although women cannot hold office as imam in the Sunni branch of Islam that prevails in Turkey. An amendment to the National Education Basic Law opened the route for graduates of imam-lycées (high schools) to enter the universities.[15] The government was obviously trying to neutralize leftist militancy in the universities. The new law both increased attendance at religious lycées and imported religious conservatism into higher education as lycée graduates became more numerous and vocal in the universities.

Not only was Atatürk's principle of a unified, secular education based on the positive sciences thereby undone, but the process added fuel to the fire. On February 16, 1969, leftists held a demonstration, "the Mustafa Kemal march against imperialism." The same day the *Bugün* newspaper called the Islamic faithful to mass prayer and cautioned them that guns might explode. Explode they did: Fanatic religious militants attacked the leftist demonstrators, killing 2 people and wounding 104. Strikes, boycotts, and demonstrations then paralleled the economic problems. Some opportunistic politicians began to blame the social and economic ills of the country on deviations from traditional religious practice. In 1970 a former engineering professor, Necmettin Erbakan, founded the National Order party, which claimed to represent the interests of Muslims and rejected Turkey's secular, Western orientation. (Between 1970 and 1983, Erbakan established three political parties, all of which were eventually banned by the Constitutional Court, the latest the Welfare party in 2000.)[16] A revival of religious brotherhoods followed, except that the brotherhoods no longer dealt with spiritual issues or mysticism. They were venues for training young minds who became religious reactionaries par excellence. Consequently, there was a ready-made pool for "Islamic" militancy and terrorism.

On March 12, 1971, the military issued a communiqué accusing the government of having led the country into anarchy, fratricidal strife, and social and economic unrest. The government resigned, to be replaced by a nonpartisan government of technocrats. The civilian politicians faced opponents who would not compromise. On the one hand, the young militants of the Left would not settle for the left-of-center position of the RPP any more than for the parliamentary socialism that TLP represented; they wanted revolution. On the other, the 1971 coup-by-communiqué was intended to settle scores among the military leadership. In the armed forces high command mutual suspicion was rampant, some fearing a socialist coup, others a rightist coup. After the 1971 coup the conservative military faction managed to retire the leftist opposition.[17]

Leftist and rightist ideological movements were thus the catalysts for terrorism during the 1970s. Left-wing activists, especially, opted for terrorism when they realized that leftist parties did not receive sufficient votes to make any difference in Turkish politics. Moreover, youth movements worldwide and theoreticians of the New Left—such as Regis Debray, Che Guevara, and Carlos Marighella—left an indelible mark on Turkish radicals.

The leftist militants had international ties. Some trained in the camps of the Palestine Liberation Organization's (PLO) al-Fatah group in Jordan. Others were trained by Kurdish rebels in Iraq. In June 1972 fourteen armed terrorists were caught after they had infiltrated into Turkey on a boat that belonged to al-Fatah and had begun rural and urban guerrilla warfare. Approximately four hundred Turkish militants had gone to the Palestinian camps alone. In May 1971 the Turkish People's Liberation Army/Front (TPLA-F) kidnapped and murdered the Israeli consul general of Istanbul, Ephraim Elrom. The TPLA-F defendants argued that their purpose was to demonstrate solidarity with the Palestinians. But Elrom had been murdered for giving the Turkish security forces the names of Turkish terrorists trained in Palestinian camps.[18]

Right-wing terrorist forces included both secular and religious groups. By 1968 the Nationalist Action party (NAP) had established commando camps to train young men, under military discipline, to combat communism. The Idealist Youth Associations (the Grey Wolves), the militant organ of the NAP, became bolder in inciting violence. The majority of their recruits were unemployed, unskilled youth from shantytowns. Ten militant religious groups existed. These included the Islamic Liberation Army, the Turkish-Islamic Liberation Union, the Turkish-Islamic Liberation Front, the Suicide Corps of the Shari'a, and the Turkish Revolutionary Shari'a Army. None of these titles pointed to peaceful intentions.

As of 1975 universities, high schools, labor unions, security forces, and political parties were polarized to the point of no return. Radical factions of leftists, ultranationalists, and religious fundamentalists murdered opponents, occupied shantytown neighborhoods and university dormitories, and robbed or extorted money from businesses big and small; the last two groups assassinated liberal and socialist intellectuals. This scene marked Turkey's domestic history between 1975 and 1980. In 1977 the minister of the interior alerted the cabinet about increased violence perpetrated by commando hit teams. Süleyman Demirel, once again prime minister, remained adamant. He would not admit that the rightists committed terrorist crimes. He was riding too wild a tiger.

The consequence was the 1980 coup, which led to an unanticipated rapprochement of forces on the Right. The 1980 military coup makers

The Revolutionary Youth organization holds an independence demonstration in Istanbul, Turkey, in March 1970. The banner bears the indignant slogan *Defol!: Get out!* (Courtesy of Fahri Aral, Istanbul Bilgi University Press.)

did not distinguish between the Right and the Left when it came to punitive action—to the chagrin of the former, whose militants had previously been protected by the government. While in jail many nationalist commandos merged their ideology with militant Islam. Religious literature was abundant in prisons whereas secular literature was limited, encouraging the widespread conversion of the formerly "pagan" Grey Wolves who served time alongside members of the Raiders Association (Akincilar), the youth branch of Erbakan's National Salvation party (NSP). Their ideology centered around an Islamic revolution, and they rejected nationalism and democracy as doctrines alien to Muslims.

One may never know how extensively the Turkish government consulted with the United States on combating terrorism, any more than one can pinpoint with exact precision whose idea it was to combat alleged Soviet influence, infiltration, and subversion by promoting Islam against "atheist communism." But a radical change was observed in the aftermath of the 1980 military coup in Turkey. The generals began citing verses from the Koran. An amorphous concept of Turkish-Islamic synthesis was introduced into the schools. Compulsory courses on reli-

gion promoted Sunni religious identity. And Saudi financial establishments that provided an alternative to banks were suddenly permitted
into the country. These establishments were not only tax-exempt; they
refused to pay and to charge interest (regarding it as usury) and distributed shares from profits—a practice that had no precedent in republican Turkey.[19] It took almost a decade of flirtation with Islam before the
policy makers realized (after having ignored the historical record) how
dangerous a force politicized religion was. In 2000, the so-called Islamic
political party, the Welfare party, was banned by the Constitutional
Court. By then Turkey was facing terrorism instigated by the Hezbollah, as well as the assassinations of renowned secular intellectuals by
other religious reactionaries. Currently, Turkish policy makers are still
trying to curb the political Islam and the terrorism, albeit subdued, that
were offshoots of their predecessors' efforts to politicize religion.

Issues Today

The history related here is relevant to at least three major foreign policy issues that should concern the United States. First, the United States
needs to overcome its history of violating the sovereignty of other nations. This requires asserting power without pretensions to hegemony.
Historically, world systems never took graciously to hegemons, be it under universal empires, a universal church, a seafaring empire over which
"the sun never set," parvenus such as Napoleon Bonaparte and Adolf
Hitler, or ideologues such as Vladimir Lenin or Joseph Stalin. International coalitions or overextension always curbed the ambitions of those
with hegemonic aspirations. By 1993 George F. Kennan, the architect
of containment policy, renounced the U.S. role in the Cold War, stat-
ing, "I should make it clear that I'm wholly and emphatically rejecting
any and all messianic concepts of America's role in the world, rejecting
that is, an image of ourselves as teachers and redeemers to the rest of
humanity, rejecting the unique and superior virtue on our part, the
prattle about Manifest Destiny or the American Century."[20] It is perhaps
the messianic attitude more than anything that Kennan is rejecting, for
that, too, feeds anti-Americanism. Projecting an image of omnipotence
usually results in higher expectations than even the United States is capable of delivering, and, ironically, it results in others' asking why the
mighty power cannot, for example, deliver justice on the Palestinian
issue.

Second, the Bush administration should rethink its proposed national missile defense system. The proposal is already domestically controversial.[21] There are indications that the administration is contemplating sharing this system with allies, that is, placing the system, or parts of it, outside the United States. Some allied leaders may jump on the bandwagon. Turkey, however, has seen the spillover effects of the Cuban missile crisis and will rightly proceed with caution if confronted with such a "defense." At certain times, deterrence can become unduly provocative, not only for regional powers such as Turkey, but for nuclear powers, however latent their animosities are today.

Third, and perhaps most important, the United States and its allies must not rely on religion to counter anti-Americanism or terrorism. Some now believe that governments should back "moderate Islam" as opposed to "radical Islam." During World War II, the Allies lambasted fascist totalitarianism while downplaying their dependence on the Soviet totalitarian state. Perhaps that victory actually made the world safe for communism, considering how rapidly it spread in the aftermath of the war.[22] It is just as dangerous to rely on "moderate Islam" and to legitimate religiously oriented power. Politicized religion generally becomes extreme. The moderation (or lack thereof) of politicized religion should not be measured by its pro- or anti-American stance. What may seem pro-Americanism on the surface may breed hostility to the pro-American leadership, and it may focus on the United States for the wrong reasons. There has scarcely been any difference between the efforts to subvert Turkey's secular regime by "anti-American" Iran and by "pro-American" Saudi Arabia, except that the latter is subtler. As early modern and modern European history attests, many struggles had at their core the confining of matters of faith to the private realm and away from the public sphere. Turkey has not remained untouched by such struggles, but it is the only majority-Muslim country to have succeeded in secularizing. While many observers in Turkey see Saudi Arabia as the most radical financial nurturer of political Islam in the country since the 1980s, Western observers, with a few exceptions, have not recognized the dangers of the Saudi version of Islamic influence.[23]

Following the dissolution of the Soviet Union in 1991, the former Soviet republics in Central Asia and the peoples of the Caucasus were often presented in terms of their alleged religious identity, that is, as Muslims. For the East, many scholars and journalists still promote religious and ethnic identities at the expense of national identities, but that is hardly the case for the West. In 1995 Graham E. Fuller and Ian O. Lesser argued that it was the refusal to extend legitimacy to Islamic movements that created polarization and radicalism. Others argue that disappointment with "secular" governments and modernization pushed many Muslims to seek social justice in Islamic movements. Add on the injustices ascribed to the United States, and one supposedly gets to the core cause of recent terrorisms.[24] But one should note the incredible similarity between the aggressors and the like-minded "moderate" political Islamists in Turkey today. Their view is that the United States is to blame for the attacks of September 11, 2001, and some American analysts, too, look for causes within and fault U.S. policies. But power, dominance, and opposition work in complex ways on the global scale. We need to assess U.S. policies critically, but we should not assume that problematic policies justify either terrorism or catering to politicized religion. The main questions are how the United States will manage the gift and the burden of power and when anti-Americanists of all shades will begin critical self-analysis, away from concepts such as the "exploiters" and the "exploited," which assume that the latter have always lacked will and agency.

In conclusion, U.S. policies as well as American messianic attitudes have fed the anti-Americanism that also results from ideological commitments. Terrorism far exceeds any anti-American sentiment; it is nihilistic and needs to be dealt with by force and legal punitive action. Yet, we should still examine its history and take whatever steps we can to prevent it.

Notes

1. Gerard Tongas, *Atatürk and the True Nature of Modern Turkey*, trans. F. F. Rynd (London, 1939), 8.

2. George S. Harris, *Troubled Alliance: Turkish-American Problems in Historical Perspective, 1945–1971* (Washington, 1972), 45.

3. Nur Bilge Criss, "U.S. Forces in Turkey," in *U.S. Military Forces in Europe: The Early Years, 1945–1970*, ed. Simon W. Duke and Wolfgang Krieger (Boulder, 1993), 331–50.

4. *Ibid.*

5. *Ibid.*

6. "The North Atlantic Treaty" <http://www.nato.int/docu/basictxt/treaty.htm> (April 25, 2002); David J. Potter and Gregory J. Stachelczyk, "The Military Relationship between the United States and Turkey since 1947" (M.A. thesis, Air Force Institute of Technology, 1981), 21.

7. Michael Beschloss, *The Crisis Years: Kennedy and Khrushchev, 1960–1963* (New York, 1991); Nur Bilge Criss, "Strategic Nuclear Missiles in Turkey: The Jupiter Affair, 1959–1963," *Journal of Strategic Studies*, 20 (Sept. 1997), 97–122; Philip Nash, *The Other Missiles of October: Eisenhower, Kennedy, and the Jupiters, 1957–1963* (Chapel Hill, 1997).

8. *Thirteen Days*, dir. Roger Donaldson (New Line, 2000).

9. George S. Harris argued that Lyndon B. Johnson's letter was convenient for the Turkish government at the Conference on Turkish Foreign Policy, Bilkent University, Ankara, Spring 1999.

10. Harris, *Troubled Alliance*, 191–98; James W. Spain, "The United States, Turkey, and the Poppy," *Middle East Journal*, 29 (Summer 1975), 295–309.

11. Bruce Kuniholm, "Turkey and NATO: Past, Present, and Future," *Orbis*, 27 (Summer 1983), 421–45; Süha Bölükbasi, "The Cyprus Dispute and the United Nations: Peaceful Non-Settlement between 1954 and 1996," *International Journal of Middle East Studies*, 30 (Aug. 1998), 411–34; U. Haluk Bayülken, "The Cyprus Question and the United States," *Foreign Policy* (Ankara), 4 (nos. 2–3, 1974); Richard Company, *Turkey and the United States: The Arms Embargo Period* (New York, 1986); Arthur Chester, "Controversy over the Cut-off of Military Aid to Turkey," *Congressional Digest*, 54 (April 1975), 99–128; Paul Y. Watanabe, *Ethnic Groups, Congress, and American Foreign Policy: The Politics of the Turkish Arms Embargo* (Westport, 1984); Albert Wohlstetter, "The Strategic Importance of Turkey and the Arms Embargo," *Journal of International Relations*, 3 (Summer 1978), 101–9.

12. On the Turkish Labor party, see Hikmet Ozdemir, "Siyasal tarih, 1960–1980" (Political history, 1960–1980), in *Çagdas Türkiye, 1908–1980* (Contemporary Turkey, 1908–1980), ed. Sina Aksin (Istanbul, 1990), 221–23. On the Turkish Association to Combat Communism, see Jacob Landau, *Türkiye'de sag ve sol* (Radicalism in Turkey) (Ankara, 1979), 305–9; and Rafet Balli, "Komünizmle Mücadele Derneklerinden Bugüne Gladyonun MHP operasyonu" (Gladio and the Nationalist Action party from the Association to Combat Communism to today), in *Bati ve irtica* (The West and fundamentalism), comp. Ferit Ilsever (Istanbul, 1999), 506–12.

13. On July 3, 1969, a Defense Cooperation Agreement (DCA) was signed between Turkey and the United States to codify previous bilateral accords. Only a few of the accords had been on paper. From 1970 onward, DCAs were renewed periodically. See Richard F. Grimmett, *United States Military Installations in Turkey* (Washington, 1984). Mehmet Gönlübol and Omer Kürkcüoglu, "1965–1973 dönemi türk dis politikasi" (Turkish foreign policy between 1965 and 1973), in *Olaylarla türk dis politikasi, 1919–1995* (External and internal events that shaped Turkish foreign policy, 1919–1995), ed. Mehmet Gönlübol (Ankara, 1996), 491–540.

14. Nur Bilge Criss, "Mercenaries of Ideology: Turkey's Terrorism War," in *Terrorism and Politics*, ed. Barry Rubin (New York, 1991), 125–50, esp. 128.

15. Halis Ayhan, *Türkiye'de din egitimi, 1920–1998* (Religious education in Turkey, 1920–1998) (Istanbul, 1999), 200–203.

16. The Constitutional Court banned the parties Necmettin Erbakan founded because they violated Article 14 of the Turkish Constitution: "None of the rights and freedoms embodied in the Constitution shall be exercised with the aim of violating the indivisible integrity of the state with its territory and nation, of endan-

gering the existence of the Turkish State and Republic, of destroying fundamental rights and freedoms, of placing the government of the state under the control of an individual or a group of people." *The Constitution of the Republic of Turkey* (Ankara, 1995), 9; or *Anayasa Mahkemesi Karari* <www.Anayasa.Gov.tr/KARARLAR/SPK/K1998/K1998-01.htm> (June 6, 2002). The European Court of Human Rights concurred with the Turkish Constitutional Court verdict. See "Affaire Refah Partisi (Parti de la Prospérité) et Autres c. Turquie" (Case of the Refah party [Prosperity party] and others v. Turkey), July 31, 2001, *HUDOC* <http://hudoc.echr.coe.int/hudoc/> (June 6, 2002).

17. Criss, "Mercenaries of Ideology," 131–33.

18. *Ibid.*, 129.

19. On compulsory school courses about religion, see Ayhan, *Türkiye'de din egitimi*, 207–8. On the Saudi financial establishments, see Enis Berberoglu, "Petrodolarlar ve islami bankacilik" (Petrodollars and Islamic banking), in *Bati ve irtica*, comp. Ilsever, 122–29. Bozkurt Güvenç et al., *Türk-islam sentezi* (Turkish-Islamic synthesis) (Istanbul, 1991).

20. Francis Stonor Saunders, *The Cultural Cold War: The CIA and the World of Arts and Letters* (New York, 1999), 413–14.

21. Steven Weinberg, "Can Missile Defense Work?" *New York Review of Books*, Feb. 14, 2002, pp. 41–47.

22. Richard Overy, *Why the Allies Won* (New York, 1996), 2–24.

23. Isabel Vincent, "How Saudis Became Extremism's Exporters," *National Post* (Toronto), Oct. 26, 2001, in *Turkistan Newsletter*, Oct. 29, 2001 <http://www.euronet.NL/users/sota/turkistan.htm#arch> (June 25, 2002); John Hooper and Brian Whitaker, "Extremist View of Islam Unites Terror Suspects: Salafi Purist Teaching Backed by Saudi Royals," *Guardian* (Manchester), Oct. 26, 2001, *ibid.*, Oct. 29, 2001; Stephen Schwartz, "Saudi Friends, Saudi Foes: Is Our Arab Ally Part of the Problem?," *ibid.*, Nov. 22, 2001; David Wurmser, "The Saudi Connection: Osama Bin Laden's a Lot Closer to the Saudi Royal Family Than You Think," *ibid.*

24. Graham E. Fuller and Ian O. Lesser, *A Sense of Siege: The Geopolitics of Islam and the West* (Boulder, 1995), 122–66; Richard Falk, "World Order after September 11: An Unmapped Minefield," *Turkish Daily News* (Ankara), Jan. 5, 2002, p. 16.

Notes on the CIA's Secret War in Afghanistan

John Prados

The 2001 campaign against Taliban and Al-Qaeda forces constituted the second U.S. war in Afghanistan. John Prados asks what we can learn from the first: the Central Intelligence Agency's efforts to fund and equip an Islamic fundamentalist and tribal insurgency against a Communist government and occupying Russian forces in the 1980s. Distilling the declassified record and recent research, Prados explores the geopolitical concerns, ethnic divisions, methods of clandestine operation, and alliances with local leaders that shaped the conflict. The lessons are chastening—nations lose heart, allies become enemies, and weapons are turned against those who supplied them. He asks us to recall those lessons as the United States plans to expand its counterterror campaigns.

The new war against terrorism has taken up where the United States left off some years ago in its campaign against the Soviet Union in Afghanistan. Events of the initial campaign of the terror war, which concluded with the fall of the Tora Bora cave complex in December 2001, as well as developments that can be anticipated in the larger conflict, can be illuminated by reference to the Central Intelligence Agency's (CIA) efforts in the anti-Soviet war of the 1980s. These notes attempt to touch on key elements of that experience that should be borne in mind today, including the purposefulness of U.S. programs, the problems inherent in hurried efforts, the crosscutting impacts of local politics and customs, the nature of modern military operations, and the tendency of the solutions of the moment to spawn later difficulties.[1]

The CIA operation of the 1980s began as a spoiling operation. In April 1978, during the Carter administration, Afghan Communists overthrew a left-leaning but moderate dictatorship that had itself resulted from a coup against the Afghan monarch. Not satisfied with the slow progress in turning the nation toward socialism, the factions of the Communist party then began to fight each other. Meanwhile, within weeks of the so-

73

called April revolution, Muslim fundamentalists and tribal groupings with no love for the Communists began a resistance movement. The CIA program sought to augment that resistance.

Soviet involvement in Afghanistan long predated both the April revolution and the antimonarchist coup of 1973. Beginning in 1955, the Russians had furnished both economic and military aid in amounts totaling $2.5 billion by 1979, and the Soviet Union had become Afghanistan's leading trading partner. At the time of the April revolution there were already a thousand Russian technical experts and military advisers in the country.[2] Much as the political machinations of local clients had deepened the American stake in South Vietnam, the Communist coups in Kabul committed the Soviet Union more deeply in Afghanistan. Washington perceived an opportunity to turn the Afghan commitment into a running sore for Moscow.

While some sources claim the American effort began very early, more concrete evidence of U.S. feelers to the Muslim guerrillas emerges only from early 1979, about the time of the kidnapping and murder of the American ambassador in Kabul, Adolph Dubs.[3] President Jimmy Carter's National Security Council (NSC) considered options for a CIA operation in March and April, and the president approved a proposal forwarded by Zbigniew Brzezinski that July. A decision to expand the project followed a meeting of the NSC Special Coordinating Committee on December 17, 1979. Thus the inception of the CIA project in Afghanistan preceded the Soviet intervention, with three motorized and airborne divisions and other units, that came on December 25, 1979.

These facts make it clear that U.S. covert operations in Afghanistan were not a direct response to a particular Soviet maneuver. Nor was the Soviet intervention a response to the CIA operation, except in the sense that Afghan Muslim guerrilla activity endured and could not be quelled by the Afghan Communist government. Equally, if not more, important motivations for the 1979 Soviet invasion were the internecine quarrels among Communist party factions and uprisings in Afghan armed forces units.[4] Many Western countries, including the United States, nevertheless perceived the invasion as a Soviet thrust toward the Persian Gulf. Carter answered by declaring what became known as the Carter Doctrine: Any attempt by any major power to seize control of the Persian Gulf would be opposed by the United States by any means necessary, including the use of force. Carter also greatly increased the impetus for the CIA's Afghan project. The Soviet intervention had the effect of transforming a spoiling operation into a crash program. Similarly, the current war on terrorism, already in progress, was transformed into a crash program by the events of September 11, 2001. In the earlier Afghan war, President Ronald Reagan and his CIA director, William J. Casey, maintained the urgency added in 1980. In the current case there is no indication that CIA activities have slowed down since September.

The character of the Reagan administration secret war remained constant. Rather than placing Central Intelligence Agency officers in the field to organize, train, and lead the guerrillas, the Americans dealt through their local allies, Pakistan and its Inter-Services Intelligence (ISI) agency. The United States had little choice. There was minimal CIA presence in Afghanistan proper, what there was remained entirely confined to the capital, Kabul, and the United States had no means of funneling arms and equipment into the country through Kabul. Working from the outside meant enlisting local allies, most prominently the Pakistanis. ISI representatives had good arguments as to why they ought to take the lead. Muslim guerrillas in Afghanistan had already forged links with Pakistan, the ISI had been cooperating with them before the advent of the CIA project, and consequently Pakistani officials knew the players and had networks in place. In addition, the inevitable Russian propaganda line would be that the guerrillas were fronting for American imperialism, and ISI leaders argued that to have CIA officers actively involved in-country would confirm Soviet claims.[5] As a result, the secret war was run through Pakistan, where even with an enlarged CIA station, a huge budget (the largest for any CIA covert program to date), and a major rebel army, the project remained among the smaller ones in terms of the agency's organizational effort.

For different reasons, in the new war on terror the United States will again have to act through local allies. Already, in the first (Afghanistan) campaign of that war, in 2001–2002, the United States has been obliged to make bilateral arrangements, including some with Pakistan, in order to effect the actions deemed necessary. As Pakistan and the ISI did during the 1980s, each of the local allies has made its best deal with Washington. Foreign aid, trade terms, international monetary assistance, and military training and equipment are not the only factors in play. The bilateral agreements will significantly tie Washington's hands in ways that will become visible only as the conflict progresses. For example, in the Philippines, where the national constitution prohibits foreign military involvement, American participation is limited and subject to potential controversy. Washington's efforts to extend the envelope, to increase its freedom of action, will simultaneously make relationships more vulnerable to local concerns. Specific problems will take different forms in different nations, but the global reach of American action and the extension of commitments over time will make difficulties inevitable.

The Afghanistan secret war of the 1980s illustrates how "difficulties" can develop. With the CIA acting through Pakistan's ISI, the latter selected the guerrilla groups to receive weapons and cash aid. Pakistan's selection was not the one Washington would have made. The ISI's favoritism for fundamentalist Muslim groups foreclosed the more moderate political evolution the United States would have preferred. At the same time the guerrillas' success strengthened the ISI's own sense of its correctness. That encouraged the agency to shift its support in the early 1990s to an even more virulent strain of fundamentalism in Afghanistan that became the Taliban, which the United States felt it necessary to combat after September 11.

Meanwhile, within the Muslim guerrilla groups, the prospect of outside support and the favoritism practiced by the states aiding the guerrillas had deleterious effects. Even favored groups experienced shortfalls in support and were encouraged to seek direct support from individuals and groups outside the arena of conflict. Brig. Gen. Mohammad Yousaf, who for four years at the height of the Afghan covert operation headed the ISI branch in direct contact with the Muslim rebels, reports that the more fundamentalist groups were the most successful at private fund raising.[6] This opened the door for individuals and groups to influence the larger conflict. Osama bin Laden, at first merely a wealthy Saudi Arabian with some dedication to radical Islam, began as one such individual. Bin Laden's evolution from supporter of the Afghan covert operation to mastermind of the attacks that kicked off the war on terrorism shows in microcosm a pattern that is likely to be replicated among nations and larger interest groups. As the war on terrorism proceeds, the United States will demand certain actions, and its allies will confront distracting political forces as they face their local realities. Degrees of allied support for the new U.S. agenda will wax and wane. It is also possible that nations or groups that at one point align with Washington may later be driven to oppose its policies.

Another effect of Afghan rebel groups' pursuit of extra funds during the CIA secret war against the Soviets was the emergence of trends entirely inimical to U.S. interests. For the Afghans raising money meant dealing—not just negotiating with outside supporters, but conducting commerce in gems and drugs. Guerrilla leaders in the interior of the country actually preferred cash to supplies in kind, which they anticipated could be freely bought in local bazaars.[7] During the CIA secret war, Afghanistan became one of the world's leading producers of heroin. Not only did this fly in the face of the war on drugs being simultaneously conducted by the Reagan administration, it created conflict between U.S. agencies involved in the Afghan and drug efforts, primarily the CIA and the Drug Enforcement Administration. Ironically, when the Taliban were in power in Afghanistan after 1995, they largely eliminated Afghan opium production, but cultivation has resumed since they were overthrown by the new U.S. allies. As did the earlier secret war, the new war on terrorism is likely to lead to conflicting interests among the agencies conducting it. The U.S. government did not resolve its internal cleavages during the 1980s secret war; unresolved conflicts in a global war in the twenty-first century will detract considerably from the stated goals of the operations.

In the CIA covert operation against the Soviets in Afghanistan, the United States necessarily accepted the interests of the local groups, such as drug trafficking, as a condition of their participation on our side. That fact entailed subsidiary ones: The allies had objectives different from those of the CIA or the United States; they had a different level of determination than did the United States; they had a far different attitude toward compromise than the CIA. Thus the war frequently disappeared from January to March, typically the worst of the Afghan winter. Similarly, cooperation among rebel field commanders remained sporadic at best. General Yousaf's account is replete with examples of attacks canceled because groups refused to coordinate and of even simple coordination activities aborted for the same reason.[8] Some U.S. allies in the Afghan campaign of 2001, particularly among the Northern Alliance, were people involved in the earlier CIA operation. This includes the former president of the country, Burhanuddin Rabbani, who headed one of the seven main resistance groups, as did Gulbuddin Hekmatyar, a former prime minister. Both of them were among the Muslim fundamentalist leaders. Abdul Rashid Dostum, now a government minister, was previously a general in the Soviet-aligned Afghan army fighting the resistance. The defection of Dostum and his troops in 1992 effectively ended the Soviet client state in Kabul. Unlike American leaders in the war on terrorism, who have enunciated their desire to get the enemy dead or alive, the Afghans happily trade in loyalties. Thus, in the denouement of the initial campaign of the terror war, in late 2001 and 2002, America's local allies in Afghanistan took thousands of surrenders and defections but kept only a few hundred prisoners to be handed over to Americans. Those released included senior Taliban officials. Such behavior is the norm, not the exception. It illustrates one important way in which the necessity for the United States to work through local allies in the terror war will reduce overall effectiveness.

Much has been made in journalistic accounts of the 2001 Afghan campaign of the military formula of using small teams of CIA and military special forces troops to summon airpower and other means of attack. It is being pictured as a new standard technique. Interestingly, that too has its parallels in the CIA secret war of the 1980s. During the latter part of that war, the Soviets changed their tactics to give the major military role almost exclusively to their own Afghan allies, focusing on helping them plan operations and prepare attacks and then backing them with aircraft and artillery.[9] The new U.S. formula is the old Russian one with the added element of reduced exposure for U.S. forces due to the sophistication of modern U.S. technology. The most important limitation on the technique is set by the effectiveness of the local forces cooperating with the United States. The key vulnerability of the system resides in its connectivity, that is, the ability of all parts of the dinosaur to communicate relevant information and to function in unison. Disruption can occur through communications failure, intelligence failure, or the coordination failure that keeps such cooperating forces as U.S. aircraft from being in place where they are needed. In the computer age there are many ways to disrupt connectivity, some of them quite innocuous, such as glitches in software or gaps in standard procedures, others purposefully sinister, such as the adversary's jamming critical communications links or spoofing (that is, faking) responses.

There has been much discussion recently of the phenomenon of "blowback," the tendency for actions to rebound and damage the initiator. In that regard, the CIA's Afghan campaign is obviously closely related to current events.[10] Osama bin Laden, as a rebel fighter from the CIA's secret war who is suddenly at the heart of the new terrorism, is the clearest example, but indeed there are many. The term "Afghan Arab" came to denote a former fighter in the CIA covert operation who went on to other causes and affairs. In the Bosnian civil war of the early 1990s an estimated five hundred to a thousand veterans of the CIA secret war served on the Muslim side. Over the course of the campaign several thousand are thought to have participated. Afghan Arabs also participated in the civil war in Azerbaijan and in the struggle against Russia in Chechnya. Several of the terrorists involved in the 1993 attempt to car bomb New York's World Trade Center were also Afghan veterans. As the first of the CIA's project leaders for the Afghan program, Charles G. Cogan, later put it, "The hypothesis that the mujahedeen would come to the United States and commit terrorist actions did not enter into our universe of thinking at the time."[11]

As with people, so too with equipment, the dangers of blowback are real. The most prominent example from the Afghan secret war is the shoulder-fired antiaircraft missile called the Stinger. The CIA provided the Muslim rebels between 1986 and 1988 with approximately 1,000 of the missiles after an intense bureaucratic battle within the U.S. government between officials worried that the technology would leak into the wrong hands and anti-Soviet (or pro-rebel) activists. About 340 of the Stingers were expended in the anti-Soviet covert operation. Once the Russians had withdrawn from Afghanistan, in early 1989, the U.S. government asked for the return of the weapons. A typical response was that of the Islamic party led by Yunis Khalis: "We will not return the Stingers. . . . We ourselves need them most."[12] Khalis was among the more moderate Muslim leaders. For a couple of years, while a Communist government in Kabul continued to resist the Muslim rebels, the United States remained quiescent. But in 1991 the CIA, which had given away the missiles, began a new covert operation to buy them back. Over the next several years, the agency spent more than $65 million on this program. Weapons that the United States had bought for $35,000 each were bought back for another $50,000 to $100,000. An estimated 200 Stingers were recovered by the CIA effort. Another 100 to 200 were believed still in Afghan hands in 2001, leaving hundreds unaccounted for.[13] Some are known to be in Iranian hands; the whereabouts of the other Stinger missiles are unknown.

Given local allies, shifting loyalties, and the fortunes of war, the new struggle against terrorism is bound to generate blowback of its own. Whether this will involve governments that change sides, nations (including our own) that lose heart, ally groups who become enemies, or weapons that are turned against their producers cannot be known. What is apparent is that the political risks are high. The CIA experience in Afghanistan gives us no confidence that those risks can be avoided.

Whether they can even be minimized remains to be seen. The Afghanistan covert operation leaves very cloudy portents for the war on terrorism.

Notes

Acknowledgments: I am indebted to colleagues at the International Center for Advanced Studies of New York University for discussions that helped clarify many of the points presented here.

1. For a detailed review of the Central Intelligence Agency (CIA) operation in Afghanistan, see John Prados, *Presidents' Secret Wars*, completely revised edition (forthcoming).

2. Amin Saikal, *The Afghanistan Conflict: Gorbachev's Options* (Canberra, 1986), 9, 19.

3. Two former Soviet military officers wrote that soon after the 1973 coup a resistance training center reportedly funded by the United States opened in Attoka, Pakistan, an initiative of the Muslim fundamentalist Gulbuddhin Hekmatyar. See Oleg Sarin and Lev Dvoretsky, *The Afghan Syndrome: The Soviet Union's Vietnam* (Novato, 1993), 53.

4. On Afghan politics of this period, see M. Hassan Kakar, *Afghanistan: The Soviet Invasion and the Afghan Response, 1979–1982* (Berkeley, 1995), 21–75.

5. Mohammad Yousaf and Mark Adkin, *The Bear Trap: Afghanistan's Untold Story* (London, 1992), 81–84.

6. *Ibid.*, 106.

7. Lieutenant Omar and Mawlawi Nezamuddin Haqani, "Zhawar One," in *Afghan Guerrilla Warfare: In the Words of the Mujahideen Fighters*, ed. Ali Ahmad Jalali and Lester W. Grau (St. Paul, 2001), 317.

8. Yousaf and Adkin, *Bear Trap*, 36, 39–40, 42, and *passim*.

9. Lester W. Grau and Michael A. Gress, trans. and eds., *The Soviet-Afghan War: How a Superpower Fought and Lost: The Russian General Staff* (Lawrence, 2002), *passim*.

10. Chalmers Johnson, *Blowback: The Costs and Consequences of American Empire* (New York, 2000).

11. Tim Weiner, "Blowback from the Afghan Battlefield," *New York Times Magazine*, March 13, 1994, pp. 52–55; Robert I. Friedman, "The CIA's Jihad," *New York*, March 27, 1995, pp. 36–47. For the statement of Charles G. Cogan, see Weiner, "Blowback from the Afghan Battlefield," 53.

12. Alan J. Kuperman, "The Stinger Missile and U.S. Intervention in Afghanistan," *Political Science Quarterly*, 114 (Summer 1999), 219–63; *New York Times*, March 14, 1989, p. A3.

13. *Washington Post*, Sept. 25, 2001, p. A15.

Rescuing Women and Children

Emily S. Rosenberg

As the United States was launching its effort to overthrow the Taliban in Afghanistan in late 2001, the Bush administration and the U.S. media focused on the need to rescue Afghan women and children from oppression. Emily S. Rosenberg draws on recent scholarship on gender and international relations to examine the competing "social imaginaries" animating such wartime calls for rescue. One imaginary takes shape within a tradition of male-coded nationalism and claims of Western superiority. Another arises in transnational networks working in culturally diverse ways to challenge the subordination of women. Although the two imaginaries may at times blur together, they coexist uneasily and point toward different futures.

Nine weeks after planes hit the World Trade Center and the Pentagon, on November 17, 2001, Laura Bush became the first First Lady to deliver the president's Saturday morning radio address to the nation. "The brutal oppression of women is a central goal of the terrorists," she explained. "Women have been denied access to doctors" in Afghanistan under Taliban rule, and they "face beatings for laughing. The Taliban threaten to pull out women's fingernails for wearing nail polish," she said. The day before, the Department of State had hosted Eleanor Smeal, head of the Feminist Majority Foundation, and representatives of several other women's groups to help publicize the release of its "Report on the Taliban's War against Women," which emphasized that the U.S. war against terrorism was, in part, a war on behalf of women and children. The report detailed measures put in place by the Taliban-controlled Afghan goverment—the enforced wearing of the burka (a loose gown that drapes the entire body), the prohibitions against women's driving or even taking taxis unaccompanied by a male, the ban on educating women over the age of eight, and the heavily restricted access to health care. "With one of the world's worst human rights records, the Taliban has perpetrated egregious acts of violence against women, including rape, abduction, and forced marriage."[1]

The First Lady's speech and the State Department's report joined a broader campaign—long waged by a diverse array of Afghan, American, and transnational women's groups—against the Taliban's rule in Afghanistan. Three weeks later, when signing the Afghan Women and Children Relief Act (a bill that had been sponsored by thirteen women senators led by the Republican Kay Bailey Hutchison of Texas), President George W. Bush received standing ovations when speaking to an audience of women activists.[2] Who, before September 11, could have imagined such a scene of common endeavor between the Bush administration and feminist leaders?

During the next several weeks, the U.S. media embraced this theme of overthrowing the Taliban in order to rescue Afghan women and children. The same day as the First Lady's address, CNN premiered a new documentary by the much celebrated team that had produced *Beneath the Veil*. First shown in June 2001, *Beneath the Veil* features Saira Shah, an Afghan now living in London. Shah, assisted by underground activists associated with the Revolutionary Association of the Women of Afghanistan (RAWA), had smuggled cameras into Afghanistan to document the plight of women and children. In a particularly dramatic scene that RAWA had filmed earlier, a Taliban official stood in the middle of a public arena in Kabul and executed a kneeling woman, shrouded in a burka, for a seemingly minor infraction of the Taliban's restrictive laws. The successor, CNN-sponsored documentary that premiered on the day of the First Lady's address, called *Unholy War*, had been filmed in October in the midst of the United States/Northern Alliance fight against the Taliban. Like *Beneath the Veil*, it mixed an adventure tale of Shah's dangerous journey into Afghanistan with an exposé of the Taliban's victimization of women and children. Adding an explicit theme of rescue, the central drama of this film was Shah's quest to find and assist three girls, featured in the earlier documentary, who had been traumatized by seeing their mother killed. Both documentaries played repeatedly in the weeks following. Major news magazines and newspapers that week also featured stories that paralleled, and drew from, the State Department reports on the plight of women; news talk shows brimmed with stories of women's sufferings; and on November 21 the PBS show *The NewsHour with Jim Lehrer* featured a panel of three Afghan women who discussed the recent history of restriction and abuse.[3]

The government and media focus on Afghan women and children, which became especially intense for the several weeks after Laura Bush's address, prompts reflection on the historical interrelationships between gender and U.S. foreign policy, an issue that has stirred considerable debate in the field of U.S. foreign relations. I want to suggest that the gender-based appeals of late November rested on, and drew resonance from, differing and often competing traditions that historians have recently illuminated. First, the trope of rescuing women and children may be viewed as emerging from a social imaginary dominated by a masculinized national state that casts itself in a paternal role, saving those who are abused by rival men and nations. Second, it may be seen as resting within the imaginary of transcultural and transnational networks (within what Charles S. Maier has called a world of declining "territoriality") that cast themselves as working in culturally diverse ways to challenge locally specific abuses based on gender. By highlighting these two imaginaries as a heuristic device, I do not mean to suggest that they constitute the only ones competing for people's allegiances, nor that they exist in completely separate realms of either rhetorical or social construction. In particular representations—such as Laura Bush's speech, the Afghan Women and Children Relief Act, Saira Shah's documentary, or the *NewsHour* panel—these two imaginaries both blur together and clash.[4]

Untangling their genealogies, however, may highlight how language and images involving gender and rescue represent no single, settled meaning in policy discussions but, rather, present a continually contested *process* of meaning formation. In other words, the language and images of rescue offer a potentially unstable set of signifiers that generate debates in which diverse parties try both to legitimate and contest assumptions and programs (although the playing field on which meanings are contested is hardly level). The imaginaries central to this analysis will each be explored in greater depth, as late November's emphasis on saving Afghan women and children is examined in the context of the historical literature on gender and foreign relations.

Striving to save women and children from the grasp of barbaric, premodern men, and then to uplift them, is a familiar theme to historians, though it seems that generations of Americans have repetitively advanced it as fresh and unique testimony to their own special enlightenment. A growing number of historical studies elaborate the ways Western evolutionary science of the late nineteenth century postulated a strong correlation between the evolved status of any group and the condition of the women belonging to it. International reformers in the United States and elsewhere often linked the eradication of male oppression (whether in the form of drunkenness, domestic violence, polygamy, patriarchal economic control, or harmful factory labor conditions) to the notion of a maternalist order—one in which women's supposedly "natural" gifts for civilizing and purifying the social order would uplift the entire nation. Reformers dedicated to americanizing new immigrants to the United States frequently targeted what they regarded as old-country patterns of gender oppression. U.S. missionaries in China, India, and Africa (as well as among American Indians at home) often made the case for Westernization and Americanization by highlighting the most visible signs of women's subordinated status, such as foot binding, suttee, and load carrying.[5]

Such historical studies, read together with seminal works of feminist criticism, suggest that the identification of Americanization with modernization and humanitarian uplift, often in the form of liberating downtrodden women both at home and abroad, has constituted a persistent trope of American exceptionalism. The almost obsessive focus on the burka recalls other practices that, in the West, emerged earlier as central symbols of barbarism and implicitly suggested the superiority of Western, Christian ways and the need for modernization (and Western nations) as women's saviors. Gayatry Chakravorty Spivak's and Chandra Talpade Mohanty's critiques of the construction of so-called Third World women in Western cultures (and within the cultures of Western feminism as well) illuminate the representations of the burka. Drawing from Spivak and Mohanty, the sociologist Shahnaz Khan argues that in American media displays, veiled women often become symbols of an invisible, passive, and undifferentiated "other." She analyzes a 1998 *People Weekly* magazine photo in which Mavis Leno (the wife of the talk show host Jay Leno), who had taken up the cause of Afghan women, stands next to a burka-clad woman, "its juxtaposition of two women, one veiled the other unveiled, suggesting other binaries as well: east/west; liberated/oppressed; and forceful/passive." The photo caption quotes Jay Leno saying "I am proud of her," but no mention is made of the anonymous woman in the burka.[6] The vision of Afghan women as passive victims (symbolized by their dress) emphasizes their need for rescue by outsiders and may, implicitly, work against the visibility of the many Afghan women activists who have struggled for years to achieve a hearing internationally. It may also connect the mistreatment of women primarily to an Eastern, Islamic tradition, obscuring the context of the twenty years of warfare in which forces from so many nations (including those in the West) played a part. The visual focus on the burka, in short, may reinforce an orientalist perspective that renders some people as exotic and wholly foreign while mobilizing the domestic emotions of humanitarian sympathy to buttress American exceptionalism.

Discourses of gender disorder and the necessity of "civilized" nations' setting things aright, recent studies suggest, can become especially emotive rallying cries in times of war. In 1898 William Randolph Hearst and other expansionists urged Americans to rescue Cuban women from Spanish brutes, and popular iconography often represented the island of Cuba as a damsel in distress. During World War I, with the Wilson administration's blessing, Hollywood portrayed Germans ravaging women and tossing children out of windows. The idea that both victimized women and brutal men assumed "improper" gender roles constituted an ever present theme of imperial enterprises during the early-twentieth-century military occupations of the Philippines, the Dominican Republic, and Haiti by the United States. Going into battle to preserve civilization and to bring the blessings of modernity, in short, often foregrounded the rescue of women and children from a social order that oppressed them.[7]

Historians have recognized that the rescue theme often works to display and reinforce notions of the superior manliness of the rescuer nation, indeed, to cast the nation itself in a manly role. The nation, in effect, is summoned to provide protection to women or to a country— emblematically feminized—that rival men are violating. A memorable moment in *Beneath the Veil* highlights the traumatized little girls who had lost their mother. The director of the film, Cassian Harrison, stated in a *Larry King Live* interview that this image of the three girls "became a metaphor for Afghanistan." As he made that statement, an image from the documentary lingered on the TV screen, showing a full close-up of one of the little girls, her beatific face punctuated by dark brown eyes brimming with tears. The picture also appears on Web sites and promotional material dealing with the film. Such a visual identification of country/woman/child/trauma seems to echo the histories of images of traumatized and brutalized women/children that have been deployed during previous wars. (Think of the harrowing images of Spanish brutality in Cuba in 1898, the "rape" of Belgium by Germany during World War I, the "rape" of Nanking by Japan during World War II, and the allegedly widespread rapes by Iraqis in Kuwait in 1991 that received coverage in the U.S. media but proved untrue.) Symbolically rendering a country as a vulnerable woman or a child without proper or effective protectors reinforces the paternalistic nationalism of the rescuer-nation and dramatizes its moral mission.[8]

Scholarship related to such gendered images implicitly suggests one way of viewing the governmental and media focus on Afghan women during late November 2001. Osama bin Laden and the Taliban had for several years claimed that they were protecting women from the ravages of the infidel West's culture of exposure and derided Americans and the ruling family of Saudi Arabia as cowardly and unmanly, especially in view of women's service in the U.S. military, which had been stationed in Saudi Arabia since the Gulf War of 1991. In an interview with Al-Jazeera television, bin Laden elaborated one of his favorite themes: "We believe that we are men. . . . We do not want American women soldiers defending [Mecca]. . . . Muslim women refuse to be defended by these American and Jewish prostitutes." The Bush administration, in turn, claimed to be saving women from the medievalism of an extremist form of Islamic fundamentalism. Framed as a fight over who had the power to free women from what each considered to be the predatory goals of rivals, the conflict assumed attributes of masculine display. The discourse of rescue, then, may cast women as emblems or pawns in a male rivalry to determine which men (or nations) have the power to save them, to restrict or expand the boundaries of their lives, and to preside over how present and future social orders will be organized.[9]

A historical analysis of how war mobilization efforts have deployed gender messages that reinforce masculinity while accentuating the dependence of women and children does not deny the real suffering and oppression of women in places where American soldiers have fought, such as Afghanistan. Nor does it demean larger wartime goals, which may certainly be independently justified on grounds of national interest or morality. But it does call attention to the provenance and the representational construction of such concerns. Where on the U.S. foreign policy agenda is the status of women and children (including reproductive health, the spread of AIDS [acquired immune deficiency syndrome], traffic in women, and education) when Americans survey foreign assistance priorities? Indeed, how secure are women and children (whose numbers have come to dominate homeless populations and poverty rolls) in the United States? Of course, no U.S. policy can provide social safety nets for every person on the planet nor dictate social arrangements to a culturally diverse world. But in a world where there is much brutality, it seems worth asking why the equality and well-being of women become highly visible on foreign policy agendas in particular times and places and invisible in others. It is also worth inquiring how seriously those agendas are pursued once they have been advanced.

Histories of the discourse of rescue suggest that it often operates to shore up visions of superior U.S. social arrangements—visions essential to rallying wartime nationalism and to presenting citizens with a sense of their nation's special benevolence. Often drawn from the imaginary of a maternalist (purified) social order and a male-coded (powerful) state, the call to rescue women and children may rework traditional sentiments of humanitarian uplift in ways that reinforce and update gender hierarchies in both domestic and foreign policies.

Discourses of gender and rescue, however, are not settled things but may be seen as continually contested processes with shifting, unsettled meanings. Although they have helped establish an arena for masculine performance and an identity between the nation-state and masculine power, it would nonetheless be absurd to imagine that every call for bettering the condition of women and children encodes only some version of gender inequality or the masculinized state. Another body of historical scholarship on gender and foreign policy has emphasized ways in which both women and men have struggled to form transnational networks concerned with enlarging the voice, the power, and the agency of diverse groups of women. Such networks attempt to make victimization visible in order to play a different game, rooted in a different global imaginary.

Many historical studies chart the growing influence of groups that have worked transnationally for ideas of universal human rights and locally for culturally specific strategies of women's empowerment. Recent studies of social activists during the 1940s, for example, show how World War II represented, in part, a struggle against a patriarchal, fascist regime that envisioned women's highest calling as reproducing soldiers for the state. Fascism's promotion of hypermasculinity and restrictively reproductive roles for women helped Eleanor Roosevelt and others argue that women's rights deserved a place on postwar agendas as a logical accompaniment to antifascism, democratization, and peace. In the spring of 1944 the First Lady and representatives of thirteen leading women's organizations organized a national conference on women in postwar planning. They subsequently assembled a "roster of qualified women" for use by the president and the secretary of state. The First Lady then promoted the plan in her "My Day" columns in the *New York Times*. (She wryly commented that men fail to appoint women, not because they oppose doing so, but because they forget. The roster would provide a reminder.) Eleanor Roosevelt and other women persistently agitated for greater representation of women in conferences planning the postwar international order and later championed creation of the United Nations (UN) and the new UN-sponsored Universal Declaration of Human Rights (1948) as ways of globally advancing women's participation as equal citizens. Although they were not completely free of maternalist or exceptionalist justifications, many of those efforts nonetheless went a long way toward imagining a world in which new forms of organization could enable women throughout the world to speak and act on their own behalf.[10]

Although those who supported such transnational networks remained a relatively small group in the world's most powerful country, with its long cultural tradition of constructing national superiority through depictions of exoticized others, historians have charted a rapid worldwide growth of transnational women's activism after World War II. Four UN World Conferences on Women, at Mexico City (1975), Copenhagen (1980), Nairobi (1985), and Beijing (1995), and the UN Conference on Population at Cairo (1994) highlighted an often conflicting variety of feminist concerns and strategies—tensions that belie any notion of a single "women's agenda." There have been persistent disagreements between those who wish a place "at the table" and those who want to overturn the table altogether. Still, emphasis on greater localized empowerment of women represents a constant theme in literature about the wide variety of women's activisms. In an elaborating network, women from all over the world now head many UN agencies, governmental bureaus, NGOs (nongovernmental organizations), and community networks that address issues relevant to women and children. Many organizations in this network had, long before September 11, mounted an anti-Taliban campaign.[11]

Scholarship on transnational activism related to women and children suggests that, as during World War II, the heightened visibility stimulated by the U.S. war against the Taliban may help those who have spent years organizing and pushing for change. Saira Shah's wide television exposure paralleled the U.S. government's informational campaign against the Taliban, for example, but Shah and other Afghan women then used the media spotlight to push for broader, transnational goals. Applauding the Taliban's overthrow, they stressed the overriding importance of maintaining a steady postwar commitment to women's empowerment (opening new schools, clinics, and jobs) within a reconstructed Afghanistan, a process that the overthrow of the Taliban and the repeal of its restrictions would only barely begin. They warned that U.S.-allied warlords often upheld similar restrictive policies toward women and suggested the difficulties of improving the lives of women and children amid the enormous instabilities wrought by war and armed warlords.[12] Advocates such as Sima Wali, president of Refugee Women in Development, an international group aiding refugee, displaced, and returnee women, and others used the new visibility of the women's issue to press for representation of women in the new interim government of Afghanistan.

Another example of an attempt to seize the momentary media attention to Afghan women to advance broader goals involved activism on behalf of the Convention on the Elimination of All Forms of Discrimination against Women (CEDAW). This "women's human rights treaty" has been ratified by 168 countries, with the United States remaining one of the few holdouts, along with Iran and Afghanistan (despite attached reservations that assure the treaty's neutrality on abortion and that prohibit it from impinging on any domestic laws). On December 18, 2001, the twenty-second anniversary of the UN's unanimous adoption of CEDAW, a coalition of women's and human rights organizations issued an open letter asking for Senate ratification. Alluding to the U.S. struggle against the Taliban, the letter invoked President Bush's promise to "always be the world's leader in support of human rights," and it asked Congress and the president to act. "CEDAW is critical to ensuring that the future of Afghanistan will have a democratic government that includes equal rights for women."[13] These small examples, which take their place within a larger historical tradition of women's transnational organizing, illustrate how contested and unstable signifiers related to gender and rescue can give rise to reformulations of the language of nationalism and paternalism on behalf of a transnational approach to achieving greater gender equity.

Such examples, however, also may illustrate the limitations of such openings. Government-led media campaigns can highlight issues but may also quickly erase them. Will the journalists who eagerly photographed women removing burkas on the streets of Kabul return to interview women about their social conditions? If a reconstructed Afghanistan remains a U.S. ally, will the many women's advocates and activists continue to find open access to CNN and the White House? National emergencies that call up rescue themes have tended to shore up the remasculinized state, projecting around-the-clock images of male-dominated military machines and relegating social conditions to a secondary, less visible arena. Even the discourse of rescue itself, connoting an act rather than a prolonged process, can diminish the attention paid to cooperative, international commitments. The scholarship on gender and foreign relations, in short, may illuminate the historical context of ongoing cultural contests over how to imagine both gender norms and world orders, but it certainly does not imply that such contests are staged on equal ground.

With the informational offensive launched during the week of November 17, 2001, the Bush administration briefly thrust the issue of women's and children's well-being into the public arena. "At long last, efforts to protect and advance women's rights are where they belong—in the mainstream of American foreign policy," proclaimed the State Department's Web site.[14] U.S. relief acts authorized dedication of special funds to women and children; the Afghan interim government appointed Sima Samar as minister of women's affairs and Suhaila Seddiqi, the country's most respected surgeon, as minister of health; and the interim government began to restore basic legal rights to women.

The genealogy and the current meanings of such proclamations and actions, however, remain complicated. Drawing upon recent scholarship related to gender and foreign relations, it is possible to position calls for the assistance of women and children within two different historical imaginaries. One of these arises from a tradition marked by nationalism, maternalist assumptions, claims of Western cultural superiority, and masculine display. In a struggle between groups of men (or male-coded nations), women and children make cameo appearances as emblems whose symbols of oppression (the burka, for example) can rally sentimentalized, self-congratulatory support. Another arises from a largely twentieth-century tradition of transnational networks, which emphasize both global issues and locally specific concerns related to human welfare and women's empowerment. Although these two imaginaries may blur together and seem allied in specific situations, they coexist uneasily and struggle toward different futures.

Notes

Acknowledgments: I wish to thank Ann Laura Stoler, Joanne Meyerowitz, and, especially, Norman Rosenberg for valuable critiques.

1. Laura Bush, "Radio Address to the Nation," Nov. 17, 2001 <http://www.whitehouse.gov/news/releases/2001/11/20011117.html> (Jan. 2, 2002); "The Bushies Unveil the Women's Issue," *Newsweek*, Nov. 26, 2001, p. 7; Feminist Majority Foundation, "The Taliban & Afghan Women: Background" <http://www.feminist.org/afghan/facts.html> (June 25, 2002); U.S. Department of State, Bureau of Democracy, Human Rights, and Labor, "Report on the Taliban's War against Women," Nov. 17, 2001 <http://www.state.gov/g/drl/rls/index.cfm?id=4804> (Jan. 2, 2002).

2. White House, "President Signs Afghan Women and Children Relief Act" <http://www.whitehouse.gov/news/releases/2001/12/20011212-9.html> (Jan. 15, 2002); U.S. Department of State, "Senate Passes Afghan Women and Children Relief Act" <http://usinfo.state.gov/topical/pol/terror/01111610.htm> (Jan. 15, 2002).

3. *Beneath the Veil*, dir. Cassian Harrison (Hardcash Productions, 2001); *Unholy War*, dir. James Miller (Hardcash Productions, 2002); *The NewsHour with Jim Lehrer* (PBS, Nov. 21, 2001). The panelists were Rina Amiri, Nafissa Mahmood Ghorwal, and Tahmeena Faryal.

4. Panels on gender and cultural approaches have, over the past five years, become regular features of the annual meetings of the Society for Historians of American Foreign Relations, and they have sparked healthy—and sometimes heated—discussions and disagreements. I adapt the phrase "social imaginary" using Charles Taylor's definition: "The social imaginary is . . . what enables, through making sense of, the practices of a society." See Charles Taylor, "Modern Social Imaginaries," *Public Culture*, 14 (Winter 2002), 90. On the rise and decline of "territoriality," see Charles S. Maier, "Consigning the Twentieth Century to History: Alternative Narratives for the Modern Era," *American Historical Review*, 105 (June 2000), 807–31.

5. These ideas are developed, for example, in Ian R. Tyrrell, *Woman's World/ Woman's Empire: The Woman's Christian Temperance Union in International Perspective, 1800–1930* (Chapel Hill, 1991); Jane Hunter, *The Gospel of Gentility: American Women Missionaries in Turn-of-the-Century China* (New Haven, 1984); Mary Taylor Huber and Nancy C. Lutkehaus, eds., *Gendered Missions: Women and Men in Missionary Discourse and Practice* (Ann Arbor, 1999); Matthew Frye Jacobson, *Barbarian Virtues: The United States Encounters Foreign Peoples at Home and Abroad, 1876–1917* (New York, 2000); and Laura Wexler, *Tender Violence: Domestic Visions in an Age of U.S. Imperialism* (Chapel Hill, 2000). For an introduction to these themes domestically, see Gail Bederman, *Manliness and Civilization: A Cultural History of Gender and Race in the United States, 1880–1917* (Chicago, 1995); Louise Michele Newman, *White Women's Rights: The Racial Origins of Feminism in the United States* (New York, 1999); and Linda Gordon, *The Great Arizona Orphan Abduction* (Cambridge, Mass., 1999). For examples of how *American* women also have become symbols in international cultural contests over alternative futures, see Emily S. Rosenberg, "Consuming Women: Images of Americanization in the 'American Century,'" *Diplomatic History*, 23 (Summer 1999), 479–97.

6. Gayatri Chakravorty Spivak, *A Critique of Postcolonial Reason: Toward a History of the Vanishing Present* (Cambridge, Mass., 1999), 312–421; Chandra Talpade Mohanty, "Under Western Eyes: Feminist Scholarship and Colonial Discourses," in *Third World Women and the Politics of Feminism*, ed. Chandra Talpade Mohanty, Ann Russo, and Lourdes Torres (Bloomington, 1991), 51–80; Shahnaz Khan, "Between Here and There: Feminist Solidarity and Afghan Women," *Genders*, 33 (2001) <http://www.genders.org/g33/g33_kahn.html>, esp. para. 9 (April 9, 2002). See also Edward Said, *Orientalism: Western Conceptions of the Orient* (London, 1979). On women in the Islamic world, see Leila Ahmed, *Women and Gender in Islam: Historical Roots of a Modern Debate* (New Haven, 1992); and Mahnaz Afkhami, ed., *Faith and Freedom in Women's Human Rights in the Muslim World* (Syracuse, 1995).

7. On issues of gender and American imperialism, see, for example, Kristin Hoganson, *Fighting for American Manhood: How Gender Politics Provoked the Spanish-American and Philippine-American Wars* (New Haven, 1998); Amy Kaplan and Donald E. Pease, eds., *Cultures of United States Imperialism* (Durham, 1993); Gilbert M. Joseph, Catherine C. LeGrand, and Ricardo D. Salvatore, eds., *Close Encounters of Empire: Writing the Cultural History of U.S.–Latin American Relations* (Durham, 1998); Mary A. Renda, *Taking Haiti: Military Occupation and the Culture of U.S. Imperialism, 1915–1940* (Chapel Hill, 2001); Eileen J. Suárez Findlay, *Imposing Decency: The Politics of Sexuality and Race in Puerto Rico, 1870–1920* (Durham, 1999); Vicente L. Rafael, *White Love and Other Events in Filipino History* (Durham, 2000); and Emily S. Rosenberg, *Financial Missionaries to the World: The Politics and Culture of Dollar Diplomacy* (Cambridge, Mass., 1999). For other literature on gender and colonialism, begin with Antoinette Burton, ed., *Gender, Sexuality, and Colonial Modernities* (New York, 1999); and Ann Laura Stoler, "Tense and Tender Ties: The Politics of Comparison in North American History and (Post) Colonial Studies," *Journal of American History*, 88 (Dec. 2001), 829–65.

8. *Larry King Live* (CNN, Dec. 26, 2001). Seminal works on gender and nationality include Anne McClintock, *Imperial Leather: Race, Gender, and Sexuality in the Colonial Contest* (New York, 1995); Anne McClintock, Aamir Mufti, and Ella Shohat, eds., *Dangerous Liaisons: Gender, Nation, and Postcolonial Perspectives* (Minneapolis, 1997); Cynthia H. Enloe, *Bananas, Beaches, and Bases: Making Feminist Sense of International Politics* (London, 1989); and Cynthia H. Enloe, *The Morning After: Sexual Politics at the End of the Cold War* (Berkeley, 1993). Studies that highlight American inattention to abuse of foreign women by U.S. troops include Katharine H. S. Moon, *Sex among Allies: Military Prostitution in U.S.-Korean Relations* (New York, 1997); and Ruth Ann Keyso, *Women of Okinawa: Nine Voices from a Garrison Island* (Ithaca, 2000).

9. Osama bin Laden interview with Al-Jazeera television network, Dec. 1998, quoted in Tony Judt, "America and the War," *New York Review of Books*, Nov. 15, 2001, p. 4. On the impact of militarism on women's lives, see Cynthia Enloe, *Maneuvers* (Berkeley, 2000); and Lois Ann Lorentzen and Jennifer Turpin, eds., *The Women and War Reader* (New York, 1998). Recent books on women in Afghanistan include Deborah Ellis, *Women of the Afghan War* (New York, 2000); Rosemarie Skaine, *The Women of Afghanistan under the Taliban* (Jefferson, 2002); and Julie A.

Mertus, *War's Offensive on Women: The Humanitarian Challenge in Bosnia, Kosovo, and Afghanistan* (West Hartford, 2000).

10. Judy Barrett Litoff and David C. Smith, eds., *What Kind of a World Do We Want? American Women Plan for Peace* (Wilmington, 2000), 16–17; Mary Ann Glendon, *A World Made New: Eleanor Roosevelt and the Universal Declaration of Human Rights* (New York, 2001); Joan Hoff-Wilson and Marjorie Lightman, eds., *Without Precedent: The Life and Career of Eleanor Roosevelt* (Bloomington, 1984); Jason Berger, *A New Deal for the World: Eleanor Roosevelt and American Foreign Policy* (New York, 1981); "Universal Declaration of Human Rights" <http://www.un.org/Overview/rights.html> (April 8, 2002).

11. On UN conferences, see John W. Foster and Anita Anand, eds., *Whose World Is It Anyway? Civil Society, the United Nations, and the Multilateral Future* (Ottawa, 1999); "United Nations Division for the Advancement of Women" <http://www.un.org/womenwatch/daw/index.html> (April 29, 2002); and "United Nations International Conference on Population and Development (ICPD)" <http://www.iisd.ca/linkages/cairo.html> (April 29, 2002). Akira Iriye, *Global Community: The Role of International Organizations in the Making of the Contemporary World* (Berkeley, 2002). On women in U.S. foreign relations, see Leila J. Rupp, *Worlds of Women: The Making of an International Women's Movement* (Princeton, 1997); Rhodri Jeffreys-Jones, *Changing Differences: Women in the Shaping of American Foreign Policy* (Rutgers, 1995); Edward P. Crapol, ed., *Women in Foreign Policy: Lobbyists, Critics, and Insiders* (Wilmington, 1992); and Estelle B. Freedman, *No Turning Back: The History of Feminism and the Future of Women* (New York, 2002). For essays on diverse topics related to women and guidance to further citations regarding activism around women's issues, see Rita Mae Kelly, ed., *Gender, Globalization, and Democratization* (Lanham, 2001). On activism by the Revolutionary Association of the Women of Afghanistan (RAWA) over the past quarter century, see Cheryl Benard, *Veiled Courage: Inside the Afghan Women's Resistance* (New York, 2002).

12. *Larry King Live* (CNN, Dec. 26, 2001); *NewsHour* (PBS, Nov. 21, 2001).

13. "An Open Letter to the Senate on Ratification of the Convention on the Elimination of All Forms of Discrimination against Women (CEDAW)" <http://www.amnesty-usa.org/news/2001/usa12102001.html> (Jan. 2, 2002). For the history and the text of, and updates to, CEDAW, see "United Nations Convention on the Elimination of All Forms of Discrimination against Women" <http://www.un.org/womenwatch/daw/cedaw/> (April 29, 2002).

14. U.S. Department of State, "International Women's Issues" <http://www.state.gov/g/wi/> (Jan. 2, 2002).

A Cultural History of the War without End

Melani McAlister

Contrary to government proclamations, the U.S. "war on terrorism" did not begin on September 11, 2001. Instead, says Melani McAlister, we need to situate that conflict in a thirty-year-long history of American encounters with terrorism that included both policy making and popular culture. McAlister traces U.S. media and cultural responses to Israeli anti-terrorist activities of the 1970s and the Iran hostage crisis of 1979–1980, placing them in the context of reactions to the U.S. defeat in Vietnam. Linking popular culture, news accounts, and public understandings of events with policy making, McAlister explores the way that narratives of public and political events are created.

In October 2001, when President George W. Bush outlined his administration's responses to the September 11 attacks on New York and Washington, he also announced that the United States was about to begin a "new and different war," a war against terrorism that would need to be fought "on all fronts." Bush argued that unlike World War II, which brought clear-cut victory, or the Vietnam War, which ended in quagmire, or even the high-tech Gulf War, the new war would be "a different kind of war that requires a different type of approach and a different type of mentality." Speaking to a reporter a few days later, Vice President Richard Cheney put it more bluntly, "It is different than the Gulf War was, in the sense that it may never end. At least, not in our lifetime."[1]

The sense of a historic rupture with previous models of understanding the world was widespread in the weeks following the attacks. Not only were the levels of destruction and the extraordinary human casualties unheard-of for Americans in peacetime, but the live television coverage had left the nation stunned. Eventually, perhaps, television's endless repetition of the second plane slicing through the south tower of the World Trade Center would become numbing, but other, more personal,

Americans memorialized those killed in the World Trade Center and Pentagon attacks by drawing on diverse histories and memories. This memorial in the Union Square area of New York City, with its powerfully reworked patriotic symbols, recalls the ritual of leaving gifts and mementos at places such as the Vietnam Veterans Memorial in Washington, D.C., Catholic churches, and personal grave sites. (Courtesy of Mirana Comstock, from *9-12: The Daze After.*)

images retained a profound emotional resonance: firefighters covered in soot, rushing to save those they could and, later, searching through the rubble. Then came the friends and family who began to arrive on the scene—and on the screen—in the hours after the attacks. They carried large photocopied photos of their loved ones and spoke to reporters, tearfully telling of their last contact or determinedly showing the pictures that they hoped would inspire rescuers. Within days, September 11 had taken on the folkloric status of the assassination of John F. Kennedy; at nearly every gathering, people would tell their stories: where they were and what they were doing when they heard—or, rather, saw—the news.

It was not surprising, then, that the Bush administration would stress what many people in the United States already felt, that the nation was facing an unprecedented crisis and that nothing in our past had prepared us for such an attack. One corollary to that sense of rupture was the ease with which U.S. officials characterized the military response in Afghanistan and the concomitant commitment to a wider, perhaps worldwide, "war against terrorism" as something entirely new. Insisting repeatedly that Americans should not look to previous military conflicts for models, administration officials failed to mention the existence of one quite relevant historical precedent: the previous "war against terror" launched by the Reagan administration in 1981, just after the U.S. hostages held in Iran had been released. That "war" was also a call for a broad and sustained commitment, one modeled in opposition to the U.S. involvement in Vietnam. Moreover, it had its own precedents in yet another "war on terror"—one waged by Israel in the 1970s.

What most Americans knew about terrorism on September 10, 2001, was shaped by those earlier wars, which had been waged on television, made meaningful through culture, and brought home through violence. U.S. involvement with terrorism and anti-terrorism emerging out of the Middle East began in the 1970s as an emotional engagement with Israel's response to Palestinian violence against civilians. These concerns expanded dramatically in 1979, with the taking of American hostages at the U.S. embassy in Iran and the ensuing hostage crisis. In the popular culture of the 1980s—particularly but not only in the emerging genre of action movies—there was a sustained fascination with the problem of terrorism and the construction of a U.S. response. As the 1980s progressed, anti-terrorism became the glue of a directly politicized popular culture, which worked to imagine American national power in a global context. By the turn of the twenty-first century, the contests and complexities of three decades of struggle with the problem of terrorism and the role of military power were all but invisible. In their place, especially after September 11, was the promise of clear, effective action against definable, defeatable enemies.[2]

Near the end of *Imagined Communities*, Benedict Anderson describes one aspect of the process of consolidating national identities in times of crisis: "All profound changes in consciousness, by their very nature, bring with them characteristic amnesias. Out of such oblivions, in specific historical circumstances, spring narratives."[3] Such narratives, born of amnesias, promise to stitch together a patchwork past. They are forged not just by policy makers, but at the intersection of news accounts, policy developments, and cultural texts such as films, novels, and even video games. Of course, the "memories" constructed and reconstructed in the public sphere are never distributed evenly or unproblematically. But they *are* powerful.

This essay explores the politics of the diverse representations of terrorism in recent decades. It is not a study of policy making per se or of public opinion, as that is measured in public opinion polls or oral histories. But it does find links between popular culture, news accounts, and public understandings of the meaning and significance of political events, though those links are neither direct nor easily measured empirically. I analyze the politics of representation, on the understanding that culture is a crucial site for the negotiation of political and moral values and for the development of an often uneven and contested public understanding of history and its significance. Cultural texts do not inject ideologies into their audiences, but they do figure in the process of constructing frameworks that help policy make sense in a given moment. Policy makers do not control representations; in fact, any given policy (or policy maker) may be deeply at odds with the views presented in contemporary news accounts or with the apparent ideology of any given cultural text. But as policy makers make difficult choices in often complex situations, they must negotiate the fractured terrain shaped by the intersection of conflicting material interests, government actions, political organizing, and cultural texts.[4] What I examine here is not a conspiracy nor a set of functionalist representations in the service of power, but a process of convergence, as historical events, overlapping representations, and diverse vested interests come together in a powerful, if historically contingent, accord that is productive of a new common sense. Cultural texts enter into that process: They are integral aspects of both history and politics. This essay traces how a history was made meaningful; that is, it explores the public activity of devising a particular narrative of anti-terrorism and U.S. power.

Beginnings: Munich

The issue of Middle East terrorism entered U.S. public life in a profound way in September 1972, when Palestinian guerrillas broke into the Israeli compound at the Olympic Games in Munich. There, they killed two members of the Israeli Olympic team and took nine hostage. Immediately, ABC, the network that televised the games in the United States, began continuous live coverage. There were tense negotiations throughout the day, but in the end the plan to capture the attackers went terribly wrong, and the Palestinians killed all of their hostages.

The massacre had an unprecedented impact in the United States, as people watched events unfold on TV and then mourned the athletes. Other terrorism had been more deadly, but nothing had quite this effect on Americans. Perhaps, as some commentators suggested, it was because the spirit of the Olympics had been destroyed. Or perhaps it was because, unlike earlier terrorist attacks, this one was covered live by U.S. television, which had crews already on the scene reporting events as they happened. But at that moment the intractable politics of the Middle East conflict also resonated unexpectedly with Americans, who in 1972 were facing their own protracted and seemingly indecisive end game in Vietnam. Israel and the Palestinians, too, were fighting a long, unconventional war over control of territory. The outcome in both cases was uncertain.

Looking back thirty years later, what is striking about the U.S. response to the Munich Olympics tragedy is that a shared outrage over brutal attacks on civilians did not lead to a uniform view of how to respond. Instead, the divided reactions to the assassinations at the Munich Olympics mirrored debates emerging out of the Vietnam conflict. Many U.S. commentators suggested that a military response would be both appropriate and effective and expressed sympathy with what they took to be Israel's inevitable counterattack (it immediately bombed villages in Syria and Lebanon that, it said, housed guerrilla bases). As one ABC news reporter explained: "Israel will not stand by while its citizens are victims of terror. . . . Time will ease their grief, but time will not weaken their determination to punish the terrorists and their supporters."[5]

Yet there was also an argument, made strongly by liberals, that in the new, multipolar world that was emerging, the battle against terrorism, like the guerrilla war in Vietnam, could not be won merely by overpowering force. This new world was one in which military victories were elusive and moral categories fuzzy. The solution to escalating violence was to respond to root causes, to negotiate, and, in the words of presidential candidate George McGovern, to "Stop the killing! Stop the killing everywhere around the world!" In this argument, specifically in the context of the mainstreamed opposition to the Vietnam War, the emergence of terrorism as a mode of conflict was one symptom of the need to rethink military power as a means for pursuing U.S. interests.

Thus liberals and some moderates pointed to Vietnam (and now Palestinian terrorism) to argue that the United States (and now Israel) relied too heavily on force in situations where political, economic, or diplomatic solutions were more likely to be effective. That argument gained considerable strength with OPEC's (Organization of Petroleum Exporting Countries) display of economic power the following year, with the 1973 oil embargo.[6]

There was also the question of how to evaluate actions such as the one in Munich—how to define what should be called terrorism, as opposed to liberation struggle, guerrilla activity, or simply war. To name something terrorism is a condemnation, distinguishing it immediately from actions against civilians that one might justify in certain contexts. Scholars and journalists have debated what kinds of actions would fall under a fully consistent definition of terrorism: Why a massacre in an airport but not a bombing of a village? When is an action terrorism, and when is it simply terrifying for the civilians under attack? Those debates are important, politically and morally, if one is to take a principled position in a particular conflict. But when we ask how the category of terrorism functioned historically in U.S. public life, we see that the definitions have mattered less than the emotions and values that swirled around the events that became exemplary. In practice, the fear and anger about terrorism in the 1970s developed from a specific set of images and stories, not through a consistent, worked-out categorization of types of violence. When an action evoked fear and horror, it was understood to be terrorism—it was as if the force of the emotion itself generated the working definition.

Entebbe

It was not until four years later, in 1976, that the terms of the debate about terrorism shifted decisively with one of the most famous hijackings in history. In June 1976 hijackers associated with the Popular Front for the Liberation of Palestine took over a flight from Tel Aviv and forced it to fly to Entebbe, Uganda. The hijackers demanded the release of pro-Palestinian prisoners held in jails in Israel and several other countries. Israel at first refused to negotiate for the hostages or to release the prisoners it held. But over the next several days, the guerrillas released 140 of the hostages, keeping only the Israelis (including dual citizens) and the French crew. On July 1, under pressure from the families of the hostages (some of whom broke into the military compound where Prime Minister Yitzhak Rabin lived and angrily demanded to see him), Israel agreed to negotiate. As negotiations opened, however, the Israeli government was also planning its military operation. Israeli commandos secretly flew to Uganda on July 4, 1976. There they attacked the airport, fought off Ugandan soldiers, killed all of the hijackers, and loaded the hostages onto planes to Israel. During the raid, three hostages and one Israeli soldier were killed.[7]

U.S. responses to the Israelis' military operation were remarkable for their level of emotional engagement. Of course, the raid *was* an impressive feat, not only technically and logistically, but also in its audacity. The Israelis not only took the political risk of invading another country to rescue their citizens; they also took the very real risk that many hostages and rescuers would be killed in the process. In the United States admiration mixed with joy, and the raid was celebrated across the political spectrum, with enthusiastic responses in the left-liberal *Nation*, the conservative *National Review*, and the mainstream *Newsweek*, among others. *Newsweek* enthused, "Once again, Israel's lightning-swift sword had cut down an enemy, and its display of military precision, courage, and sheer chutzpa won the applause and admiration of most of the world." The *Nation* declared, "The fact is that Israel was doing the work of the rest of the so-called civilized world when it staged that coup against the hostage-holding hijackers."

How-they-did-it stories, complete with detailed maps and illustrations, were produced in virtually every major newspaper and magazine in the country, where they competed with television specials, quickie books, and a spate of movies immediately put into production. The response to terrorism had hardened considerably since Munich. When the eleven athletes were killed, there were calls for Israel and the Palestinians to negotiate. Four years later, when scores of people were taken hostage, but no one killed (until the rescue raid), the enthusiasm for military response had increased considerably. Some of the responses suggested not only enthusiasm, but an appropriation of the Israeli success as a shared victory.[8]

While analogies to Vietnam remained very much a part of the public response to Entebbe, the general tenor of U.S. understandings of Vietnam had shifted. Americans had witnessed the disastrous final pullout from Saigon the year before, and comparisons were everywhere. By 1976, conservative intellectuals were already promoting the concept

Americans responded enthusiastically to the Israeli rescue of hostages at Entebbe, Uganda, in July 1976. This cartoon is one of many that celebrated Israeli military prowess and suggested a biblical mandate for the response to terrorism. (Courtesy of Steve Greenberg, from *Los Angeles Jewish Federation Bulletin*, 1976.)

of the "Vietnam syndrome," which suggested that not only had the United States failed to use adequate force to win the war, but that in the wake of the failure, the nation suffered from a failure of nerve, an unwillingness to act decisively. Israel's decisive action in *its* unconventional war was taken as an example of the successful use of force. It became a commonplace after 1976 that the United States should not only act *with* Israel on foreign policy but *like* Israel in matters of unconventional war.[9]

The engagement with Israel's war against terrorism was evident on another front in the summer of 1976. That year was the beginning of an avalanche of popular "true spy" books that featured Israel's intelligence agency, the Mossad, and its special forces as lead characters. *Hit Team*, by the *Time* reporters David B. Tinnin and Dag Christensen, was published that year. In it they describe the actions of a secret group of Israeli operatives who, from 1972 to 1974, had assassinated twelve or thirteen Palestinian leaders. Some of those Palestinians were implicated in the planning of the Munich massacre; others were believed to be important Palestinian operatives or spokesmen linked to various factions. The team (or, according to some reports, teams) used new technologies then being perfected by Israel, including radio-controlled bombs and telephone bombs, which could be activated when the intended target picked up the phone. Soon thereafter, several other adoring accounts of Israeli covert operations methods were published, with such titles as *The Spymasters of Israel, The Israeli Secret Service,* and *Every Spy a Prince;* all included long sections on the "reaction to Munich." Though this literature rarely reached the best-seller list, the sheer proliferation of titles suggested a substantial subcultural interest, one that was far from idiosyncratic in its fascination with the Mossad and the Israeli military as exemplars of effective, no-holds-barred action.[10]

Yet even with this level of enthusiasm, there remained a genuine debate about whether Israeli tactics could or should be a model for the United States. Two weeks after the Entebbe rescue, the journalist Judith Miller (who fifteen years later wrote a well-publicized exposé of Saddam Hussein) reported in the *New York Times Magazine* that many diplomats were concerned about the uncritical embrace of a get-tough-with-terrorists policy. Faced with the mixed results of such policies in the early part of the 1970s, the Ford administration hired the RAND Corporation (a conservative think tank generally tied to the U.S. Army) to review U.S. policies. Brian Jenkins, a senior RAND analyst, concluded that U.S. policy makers should show flexibility in dealing with terrorism. The United States had a firm policy not to negotiate with terrorists; the assumption was that such refusals would deter other terrorism in the future. Jenkins argued that evidence for that assumption was "'squishy' at best." The wringing of concessions is only part of what terrorists want, he argued, and it may not be the most important thing. Describing well the emerging consensus about the impetus to and meanings of terrorism, he surmised that most hijackers and hostage takers did not want mass murder. Instead, "terrorists want a lot of people watching and a lot of people listening, not a lot of people dead." Their target was not so much the hostages as it was the larger audience. "Terrorism is theater," he said. Some U.S. officials argued that the types of raids or assassinations that Israel could carry out would never be possible, politically, for a superpower. But the appeal of quick, clean military action, particularly in hostage situations, was undeniable. Shortly after President Jimmy Carter took office in 1977, he directed the Pentagon to develop anti-terrorist capabilities similar to those of Israel and West Germany (which had just pulled off a successful rescue at Mogadishu, Somalia). Within a month, the Delta Force was created—the first special forces detachment specifically organized to fight "unconventional warfare" against terrorism.[11]

The United States was not often targeted by Arab guerrillas in the 1970s, but Palestinian terrorism against Israel had a cultural salience far beyond its limited strategic importance. Redeploying Israel's war against terrorism from the context of the Israeli-Palestinian conflict, American observers used it to do the cultural work of reimaging U.S. power after Vietnam. Thus Israeli actions mattered in U.S. public culture largely due to internal considerations—*not* the political influence of American Jews, but the legacy of Vietnam and fears of U.S. weakness.

Iran

The presumption of a single appropriate response to the terrorist violence of September 11 evoked the embrace of Israeli tactics but ignored the layered debates that had linked responses to terrorism to the changing understandings of U.S. global power after the Vietnam War. In addition, Bush's notion of an entirely new kind of war depended on a similar mix of memory and forgetting in the face of the most significant American encounter with terrorism in the late twentieth century, the Iran hostage crisis.

In November 1979 Iranians loyal to the Ayatollah Ruhollah Khomeini overran the U.S. embassy in Tehran and took fifty-two Americans hostage. For 444 days the hostages remained captive, while the Carter administration worked furiously to gain their release. And every night for more than a year, Americans watched as Iranians held demonstrations outside the embassy, chanting their anger at the United States and burning U.S. flags.

Television news coverage of the Iran crisis was remarkable for being at once absolutely ubiquitous and remarkably innocent of any historical sense. The long history of U.S. involvement in Iran—thirty years of military and political support for the ruthless Mohammed Reza Shah Pahlavi, who had just been overthrown by a coalition of Islamic activists and leftist opponents—was subordinated to a story of the Iranians' irrational rage. U.S. soil (the embassy) had been attacked and Americans had been made victims; the fate of the hostages became the single most discussed issue in U.S. public life. Television news highlighted the personal aspects of the crisis, focusing particularly on the family members of the hostages. Gary Sick, an official in the Carter administration, de-

In April 1980 Desert One, the U.S. mission to rescue the hostages in Iran, failed. Here, Iranian soldiers and Ayatollah Sadegh Khalkali, a member of Iran's revolutionary government, survey the wreckage of U.S. aircraft from the mission in the desert outside Tehran. Americans responded with furious outrage to the mission's failure, which seemed one of many symptoms of U.S. decline in the post–Vietnam War era. (Courtesy of Michael LeTourneau, Wide World Photos.)

scribed the coverage as "the longest running human interest drama in the history of television." The hostage families became a collective icon in the U.S. media: They gave interviews, held their own press conferences, and confronted political officials.[12]

The hostages soon became a national symbol, but their public status came about precisely because they were understood first and foremost as private individuals—in part, because they were represented first and foremost by their families. Though all of those held were "official Americans," embassy employees or marine guards, that was not what mattered about them: It was just the opposite. They represented the United States because they were ordinary. Television helped to render them as such, identifying them with a private sphere, allied with family, emotions, and domesticity and thus imagined as outside of politics.

In popular culture anti-Arab stereotypes were recycled to apply to (non-Arab) Iran, from the "rich oil sheik" rhetoric that emerged out of the oil crisis in the mid-1970s to the images of the fanatic Arab terrorist. Americans could buy "Nuke Iran" or "Don't Waste Gas, Waste Khomeini" bumper stickers or dart boards and toilet paper with Khomeini's image. (After September 11, there was a similar but smaller-scale business in items such as Osama bin Laden piñatas and "Osama Yo' Mama" hats.)[13]

The small but now highly visible population of Iranians living in the United States also became a charged political issue. Most of the Iranians were students; some were exiles from the Khomeini regime, but many had been deeply opposed to the rule of the shah. From the first weeks of the crisis, the presence of these immigrants and visitors was a source of anger and outrage. Tensions only increased when, on several occasions during the year, Iranians demonstrated to call for the return of the shah to Iran or in support of Khomeini. There were calls to deport all Iranians in the United States, but as one CBS reporter wearily announced, quoting a Justice Department official, "The Constitution protects even visitors to this country, and some Iranians have learned to take advantage of that."[14]

On April 24, 1980, about six months after the hostages were taken, President Carter appeared on national television to announce that the Delta Force special operations team had aborted an attempted rescue mission after several of the helicopters that were supposed to evacuate the hostages had malfunctioned. As the rescue team was preparing to withdraw from the desert outside Tehran, a helicopter accidentally collided with a transport plane, and eight military personnel were killed. Those deaths and the failure of the rescue ignited a storm of protest from all over the political spectrum, and media coverage of the events was notable for its overt expressions of outrage. Many policy makers and pundits had strongly supported the idea of a rescue but now angrily discussed the mission's failures of planning and execution. Meanwhile, both television and print media produced detailed accounts of the planned raid, with detailed maps, step-by-step illustrations, and charts and arrows explaining what went wrong, where, and why. A special commission was formed to investigate the failure; after it released its report in August 1980, a new flurry of articles appeared. No one who had seen the gleeful enthusiasm that greeted similar illustrations after Entebbe, three and a half years earlier, could have missed the contrast. With the onset of the Iran crisis, the embrace of Israel's military actions did not disappear, but Israeli success could no longer serve a prosthetic function: Now Americans were not vicarious victors, but victims.[15]

The hostages were finally released, after intense, final-hour negotiations with the Carter administration, on January 20, 1981, the day Ronald Reagan was inaugurated president. Reagan used his inaugural address to announce that "terrorism" would replace Carter's focus on "human rights" as the nation's primary foreign policy concern. Over the next decade, that first U.S. "war against terrorism" had many fronts. There was continued instability in the Middle East, and Arab- or Iranian-sponsored attacks on U.S. targets increased noticeably. Hijackings and airline bombings were the most visible: In 1985 a TWA flight carrying mostly American passengers was hijacked from Athens to Beirut and one American was killed, and the cruise ship *Achille Lauro* was hijacked, also with one passenger killed. In 1988, Pan Am flight 103 was blown up over Lockerbie, Scotland, killing 270 people, mostly Americans.

The campaign against such terrorism was a major component of the theoretical structure that supported the Ronald Reagan–George Bush military buildup in many parts of the world (including Latin America and Europe) and the determined reassertion of U.S. political and military hegemony in the Middle East. That reassertion included, among other things, military intervention in Lebanon (1981–1983)—effectively ended by the bombing of the U.S. Marine barracks in Beirut by Shiite militants, in which 243 marines were killed. Other U.S. involvements centered on political and military interventions in the Iran-Iraq war (1980–1988), including political and logistical support for Iraq (1980–1984) and the sale of arms to Iran (the Iran-Contra deal, 1985–1986). In addition the United States expanded arms sales to Saudi Arabia (1985–1988) and in 1986 bombed Libya in retaliation for what the Reagan administration said was Libya's involvement in the bombing of a disco in Berlin.[16]

Moreover, throughout the 1980s, Middle Eastern terrorism was a major concern of foreign policy makers and pundits, and rescue from terrorists was a primary theme in U.S. popular culture. Yet this concern differed in important ways from the focus on Israel in the 1970s. First, the focus was no longer on Israel, but on the United States, which was now represented as the primary victim and the most important warrior in a worldwide battle against terrorism. Second, professional definitions of terrorism took on a new political and cultural force. By the mid-1980s, a new public figure had emerged, the "terrorism expert," and the production of literature on terrorism had become its own industry. There was, among those professionals, a marked change in the moral geography of the Middle East, one heralded by a reclassification: Islam, rather than Arab nationalism or political radicalism, became highlighted as the dominant producer of terrorism. Of course, Islam had indeed become more important as a political force in the Middle East, as the hopes for secular nationalism failed and religious revivalism became one response to the new pressures of globalization, the reach of superpowers, economic crises, and the displacements of modernization. But there was a tendency, especially among experts promoted by the conservative foundations and think tanks, to reassign political struggles as religious ideology and then to search for the "nature of Islam" as the source of the problem. The task was then to discover *How the West Can Win*, to quote the subtitle of one of the best-known anti-terrorism studies.[17]

Third, the sheer proliferation of policy studies was replicated in popular culture, from films to television specials to popular books. In the 1970s, terrorism had been quite visible—when there was a crisis, newspapers and television covered it intensively—but the focus was periodic rather than sustained. By the 1980s, terrorism, particularly the rescue of hostages taken by Middle Eastern terrorists, became a near obsession. These stories inevitably took the Iranian hostage crisis as their reference point, either directly or indirectly, but they enacted a crucial transformation: Now, the hostages in question were rescued, not negotiated for. In these cultural texts, hostages returned home as symbols of victory; they *did not* linger as nightly reminders of the impotence of the United States.

Terrorism had certainly been represented in films before the Iran hostage crisis. Terrorist attacks, often from domestic groups, figured centrally in the plots of several well-known films in the 1970s, such as *The Taking of Pelham One Two Three* (1974), about the takeover of a New York City subway, and *Black Sunday* (1977), about a terrorist plot to explode the Goodyear blimp over a Super Bowl game. And in 1976, the critically acclaimed *Network* included a running joke about a terrorist sitcom, in which a radical terrorist group (a parody of the SLA [Symbionese Liberation Army] of Patty Hearst fame) contracts to get a weekly half-hour show to broadcast their attacks on television. After 1980, however, terrorism and the rescue of hostages became a stock trope in a new and popular style of action thriller. The theme of hostages and terrorism structured action films ranging from the B-movie military genre— *Missing in Action* (1984), *Iron Eagle* (1986), *Navy SEALS* (1990), *Rambo III* (1988)—to big-budget thrillers such as *Patriot Games* (1992) and the film version of John Le Carré's best-selling novel, *The Little Drummer Girl*

(1984). The Chuck Norris vehicle *The Delta Force* (1986) opened with a scene of the failed rescue of U.S. hostages in Iran. The film then unfolded a hijacking plot almost identical to that of the 1985 Athens-Beirut TWA hijacking, except that this time, rather than the hostages being freed by negotiation, they were rescued by the Delta Force team in an impressively pyrotechnic operation.[18]

There were, of course, many negative stereotypes of Middle Easterners in those films—they were awash in cartoonish portrayals. But that is not the most interesting or most important aspect of the anti-terrorist action genre. Instead, the cultural work emerges from the fact that, of all the potential "actions" in the action genre, the predominant theme is hostage rescue. In other words, unlike action films in the late 1990s, which might have focused on efforts to prevent a bombing or on vengeance for a previous act of violence, the issue for many of these films was not just terrorists, but hostages—particularly, hostages who were marked by their positions in families. In *The Delta Force*, the hostages aboard the TWA flight are carefully delineated in terms of their personal relationships: the father with a little girl, the happily married older couple, the two nuns and the priest who love each other. In *Die Hard* (1988), the people being held are not a family; they work together in an office building. But the most important hostage is the estranged wife of Bruce Willis's character; he will rescue her, and their marriage will be saved. In these films, the uncertain and messy outcomes of real-life hostage and terrorist situations were reimagined in the simpler language of defined threat and unambiguous victory. The rescue of families from terrorists becomes so common, so banal, that its origins as a response to a specific event are submerged and invisible.[19]

What made the terrorist-rescue films *work* so powerfully in this period was not their policy statements, nor their images of Arabs, nor even the military solutions inevitably posited for the problems they depicted. Instead, it was a deep commitment to this simple proposition: It is time to get our people out of there. The presentation of American identity as essentially private, located in family ties and protected by love, means that even films that seem to have deeply political commitments—whether *Rambo III* or *Navy SEALS*—make their most profound political statements in their *depoliticization* of the activities they depict. In U.S. political culture, emotions are imagined as spontaneous and internal to the self; they are naturalized. Thus the desire, the right, to save loved ones by any means can be presented as if it falls beyond explanation.

Loved ones return home, and hostage rescue works in their service. Of course, such rescue requires military and political action, but that action is framed as an essentially personal matter, one located in the family and in affect—both love and anger—and therefore outside history.

What the hostage films imagined, the political world eventually provided. With the 1990–1991 Gulf War against Iraq, the United States was able to put together a large multinational coalition to launch one of the largest military operations of the postwar period against Iraq, which had invaded Kuwait. That war was not a hostage rescue (though there was a brief hostage incident) but it was an answer to the hostage story. The Gulf War was understood by almost everyone, its supporters and its opponents, as proof that U.S. military power was back in force—and that it could, and would, be used to shape the political landscape of the Middle East.

Conclusion

In the immediate aftermath of September 11, many Hollywood executives suggested that there could be no more violent action movies after such a national trauma. The planned releases of several action films were delayed, as producers predicted a return to musicals and family drama. But those predictions soon proved wrong. In December 2001, *Entertainment Weekly* previewed winter film releases with a simple summary: "Hollywood Goes to War." This return to the action genre would not have been a surprise had Hollywood remembered its own history. It was the national drama of the Iran hostage crisis that had helped fuel development of the new hyperviolent action films, which promised military action without the constraints of public debate.[20]

But the two most prominent action films of early 2002 seemed to offer diametrically opposed visions of the nature of U.S. power, and they received quite divergent public responses. The Arnold Schwarzenegger vehicle *Collateral Damage* had received a great deal of publicity when its planned October 2001 release was postponed due, producers said, to the sensitive nature of several scenes. The plot revolves around a fireman (Schwarzenegger) whose wife and child are killed in a terrorist attack by Colombian drug lords. Realizing that the incompetent and/or unconcerned agencies of the U.S. government will never catch the man who killed his family, Schwarzenegger goes on a one-man revenge mission to Colombia, where, without carrying a gun or speaking Spanish, he manages to find the terrorists, destroy a cocaine plant, and get his revenge. The film makes some perfunctory efforts to show "both sides of the story" by giving the terrorists a chance to make statements criticizing U.S. policy, but political nuance quickly disappears as the bad guys reveal themselves to be fundamentally evil and Schwarzenegger enacts justice with "his bare hands and a handy ax." When the film opened in early February 2002, the box office was middling (the film opened at number one, but the receipts plummeted 40 percent in the second week) and the reviews were worse. Reviewers almost uniformly referred to the resonances to September 11 in negative terms (for example, the fact that the hero is a firefighter, and the film's untimely reference to "the first terrorist attack on our nation's capital"). If the filmmakers could not have known what kind of terrorism would happen in the real world, the painful realities had nonetheless, it seemed, rendered the simplicities of Schwarzenegger's trademark action formula unpalatable. One might have expected the opposite, and some audiences did seem to revel in the sense of moral and satisfying violence. Yet reviewers seemed to be speaking for a rather unimpressed public when they announced that the basic story, of one man seeking revenge for his family, making his justice into a personal affair yanked from the jaws of indifferent police and security agencies, "had been played out even back when everyone thought exploding buildings were cool." As Paul Clinton wrote for *CNN.com*, "Without September 11, *Collateral Damage* would have been just another bad movie. Now it's a bad, embarrassing movie."[21]

While *Collateral Damage* was postponed as potentially too painful for viewers, Ridley Scott's *Black Hawk Down* was moved up several months before its planned March 2002 release, appearing on December 28, 2001, just in time both to qualify it for the Oscars and to cash in on the more militaristic mood of a country that had just routed the Taliban from Afghanistan. The plot was based on the *Philadelphia Inquirer* reporter Mark Bowden's account of the October 1993 raid by the U.S. Army Rangers and Delta Force into Mogadishu. While participating in a United Nations program responding to large-scale famine, they attacked and attempted to capture two deputies of the warlord Mohammed Farah Aidid. What was supposed to be a simple strike turned into a large-scale day-long street battle, in which 18 American soldiers and perhaps 1,000 Somalis were killed.[22]

The film did extremely well at the box office (it was number one for five weeks, far outgrossing *Collateral Damage*), and although reviews were mixed, there was a broad sense that *Black Hawk Down* presented much of the complexity of fighting in a war, particularly the horror and the camaraderie. Many reviewers commented on the arresting spectacle of the battle scenes—beautiful in their staging and use of color as well as nightmarish in their intensity. "*Black Hawk Down* has such distinctive visual aplomb that its jingoism starts to feel like part of its atmosphere," wrote the *New York Times* reviewer Elvis Mitchell, echoing a common sentiment that while the movie showed images of war particularly well, it was so focused on presenting the battle that the political background remained undefined and the characters of the U.S. soldiers were virtually indistinguishable. Scott himself was not unaware of the issue, insisting that his movie was not about the political issues at stake in Somalia or the soldiers' lives back home, but about the valor of those who, in the face of danger, found courage and performed their duty.[23]

Of course, no one missed the wartime political resonance of this "apolitical" approach to the story. The Pentagon fully cooperated with the film, providing helicopters, technical support, and even soldiers to serve as extras. The political valence did not come simply or even primarily from the fact that Somalia had been named by the Bush administration as a potential hiding place for Osama bin Laden and thus as a potential target in the next stage of the U.S. war on terror. Instead, it was the film's view of the moral righteousness of U.S. motives and the inherent honorableness of military virtues that made it so seemingly right for its moment. In fact, the film makers themselves had considered adding a postscript to the movie that explicitly linked it to the September 11 attacks, suggesting that the Clinton administration's decision to remove the troops in the wake of the raid and the subsequent "irresolution" in Rwanda, Bosnia, and Kosovo had emboldened U.S. enemies. In the end, they removed the explicit statements, asserting that the connection was clear enough for those who wanted to make it.[24]

Yet others saw a different lesson. Andrew O'Hehir, writing for *Salon.com*, suggested that *Black Hawk Down*'s refusal to develop the political background to the action in Somalia had reproduced an American tendency to assume that good motives are enough to justify any action. Early in the movie, one earnest young sergeant speaks in favor of the U.S. presence, saying, "Look, there are two things we can do. We can help these people or we can watch them die on CNN." O'Hehir comments, "There was a third option, as it turned out. Armed with good intentions and expensive weaponry, we could blunder into a situation we only partly understood, causing a lot of death and destruction and making a bad situation even worse."[25] It is notable that it was on the Internet, and not on television or in print media, that this dissenting voice appeared.

Yet, by January 2002, enthusiasm for the war against terrorism was beginning to be mixed with precisely such doubts about its long-term outcome. In the immediate aftermath of the attacks, statements of doubt or dissent were often treated as traitorous, as when Attorney General John Ashcroft remarked that those who criticized U.S. policy were only aiding the terrorists. But in December reports about the number of civilian deaths in Afghanistan led one *Time* columnist to suggest that the danger to American troops arose when locals did not share Americans' views of their own actions, especially given that, in Afghanistan, the "collateral damage" that resulted from U.S. bombings was every bit as horrifying for its victims as the attacks on New York and Washington had been for the Americans who died. The fear of a long Vietnam-style entanglement (a fear shared, in different ways, by liberals and conservatives) began to merge with a conservative political discourse that increasingly warned against peace keeping and nation building, indeed *any* humanitarian involvement by U.S. troops.[26]

This layered discourse of refusal and remembrance suggests that when Bush administration officials insisted that there was no relevant history for the "new war" against terror, they did not intend that Americans forget entirely the conflicts outlined here. Indeed, they could operate confidently from the assumption that the sedimented cultural impact of those earlier encounters would help focus Americans' deep moral outrage and desire for justice toward support for a specific policy that called for immediate and far-reaching military action, including a bombing campaign, removal of the Taliban, and, ultimately, military action that would reach well beyond Afghanistan. The narratives that had emerged from the wars against terrorism of the 1970s and the 1980s were personalized tales, organized around captivity and rescue, in which the protection of private life, even the promise of a right to be protected from politics itself, appeared as the preeminent value for the very public activities of the state and the military. They were, at their heart, displacements: Israeli rescues appropriated as part of U.S. responses to Vietnam, the claim to private life pushing aside the political nature of the embassy in Iran, and the promise of valiant rescue displacing the reality of limited military success.

At the same time, neither the public statements of official policy makers nor most of the media have engaged just how politically and militarily complex those earlier battles against terrorism really were. A public acknowledgment that there *had* been a debate, not only about how to respond to terrorism but about the nature of Middle East politics and the terms of U.S. world power, might have opened up the possibility for an expanded political discussion—about the military and diplomatic options available and about the possible long-term political effects of U.S. actions.

If, after September 11, such a discussion seemed impossible for most people to imagine, that boundary of thought was forged in part by our narratives of the past. With the memory/forgetting of captivity and rescue behind us, it became time for Americans to win the thirty years' war—by pretending it had just begun.

Notes

1. *Boston Globe*, Oct. 12, 2001, p. A28. Sections of the argument that follows draw from my analysis in Melani McAlister, *Epic Encounters: Culture, Media, and U.S. Interests in the Middle East, 1945–2000* (Berkeley, 2001), chaps. 4 and 5. *Washington Post*, Oct. 21, 2001, p. A01.

2. On the politics of "certainty" as it emerged after September 11, 2001, see Peter Alexander Meyers, "Defend Politics against Terrorism," *Social Science Research Council* <http://www.ssrc.org/sept11/essays/meyers.htm> (May 15, 2002).

3. Benedict Anderson, *Imagined Communities: Reflections on the Origin and Spread of Nationalism* (New York, 1991), 204.

4. In recent years, foreign policy scholars have increasingly analyzed the importance of culture to studies of international relations. See, for example, Emily Rosenberg, *Financial Missionaries to the World: The Politics and Culture of Dollar Diplomacy, 1900–1930* (Cambridge, Mass., 1999); John Dower, *War without Mercy* (New York, 1987); Penny Von Eschen, *Race against Empire: Black Americans and Anticolonialism, 1937–1957* (Ithaca, 1997); John Fousek, *To Lead the Free World: American Nationalism and the Cultural Roots of the Cold War* (Chapel Hill, 2000); and Robert Vitalis, "The Graceful and Generous Liberal Gesture: Making Racism Invisible in American International Relations," *Millennium*, 29 (Sept. 2000), 331–56.

5. *ABC Evening News*, Sept. 7, 1972 (videotape), Television News Archive (Vanderbilt University, Nashville, Tenn.).

6. *ABC Evening News*, Sept. 6, 1972 (videotape), Television News Archive; *Atlanta Constitution*, Sept. 7, 1972, p. A20. For others who drew the connection between Munich and Vietnam, see *New York Times*, Sept. 8, 1972, p. A22; *Washington Post*, Sept. 8, 1972, p. B1; and *ibid.*, Sept. 10, 1972, p. B7. For the argument about the reliance on force, see Jerry Wayne Sanders, *Peddlers of Crisis: The Committee on the Present Danger and the Politics of Containment* (Boston, 1983), 191–276.

7. Edgar O'Ballance, *Language of Violence: The Blood Politics of Terrorism* (Novato, 1979). See also *Atlanta Journal-Constitution*, July 4, 1976, p. 1.

8. Milton R. Benjamin, "The Fall Out from Entebbe," *Newsweek*, July 19, 1976, p. 41; "Israel's Skill and Daring," *Nation*, July 17, 1976, p. 37. Newspaper and magazine coverage included James Burnham, "Reflections on Entebbe," *National Review*, Aug. 6, 1976, p. 834; Raymond Carroll, "How the Israelis Pulled It Off," *Newsweek*, July 19, 1976, pp. 42ff.; *New York Times*, July 11, 1976, sec. 4, p. 7; and "Rescue at Entebbe: How the Israelis Did It," *Reader's Digest*, 109 (Oct. 1976), pp. 122–28. Books included William Stevenson, *Ninety Minutes at Entebbe* (New York, 1976); and Ira Peck, *Raid on Entebbe* (New York, 1977). The race to make movies about the event is discussed in "Entebbe Derby," *Time*, July 26, 1976, p. 82.

9. For a discussion of the idea of a "Vietnam syndrome," as it developed among conservatives, see Sanders, *Peddlers of Crisis*, 235–311. See Robert Holtz, "Israel Points the Way," *Aviation Week and Space Technology*, July 12, 1976, p. 7; and "When the U.S. Rescue Mission Fizzled," *U.S. News and World Report*, July 19, 1976, p. 32. See also my more detailed analysis of this admiration for Israel in McAlister, *Epic Encounters*, 178–97.

10. David B. Tinnin and Dag Christensen, *The Hit Team* (Boston, 1976); Steven Stewart, *The Spymasters of Israel* (New York, 1980); Richard Deacon, *The Israeli Secret Service* (New York, 1978), 227–56; Dan Raviv and Yossi Melman, *Every Spy a Prince: The Complete History of Israel's Intelligence Community* (Boston, 1990), 163–94. See also George Jonas, *Vengeance: The True Story of an Israeli Counter-Terrorist Team* (New York, 1984); and Steve Posner, *Israel Undercover: Secret Warfare and Hidden Diplomacy in the Middle East* (Syracuse, 1987).

11. Judith Miller, *Saddam Hussein and the Crisis in the Gulf* (New York, 1990); Judith Miller, "Bargain with Terrorists?" *New York Times Magazine*, July 18, 1976, pp. 7ff.; David C. Martin and John Walcott, *Best-Laid Plans: The Inside Story of America's War against Terrorism* (New York, 1989).

12. Gary Sick, *All Fall Down: America's Tragic Encounter with Iran* (New York, 1986), 258.

13. The anti-Khomeini items are mentioned both by Edward Said, *Covering Islam* (New York, 1981), 117; and Hamid Naficy, "Mediating the Other," in *The U.S. Media and the Middle East*, ed. Yahya Kamalipour (Westport, 1995), 81–82. On bin Laden items, see *St. Petersburg Times*, Oct. 28, 2001, p. 1F.

14. CBS *Evening News*, Aug. 7, 1980 (videotape), Television News Archive.

15. *Washington Post*, April 26, 1980, p. A1; "Tragedy in the Desert: Rescue That Failed," *U.S. News and World Report*, May 5, 1980, pp. 6ff.; Alan Mayer et al., "A Mission Comes to Grief in Iran," *Newsweek*, May 5, 1980, pp. 24ff. See also *New York Times*, Aug. 24, 1980, p. 1; and *Washington Post*, Aug. 24, 1980, p. A1.

16. Edward Herman and Gary O'Sullivan, *The Terrorism Industry: The Experts and Institutions That Shape Our View of Terror* (New York, 1989), 44. See also Marc Celmer, *Terrorism, U.S. Strategy, and Reagan Policies* (Westport, 1987).

17. On the development of expert ideologies about terrorism, see McAlister, *Epic Encounters*, chap. 5. A collection developed from an anti-terrorism conference held in Washington, D.C. in 1984 included contributions from Israelis, Europeans, and Americans. Prominent U.S. contributors included George P. Schultz, Daniel Patrick Moynihan, Jeane J. Kirkpatrick, Bernard Lewis, Charles Krauthammer,

Daniel Schorr, and Edwin Meese III. See Benjamin Netanyahu, ed., *Terrorism: How the West Can Win* (New York, 1986).

18. *The Taking of Pelham One Two Three*, dir. Joseph Sargent (Palladium Productions, 1974); *Black Sunday*, dir. John Frankenheimer (Paramount Pictures, 1977); *Network*, dir. Sidney Lumet (MGM/United Artists, 1976); *Missing in Action*, dir. Joseph Zito (Cannon Group, 1984); *Iron Eagle*, dir. Sidney J. Furie (TriStar Pictures, 1986); *Navy SEALS*, dir. Lewis Teague (Orion Pictures Corporation, 1990); *Rambo III*, dir. Peter MacDonald (Carolco Pictures, 1988); *Patriot Games*, dir. Phillip Noyce (Paramount Pictures, 1992); *The Little Drummer Girl*, dir. George Roy Hill (Warner Bros., 1984); *The Delta Force*, dir. Menahem Golan (Golan-Globus, 1986). There were also several docudramas, including at least one made-for-television film, about the Munich massacre (*21 Hours at Munich*, dir. William A. Graham [Filmways Motion Pictures, 1976]), as well as several movies about the Israeli raid on Entebbe.

19. *Delta Force. Die Hard*, dir. John McTiernan (20th Century Fox/Silver Pictures, 1988).

20. *Chicago Tribune*, Sept. 13, 2001, p. 13. Dave Karger, "Calling Out the Troops," *Entertainment Weekly's EW.com*, Dec. 3, 2001 <http://www.ew.com/ew/report/0,6115,186560~1~~,00.html> (June 11, 2002).

21. *Collateral Damage*, dir. Andrew Davis (Warner Bros./Hacienda Productions, 2002). *Seattle Post-Intelligencer*, Feb. 8, 2002 <http://seattlepi.nwsource.com/movies/57462_collateral08q.shtml> (May 15, 2002); "Box Office Preview: Mommy Dearest," *Entertainment Weekly's EW.com*, Feb. 15, 2002 <http://www.ew.com/ew/report/0,6115,203263~1~0~,00.htm> (June 3, 2002); Dave Karger, "Box Office Report," *Entertainment Weekly's EW.com*, Feb. 18, 2002 <http://www.ew.com/ew/report/0,6115,203642~1~~,00.htm> (June 3, 2002); Mark Caro, "Movie Review: *Collateral Damage*," *Metromix* <http://www.metromix.com/top/1,1419,M-Metromix-Home-X!ArticleDetail-15175,00.html> (May 15, 2002); Paul Clinton, "Review: New Schwarzenegger 'Damaged' Goods," *CNN.com*, Feb. 7, 2002 <http://www.cnn.com/2002/SHOWBIZ/Movies/02/07/review.collateral/index.html> (May 15, 2002).

22. *Black Hawk Down*, dir. Ridley Scott (Columbia Pictures/Jerry Bruckheimer Films/Revolution Studios, 2001); Mark Bowden, *Black Hawk Down: A Story of Modern War* (New York, 1999).

23. Elvis Mitchell, "Film Review: Mission of Mercy Goes Bad in Africa," *New York Times*, Dec. 28, 2001, sec. E, p. 3, available from the *New York Times* Premium Archive <http://www.nytimes.com/premiumproducts/archive.html> (May 15, 2002). Jamie Malanowski, "Film: War, without Any Answers," *ibid.*, Dec. 16, 2001, sec. 2, p. 3, available from the *New York Times* Premium Archive

24. Rick Lyman, "An Action Film Hits Close, but How Close? Second Thoughts Prevail against a Political Message," *New York Times*, Dec. 26, 2001, sec. E, p. 1, available from the *New York Times* Premium Archive.

25. Andrew O'Hehir, "Fog of War: *Black Hawk Down*'s Gripping Images of U.S. Military's Missteps in Somalia Grope About in a Context-Free Void," *Salon.com*, Dec. 28, 2001 <http://www.salon.com/ent/movies/review/2001/12/28/black_hawk_down/> (May 15, 2002).

26. "Ashcroft: Critics of New Terror Measures Undermine Effort," *CNN.com*, Dec. 7, 2001 <http://www.cnn.com/2001/US/12/06/inv.ashcroft.hearing> (May 15, 2002). Tony Karon, "What the Army Can Learn from *Black Hawk Down: Danger*

Lurks When the Locals Don't Share the U.S. View of Its Own Actions," *TIME.com*, Feb. 12, 2002 <http://www.time.com/time/columnist/printout/0,8816,202706.00. htm> (June 3, 2002). On the number of civilian deaths, see Carl Conetta, "Operation Enduring Freedom: Why a Higher Rate of Civilian Bombing Casualties," *Project on Defense Alternatives Briefing Report #11*, Jan. 18, 2002 <http://www.comw.org/pda/0201oef.html> (May 15, 2002).

The September 11, 2001, Oral History Narrative and Memory Project
A First Report

Mary Marshall Clark

Within days of the September 11 attacks, Columbia University's Oral History Research Office and its Institute for Social and Economic Policy jointly inaugurated the September 11, 2001, Oral History Narrative and Memory Project. Over the next several months the project staff interviewed almost four hundred people, some of whom will be interviewed three times over the course of three years. The longitudinal study allows interviewees to reconstruct their varying experiences without reducing them to formulaic, static, or homogenized "media-sized" stories and without erasing "ambiguity, uncertainty, and contradiction." Yet, as Mary Marshall Clark describes, certain narrative themes—consolation and solace, flight and refuge, patriotism, and apocalypse—appear repeatedly in the early-stage interviews.

One of the dilemmas in the debate over whether memory or history dominates the interpretation of major events is that few opportunities exist to study how people reconstruct the past before a dominant public narrative has been created by those who have a vested interest in defining the political meaning of events. Oral historians have often claimed that the lived experience of history is more complex than subsequent interpretations reveal. Rarely do we have the opportunity to document the historic evidence of that complexity through first-person interviews collected close to a historical event that has the power to transform our ideas about history. As a result, debates over the relationships between memory and history and between individual and collective memory often remain abstract and theoretical. In the case of an episode such as the terrorist attacks of September 11, 2001, which immediately stirred a public debate over the ultimate significance of the events for American history and foreign policy, the stakes over how and by whom memory is shaped were particularly high.

Given the nature of the attacks and the need for government response to them, it is no surprise that an official public interpretation of the meaning of September 11 was generated soon after the events occurred. This dominant account portrayed a nation unified in grief; it allowed government officials to claim that there is a public consensus that September 11 was a turning point in the nation's history that has clear implications for national and foreign policy. It is important to remember that this consensus was constructed not by those who lived through the terrorist attacks and their aftermath, but by those who observed it and had political reasons to interpret it as they did.

Columbia University's Oral History Research Office and the university's Institute for Social and Economic Research and Policy created the September 11, 2001, Oral History Narrative and Memory Project within days of the attacks to explore a variety of memories and interpretations of the events and their aftermath that we believed could only be constructed over time through personal accountings of the catastrophe. Peter Bearman, a sociologist interested in the formation of identity in the wake of such events, and I co-founded this longitudinal oral history study in which sample groups from a pool of four hundred people will be interviewed three times over a three-year period. The project's purpose is to understand whether the catastrophe and its aftermath constitute a turning point in the lives and the imaginations of those both directly and indirectly affected. We used a modified life history approach in which we asked interviewees to talk about the meaning of the terrorist attacks in the context of their life stories and their understanding of the historical importance of September 11. In an effort to expand beyond the predicted formation of a unified collective memory based only on the experiences of those who were most dramatically affected by September 11, we attempted to interview people with widely different experiences, including many who were not close to the site of ground zero and some who were discriminated against in the aftermath. While most of the interviews were conducted in New York, we also collected interviews in New Jersey, Boston, and Washington.

Given our determination to allow a broad range of people to interpret the impact of the catastrophe, we spread our thirty interviewers around New York City in the first few weeks following September 11.

We approached people on the streets in Union Square, an impromptu memorial site, and other public gathering places to invite them to be interviewed. After that we approached people through community organizations, mosques, temples, churches, firehouses, restaurants, small businesses, and other institutions or associations to let them know about our project. Rarely did we approach individuals directly after the first few weeks. Our project was announced through formal networks, organizations, and associations and through informal networks. Generally, people volunteered to be interviewed because they wanted their experiences recorded for history. While we offered all those we interviewed information about counseling services, we are not affiliated with or supervised by a clinic or psychological center. We also provided interviewees the opportunity to remain anonymous. With few exceptions, those we interviewed elected to become a part of the permanent record through depositing their interviews at the Oral History Research Office, a public archive.

In the seven weeks following September 11 we conducted interviews with nearly 200 people. Over the next six months, we conducted another 200 interviews and began to read and analyze transcripts. So far, we have interviewed approximately 170 eyewitnesses, survivors, rescue workers, volunteers, and others who lived and worked within an approximately six-block area around ground zero. Fifty of those worked in the World Trade Center. Among interviews conducted at ground zero and throughout the New York City region, we have interviewed 50 Muslims and 10 Sikhs from a range of backgrounds and over 60 Latinos representing many different countries of origin. We have interviewed immigrants from over thirty different countries, including 25 Afghan Americans or refugees. We have also interviewed over 30 artists whose lives and work were directly and indirectly affected by the events of September 11 and its aftermath. We have interviewed those who have been bereft of relatives, friends, and social networks. We have conducted interviews with health workers, transportation workers, and construction workers who worked in or near ground zero and individuals who lost their housing or work.

In analyzing the interviews, we are especially interested in understanding how individual and social memory is constructed. Specifically, how did the media and government help to define impressions and interpretations of the September 11 events? What was the impact of September 11 on individual relationships and on social networks? What did the terrorist attack mean to immigrants and refugees who looked the way officials portrayed "the enemy"? We also explored how political responses that ranged from patriotism (belonging) to alienation (exile) affected the construction of memory in relation to identity, both personal and social, and how memory was formed in response to a historic event that most considered was "unique" and without parallel. As our work has developed, we have also become interested in the role of grief and trauma in defining the political as well as the cultural legacy of September 11 on national and international levels. Our underlying question was: Is September 11, 2001, a historic moment that qualifies as a turning point in American history? If so, will the continuing threat of terrorism itself spark new interpretations of history that will transform our national self-understanding and how we also view the future?

Initial Findings

> To speak is to preserve the teller from oblivion.
> —Alessandro Portelli

Given the speed with which images and narratives have combined to form definitive impressions of the September 11, 2001, attack as the beginning of "America's new war," it is hard to remember that in the first days and weeks after the events there was confusion about the origin and meaning of the attacks, which promoted a deep disquiet over the definition of the enemy in cultural as well as ideological terms. During this period, the government and the media rushed to consolidate an impression of "the enemy" that was precise enough to rationalize a wholesale invasion of Afghanistan and yet broad enough to stimulate a climate of fear of anyone who "looked like" the enemy at home.

Through our interviews with clusters of communities both directly and indirectly affected by the catastrophe, we found that a climate of fear dominated the responses of those we interviewed in at least two ways that were not reflected in mainstream media accounts. First, those interviewees who experienced the most direct and traumatic aspects of the disaster, through either proximity or loss, often feared that the violence they lived through would spark greater violence. Many whom we interviewed before October 7, 2001, the date of the first air strikes in Afghanistan, wanted publicly to record their reluctance to pinpoint the enemy in a way that would rationalize an invasion. They were particularly afraid not only of retaliation but of a technological war in which civilian populations might accidentally be attacked and falsely targeted. These statements rejected revenge as the only official response and revealed how the vulnerability of eyewitnesses and survivors translated into sympathy for other potential victims. The most striking example of the "resistance" to this fear of oblivion in which the individual point of view would be lost and terrorism would perpetuate itself through war was a plea I received from a man who described himself as a "part-time" (reservist) soldier at ground zero. He claimed to have taken over two hundred oral history interviews with workers, including police officers and others, and asked me if I would help him organize an oral history project in Afghanistan if he were assigned there, "to show the American people how easily civilians could be harmed there."[1] Most of those we interviewed expressed their desire for peace even when they spoke of patriotism and their fear that their stories might be misused by the media and others to justify an international war.

A second illustration of the extreme climate of fear not fully reported by the media was demonstrated in our interviews with immigrants and refugees, particularly those who by skin color or dress might be confused with the enemy; those interviews reveal the frightening degree to which terror continued to dominate their lives in the aftermath. In the interviews we conducted with Afghans, Pakistanis, Muslims, and many Latinos, the dread of oblivion that September 11 occasioned emerges from two distinct sources. The first is the trauma produced by the catastrophe itself, especially in those who migrated to the United States to flee terrorism or war. The second anxiety, at times taking preeminence over the first, was the fear of retaliation within the United States at the hands of the government, hate groups, and individual citizens. This constituted a double catastrophe for immigrants and refugees, which led to withdrawal and isolation in the aftermath of September 11 and, in a striking number of cases, to attacks and threats on those we interviewed or their friends and families. The *Washington Post* poll conducted on September 13, 2001, which revealed that 43 percent of Americans polled thought the attacks would make them "more suspicious" of people who "appear to be of Arab descent," was tragically prescient for New York as well as for the rest of America.[2]

Some of the threats were direct, and others were subtle. One Latino Muslim we interviewed spoke of his fear of a "collective herd" mentality that he was afraid would "trample him," and he reported on the experience of a pregnant Muslim woman friend who was beaten in the streets of the Bronx. Like others of Arab descent, a business executive from Pakistan who escaped one of the towers and believed that his father had perished in the other declared that the terror of September 11 paled in comparison to the terror of the aftermath. (The father escaped, and he was interviewed for the collection.) The interviewee refused to leave his neighborhood for two weeks and shaved his beard for a month and a half, all of which he described as "complications from the moment of national [collective] mourning." Taxi drivers of Arab descent reported to us that almost everyone they knew from Arab lands experienced threats and described their double anguish over not being considered Americans and living in a climate of fear. One individual described his "triple trauma" of living through the attack, then being betrayed not only by his country but by his beloved city, in which he had previously felt safe in exile.[3]

For many of the immigrants and refugees we interviewed, September 11 was interpreted as not only a national but also a global event with far-ranging political implications. One man, born in Kabul, was angry because he said most Americans did not understand how the Taliban devastated Afghanistan (a view reflected by many Afghan women we interviewed) and that an American invasion would lead to many civilian deaths. He explained, "This is not a war. This is something small. Once you are bombed on a regular basis and you are targeted as a people you know what war is. This was just a single act of terrorism." Later, he defined his view of patriotism: "For me patriotism means not staining the blood of American soldiers with innocent Afghan blood." Most upsetting was evidence of a new and pernicious level of xenophobia in which women and children of Arab descent were threatened and attacked. An Afghan American teacher we interviewed said she often tried to get her students to examine the complexity of an American invasion of Afghanistan, despite her own belief that some intervention was necessary. Despite her attempts to portray herself as a concerned American citizen to her students, she later found a swastika drawn on the windshield of her car with the words "America rules" scrawled in red underneath.[4] These stories tragically confirm a report by the National Asian Pacific American Legal Consortium, "Backlash: When America Turned on Its Own," that after September 11 hate crimes that were previously reported as targeting young males were now being reported as targeting a high number of women, senior citizens, and even children.[5]

These incidents confirm my reading of interviews that after September 11, 2001, there has been a paradigm shift in racial profiling in which immigrants are perceived as a national security threat by a culture that once welcomed them. It is no surprise that many of those we interviewed feared that the closest analogy to the legacy of September 11 in American history was the experience of Japanese American citizens during World War II or the political repression of the McCarthy era. Incidents we found in our interviews that confirmed this possibility included stories of middle-of-the-night raids by police and federal agents in immigrant communities of Queens and Brooklyn, where family members were taken to detention centers without explanation or recourse, and graphic accounts of violence against people who tried to speak out against the war in Afghanistan.

It is clear from interviews conducted with immigrants and refugees that displacement, exile, loss, and insecurity about the future were common experiences that were not unique to September 11, 2001. The impression created by the media that September 11 constituted a "loss of innocence" for the nation did not apply to its most recent citizens and prospective citizens who had sought refuge from previous trauma. Neither did it apply to the millions of refugees around the world who have been prevented from entering U.S. borders since September 11. A hopeful sign that this double standard was noticed and taken seriously is reflected by the concerns of many people we interviewed (across communities and generations) that a widespread climate of fear would result in the profiling of refugees and others who were clearly going to be targets in the wake of the events. On the other hand, there is a frightening degree of evidence in the stories we collected, especially in the first few weeks following September 11, that the "upsurge" of patriotism following the attacks also led to a pernicious inability to discriminate.

Other findings are equally revealing. The September 11 attacks caused fear, confusion, and disorientation among almost everyone we interviewed. The media amplified the trauma and at the same time suppressed it by conscious decisions not to convey graphic scenes of people jumping from buildings, the sounds and sights of bodies hitting the ground, and stories about the violence against individuals, families, and community centers in the weeks and months following the disaster. For many whom we interviewed, the invitation to participate in a longitudinal oral history project was the first real opportunity they had been given to explore the meaning of such experiences and the sights they witnessed without having to reduce their memories to a media-sized story. As a result, long before the media began to report on the true scope of the catastrophe (and before many of us working on it understood it ourselves), our interviewers gathered evidence of massive and overwhelming trauma from people who suffered from isolation and despair, responding to an environment in which there was little public understanding of their experiences.

The experience of isolation often translated into that of exile, not only for immigrants and refugees but also for those whose familiar territories of home, work, and neighborhood were assaulted directly or indirectly. This primary disruption had an impact on social networks created by home, family, and community, further deepening the isolation of many. While we have collected many "heroic" stories, which cohere with the narratives profiled of September 11 survivors and rescuers, we also gathered many more ordinary stories in which the struggle to survive was the primary theme of the interview. There are stories of some who pushed aside others to survive themselves or left behind co-workers in a race to exit the towers—"unheroic" moments that are part of the tragic legacy of September 11 (and that must be included in historical accounts). While many of the genuinely heroic stories did indeed help promote unity in grief for the short term, they failed to account for long-range trauma and loss on both collective and individual levels. These stories included portraits of the September 11 rescuer as national hero/patriot, of New York City as "wounded" but bouncing back, and by extension of the September 11 survivors as "one in grief and mourning."

Methodology

The challenges of interpreting the events and aftermath of September 11, 2001, in close temporal and physical proximity to the catastrophe are manifold. First and foremost, oral history relies upon memory not only as a source of details but also as a rich repository of thoughts, beliefs, and impressions of self-understandings and historical understandings that have evolved over time. We still know little about how trauma affects memory in general or that of the traumatic event itself.

A second challenge stems from the lack of historical research sources and interpretive paradigms. Oral historians usually conduct research in primary and secondary sources before inviting people to construct their own life stories. Moreover, when documenting the history of political events that have had great impact on society and count as an experience of mass culture, there are historical analogies and frameworks of experience that allow us to speculate about the dimensions of the stories that we will collect—allowing us to refine our interviewing approach and tailor our expectations appropriately.

The events and aftermath of September 11 offered us no prototypes, methodological or historical, that would have allowed us the benefit of prior research. Our interviews revealed the absence of comparisons and analogous historical experiences on the part of most of those we interviewed. Moreover, with the exception of those who had fled to this country to escape oppression, there were almost no "collective" experiences of prior trauma among people we interviewed that had been passed down in living memory. This meant that oral culture itself was not a resource from which to create a story or stories by historical comparison.

Accordingly, our interviews are characterized by ambiguity, uncertainty, and contradiction, as well as meaning, form, and purpose. This argues for the lack of a "collective" story as it emerges from within the communities most affected by the terrorist events and raises profound questions for all of us who have documented or written about September 11. The questions include: Is this history yet? Is it memory? And, for those of us offering the solace of the interview as a means for people to bring coherence to catastrophe, we must also ask ourselves: Is it therapy?

Despite such limitations, the life history interviews provide important context for narratives about September 11. Our interviews are distinguished by the degree to which people could find—within themselves and their life stories—the frameworks through which to interpret the chaos they experienced on the day of September 11, 2001, and thereafter.

Themes and Interpretations

The past is not dead. It is not even past yet.
—William Faulkner

The dimension of time and memory through which our reminiscences of historic events are framed and filtered is broken, is occasionally fractured by events that could be described as larger than life. In some cases, these events become a "turning point" from which the history of the past and the understanding of the future are rewritten. But the very phrase turning point implies that, for most of these events, there is a before and there is an after, an axis from which a rotation from one set of understandings to another is accomplished. As many of us who lived through and documented the events and aftermath of September 11, 2001, know, the story we are engaged in recording and constructing may have a beginning (as a national story), but it is still unfolding and has no clear end—giving the future far more power than the past. The interpretations we have gathered, reading across the first sessions of the oral histories we have taken to date, reveal the complex and delicate ways in which September 11 still stands outside history as we know it, exploding the frameworks of urban and national consciousness and inviting us to interpret the terrorist attack as a global event with consequences and demands that must cause us to listen and think in new ways. The interviews that we have collected reveal the first whispers of what is possibly a new era in America, one that is defined not only by the reality of terrorism but by the necessity of realizing we are living in a fragile and interdependent world.

The role of the political imaginary, always of interest to oral historians who attempt to derive meaning from the subjectivity of a major historical event, is profoundly important in understanding the events and aftermath of September 11. Because there was no close analogy to the terrorist attack and its legacy in living memory of many of those we interviewed, in concert with the surreal dimensions of the experience itself, people had to search for ways to interpret their experiences outside established frameworks. While the attack on Pearl Harbor was offered as one analogy by the media, the fit was wrong for the lived experience of September 11 because the latter attack was targeted for a civilian population in a major urban center that in some ways represented America's connection to the rest of the world. The sinking of the *Titanic* was an analogy used far more frequently by many we interviewed, drawing people's attention to the myth of invincibility, which was difficult for people to reject as a reality in both cases. The analogy fits in some ways as a literal one, as both the ship and the twin towers were reputedly indestructible (in fact, many people in both situations died because they were told that they should not try to escape). But the *Titanic* and the myth of invincibility it represents in mainstream American culture was also used as a metaphorical analogy, demonstrating the degree to which many of those we interviewed were still in a state of shock and disbelief that international terrorism could have such a tremendous impact within U.S. borders.

For most people, the interviews represented an opportunity to try to make sense of what was senseless where there was apparently no analogy. Still, the meaning and the structure of their stories yield many important insights into how September 11 will be remembered in its uniqueness by eyewitnesses, survivors, and those who have suffered in the aftermath. While at this time it is impossible to make conclusions about how the people we have interviewed will eventually interpret the legacy of September 11, in political as well as personal terms, we have begun to find some themes that connect people across generations, classes, and ethnic categories.

Among these are narratives of consolation and solace, in which those we interviewed described a search for meaning that began with stories of survival of the September events but continued to define a social response weeks and months afterwards. These stories included expressions of wishes for world peace, a desire for increased humanitarianism and tolerance at home, and the search for personal fulfillment and meaning that included changes in relationships and patterns of living. As mentioned earlier, in sheer number these narratives dramatically exceed the narratives of revenge that are so commonly reported on and that are used to suggest a national consensus.

We have also found that the themes of flight and refuge connected those who had to run for their lives on September 11 with those who fled terror in their own countries but experienced it again in the aftermath. For many we interviewed this connection provided the link between understanding September 11 as a national event and as a global event, reminding New Yorkers of the identity of the city as an international center. A public interest in the political dimensions of the aftermath and the international nature of the events was reflected in the high rates of attendance at museums and community centers where the plight of Muslim immigrants was profiled.

Finally, patriotism was itself a category of interpretation, and perhaps the most contested and yet important domain in which we began our explorations. We found that for most people prior assumptions about national identity and a collective sense of belonging were often not enhanced, but shaken, by September 11. The meaning of flying flags differed dramatically in various communities, offering protection to many who feared being cast as the enemy in the drama of September 11 as it was played out in the collective culture. For others, the flag was a symbol of mourning, collective grief without any explicit political implications. For most people we interviewed, including those for whom the flag reflected a genuine rise in patriotism, it held different meanings at different times and in different contexts.

Perhaps most important for our ultimate considerations of the significance of September 11 as an axis of national as well as international understanding, the attacks were perceived in direct and indirect ways as an apocalypse. It was registered, in that sense, as a moment that stood outside of time and an event that ended history as we had previously understood it. The interviews we conducted with survivors and eyewitnesses were frequently shot through with religious analogies and metaphors and with apocalyptic imagery from films and movies, demonstrating the ways that many wrestled with questions of good and evil, life and death outside the frame of history as they had previously understood it. Of all of our interviewees, the people who had the most "complete" framework with which to understand the catastrophe were themselves already religious or apocalyptic thinkers. For them, the attacks of September 11 were a confirmation of their view of history and the world we live in. The narratives in which apocalyptic imagery and vision dominate descriptions of life "before and after" September 11 come closest to linking us to an understanding of the nature of the catastrophe itself —and its symbolic intent and purpose. As our primary purpose in the first round of interviews was to capture a sense of what the lives of those we interviewed was like before September 11 and what the immediate impact of the catastrophe and its aftermath was, we did not spend a lot of time exploring patriotism in the complex ways it deserves. We look forward to returning to this theme in our follow-up interviews.

It also tells us that in some ways for many of those we interviewed September 11, 2001, is not yet history, for it is the antithesis of history, of continuity, and of time as we understand it. For others, it was of course a tragic continuation of history and of traumas escaped. As a result, an early reading of our interviews reveals a great range and variety of experiences, thoughts, and emotions in which the contradictions we expect to find in historical accounts exist not only across communities but within individuals. These tensions and ambiguities are evidence not only of massive trauma but of the genuine impossibility of defining a moment of the magnitude of September 11 too quickly. For most of those we interviewed, the task of interpreting the political and cultural legacy of the events and their aftermath was premature given the scope of both the catastrophe and the United States response to it.

The ways in which September 11 will influence the course of human events and our imagined future cannot be predicted. But, if consensus can be claimed as one outcome of a collective memory in formation, the September 11, 2001, Oral History Narrative and Memory Project reveals that it does not yet exist within the communities most directly affected. There is ample evidence to suggest, however, that a battle for democracy is being fought at home as well as abroad.

Appendix: Organization of the Project

The September 11, 2001, Oral History Narrative and Memory Project was launched within a week following the terrorist attacks. Most of the interviewers we hired or accepted as volunteers had previous training or experience in oral history or journalism. We established a large team of interviewers, ranging in number from twenty to thirty throughout the first year of the project, to conduct ten interviews each. A third of our interviewers were volunteers, some of whom had previously interviewed for the Survivors of the Shoah Visual History Project in Los Angeles. At least five of our interviewers were fluent in Spanish, and we later hired an interviewer who was fluent in Arabic and Arabic dialects. We had to turn away fifty or more volunteer interviewers. We held weekly meetings for interviewers that ran two to three hours. Interviewers were given general instruction in the art of the oral history interview and were provided with a list of the overarching questions and topics we were interested in: interviewees' memories of the event and how those memories supported or differed from public accounts generated in the media; their networks of communication (how people learned about the event, in what medium if they did not witness it directly, and how they talked about it with others); changes in their personal and social relationships; changes in their geographical or work location; the role of the media as a shaping influence; and their views of the future. Interviewees were told that we were conducting a longitudinal study and that, if resources and circumstances permitted, we would be able to conduct at least one and possibly two additional sessions with each of them. They were also told that they would have the opportunity to deposit their tapes and transcripts in the Oral History Research Office Collection, subsequent to their review and editing of the transcripts of their recorded interviews.

The second phase of the project is scheduled to begin October 1, 2002.

The interviews for the September 11, 2001, Oral History Narrative and Memory Project have been conducted on audiotape, in digital form, and transcribed. Sixty interviews were conducted in Spanish; several were conducted in Farsi; and one was conducted in Dari. Tapes will be preserved in analog and digital formats and will be made available at the individual discretion of interviewees. We hope to begin a program of videotaping in the second year of the project, and interviewees will be able to choose whether to be interviewed on audio or video.

The project is funded by the National Science Foundation, the Rockefeller Foundation, and Columbia University. The Oral History Research Office has most recently received a grant to support additional interviews from the *New York Times* Neediest Fund. That new project, the September 11, 2001, Response and Recovery Oral History Project, will explore long-term issues of recovery and response in the areas of psychological trauma, economic rebuilding, civil liberties, philanthropy, education, and the arts.

Notes

1. The interviews quoted here have not yet been fully prepared for the permanent Oral History Research Office Collection; therefore, only descriptions of interviewees and dates of interviews are provided here. The reservist at ground zero sent an e-mail in December 2001.

2. ABC News/*Washington Post* Terrorist Attack Poll #2, Sept. 13, 2001 <http://www.icpsr.umich.edu:8080/ABSTRACTS/03290.xml> (June 27, 2002).

3. The Latino Muslim of the United States, who has lived in Puerto Rico, was interviewed Oct. 18, 2001. The Pakistani business executive, an immigrant, was interviewed Nov. 6, 2001. The "triple trauma" was described by a Pakistani Sikh immigrant in an interview on Jan. 20, 2002.

4. The Afghan American immigrant born in Kabul was interviewed Nov. 8, 2001. The Afghan American immigrant teacher was interviewed Nov. 6, 2001.

5. National Asian Pacific American Legal Consortium, "Backlash: When America Turned on Its Own" <http://www.napalc.org/literature/annual_report/9-11_report.htm> (June 27, 2002).

"Anti-Americanism" in the Arab World

An Interpretation of a Brief History

Ussama Makdisi

Ussama Makdisi historicizes the rise of anti-American sentiment in the Arab world by exploring Arab-American interactions over the past two centuries. He suggests that such sentiment is grounded, not in an epochal confrontation of civilizations, but in modern politics. Thus anti-Americanism is not ideologically consistent—its intensity, coherence, and evidence vary across the Arab world. Most Arab expressions of anti-American feeling stem less from blind hatred of the United States or American values than from profound ambivalence: The United States is at once admired for its affluence and technology (and by some for its secularism, law, and order) and resented for its contribution to a repressive Middle Eastern status quo.

"I think that anger in the Arab street is real. It is produced by a number of different factors. But in the end, what matters is not whether they hate us or love us—for the most part, they hate us. They did before. But whether they are going to respect our power." With these words addressed to the U.S. House of Representatives in 1991, in the aftermath of the Gulf War, Martin Indyk, then executive director of the Washington Institute for Near East Policy and later one of the architects of the failed Middle East policy in the Clinton administration, dismissed the history of anti-Americanism in the Arab world. "The antipathy towards the West that is likely to follow this war," added Indyk in a prepared statement he also submitted, "has *long* been present in the Arab world. It cannot be resolved through accommodation."[1] Indyk's assumption that "they" hate "us"—and that the reasons for it are essentially immaterial and obscure—has appeared elsewhere in the recent discourse of American policy makers and pundits, as if Arabs and Americans have always been and will always be doomed to a relationship of mutual antagonism.

131

In contrast, this essay turns to history to answer the oft-asked question "Why do they hate us?" It offers a brief, synthetic, interpretive account of Arab and American interactions over the past two centuries. I recognize from the outset the limits of generalizing about 280 million Arabs, living in a host of Arab countries, each with its own tradition and history. Nonetheless, I seek to place the rise of anti-American sentiment in the Arab world within a historical and political context often neglected, misunderstood, or ignored by proponents of a "clash of civilizations" thesis.[2]

Anti-Americanism is a recent phenomenon fueled by American foreign policy, not an epochal confrontation of civilizations. While there are certainly those in both the United States and the Arab world who believe in a clash of civilizations and who invest politically in such beliefs, history belies them. Indeed, at the time of World War I the image of the United States in the Arab provinces of the Ottoman Empire was generally positive; those Arabs who knew of the country saw it as a great power that was not imperialist as Britain, France, and Russia were. Those Americans who lived in the region—missionaries and their descendants and collaborators—were pioneers in the realm of higher education. Liberal America was not simply a slogan; it was a reality encountered and experienced by Arabs, Turks, Armenians, and Persians in the hallways of the Syrian Protestant College (later renamed the American University of Beirut), Robert College in Istanbul, the American College in Persia, and the American University in Cairo. But over the course of the twentieth century, American policies in the region profoundly complicated the meaning of America for Arabs.

Among the vast majority of Arabs today, the expression of anti-American feelings stems less from a blind hatred of the United States or American values than from a profound ambivalence about America: at once an object of admiration for its affluence, its films, its technology (and for some its secularism, its law, its order) and a source of deep disappointment given the ongoing role of the United States in shaping a repressive Middle Eastern status quo. Anti-Americanism is not an ideologically consistent discourse—its intensity, indeed, its coherence and evidence, vary across the Arab world. Yet to the extent that specifically anti-American sentiments are present, never more obviously so to Americans than in the aftermath of the attacks of September 11, 2001, it is imperative to understand their nature and origins.

Benevolent America

American involvement with the Arab world began inauspiciously in 1784 when an American ship, the *Betsey,* was seized in the Mediterranean Sea by Moroccan privateers. A year later Algerians captured more American vessels and imprisoned their crews. Thus were inaugurated the negotiations, skirmishes, and legends known collectively as the Barbary wars, which culminated in the capture of the U.S. frigate *Philadelphia* in 1803, Stephen Decatur's famous but quite ineffectual raid on Tripoli in 1804, and the ransom and release of the American captives in 1805. The episodes sparked debates between Thomas Jefferson and John Adams about whether it was necessary to go to war, rather than pay ransom to the Barbary States, in order to uphold the values of the newly independent republic. As Robert J. Allison has noted in his work on the image of Islam in the early-nineteenth-century United States, the Barbary wars, and especially the myriad captivity narratives that emerged from them, crystallized existing negative Western images of the Muslim and Ottoman world. The discourse of the despotic "Turk" functioned as one foil to early republican identity just as the more entrenched discourse of "Mohammedanism" as imposture signified the antithesis of true religion, that is to say, Christianity, at a time when complex political and sectarian battle lines were being etched into a rapidly changing American landscape.[3]

Such perspectives were amplified in the nineteenth century by the advent of U.S. travelers' discourses of the Orient and, specifically, of Palestine. Hilton Obenzinger has described a "Holy Land mania" that gripped American travelers, artists, and writers who toured and laid claim to Palestine. The Arab inhabitants of Palestine (and the surrounding areas) were acknowledged to be paradoxically there—animating accounts of the Holy Land as Levantine dragomans, dirty natives, impious Mohammedans, or "nominal" Christians—yet not there in any meaningful historical or spiritual sense. During his post–Civil War tour of the Ottoman Empire, for example, Mark Twain irreverently satirized American travelers' religious obsession with Palestine and their enchantment with the East more generally.[4]

In the United States itself books by Twain and by missionaries, landscapes by such artists as Frederic Church, as well as novels such as Robert Smythe Hichens's 1904 *The Garden of Allah* (which went into forty-four editions over the next forty years), contributed to the rise of a specifically American genre of orientalism. It exoticized the East as premodern, conceived of it as dreamy yet often experienced it as squalid, separated the sacred landscape of the Holy Land from its native Arab inhabitants, and commodified the Orient though promotions, advertisements, trinkets, novels, photographic exhibits, postcards, and ultimately films.[5]

There was, however, an American encounter with the Arabs that was far more direct and had a far greater impact on early Arab attitudes toward the United States. This was the missionary encounter led mostly by New England men and women. They shared many of the prejudices that characterized nineteenth-century American travelers; indeed, the roots of their missionary effort lay in part in their disavowal of a growing liberalism in New England religious thought. They were impelled by a sense of patrimony in the Holy Land and feelings of superiority to the natives as they sought to reclaim the lands of the Bible from Muslim and Eastern Christian control. Yet, motivated by "disinterested benevolence," they were also the first Americans to engage with the local populations in a serious and sustained manner—they wanted to change the Ottoman world, not just to describe or experience it. Their spiritual preoccupation with the Holy Land was premised, not on overlooking the natives, but on recognizing their presence on the land and on proclaiming the urgent need to save the "perishing souls" of the East. The first American missionaries to the Arab world were associated with the American Board of Commissioners for Foreign Missions. They departed Boston in 1819 and arrived in the Levant in 1820. Failing to establish themselves in Jerusalem, they settled on Beirut as the center of a missionary enterprise to Syria in 1823.[6]

Initially, the Eastern churches and local Ottoman officials described the Americans as "English," reflecting both their dim awareness of the United States and the protection afforded by British consuls in the Levant to the missionaries. There was sporadic local interest in the evangelical message of the missionaries and in their new and seemingly unmediated approach to the Scriptures in an era of increasing Western power over the Ottoman Empire. But for the most part evangelism fell on deaf ears and was effectively countered by the native churches, which repeatedly warned their respective communities of the spiritual and political dangers allegedly posed by the missionaries. A Maronite Christian was the first Arab convert to Protestantism, but he was imprisoned by the Maronite Church and subsequently disappeared in the late 1820s.

Most indigenous Christians, Jews, and Muslims refused to accept the missionaries' claim that theirs was the only correct path to salvation. Evangelically speaking, the American mission to the Arab world was largely a disappointment.[7]

Had the missionaries devoted themselves only to direct proselytizing, their impact on the region would have been scarcely noticeable and their later achievements impossible. But the missionaries also functioned as a bridge between cultures. Not only did they seek to introduce the Ottoman Arab world to Protestant notions of piety and individual salvation, they also brought with them American manners and customs, clothes, education, and medicine. Simultaneously, they sought to introduce Americans to a world unknown to them—to actual inhabitants, societies, histories, and geographies normally excluded by the alternatively sacred and exotic discourse of American orientalism. Intrinsic to the missionaries' endeavor was a sincere desire to know and evangelize the Arabs—to establish Christian fellowship—mixed with a paternalism that would remain a hallmark of their enterprise. Eli Smith, a famous American missionary to Syria, explained to an audience in New York in May 1840 why he considered the Arabs a peculiarly fascinating and promising object of missionary endeavor:

> [They] are a very talented race. I have examined all their books of science, mathematics, etc., and it is curious to see how they have started from points totally opposite to our scientific land marks, and yet have arrived at precisely as accurate results. Again, there is Algebra, which owes its origin to them; its name is Arabic. In astronomy they are proficient. . . . In philosophy they often reason more accurately than the most civilized nations of Europe. They generally tell all the facts of the case, insist on no dogmatic inferences, but leave you to judge conclusively for yourselves.
>
> Their history is like the Hebrews, full of romance, and chivalry, and high and lofty achievements. Their poetry is like ascending from earth to heaven; it is the soul of sublimity. . . . In literature they excel all other nations, for there is no country which possesses so many different books in the native tongue. . . . We love our language, and think very highly of its beauty, and force, and finish. But it sinks into insignificance before the beauty and force, and finish of the Arab tongue.[8]

Missionaries such as Smith learned Arabic; others mastered Armenian or Turkish. Smith devoted himself to revitalizing the Arabic language and Arab history and to studying Arab manners and customs. He pioneered the development of modern Arabic printing fonts, which set the standard for nineteenth-century Arabic printing. He thereby made a powerful and enduring impression on many educated inhabitants of Beirut, such as the Maronite-turned-Protestant educator, writer, and encyclopedist Butrus al-Bustani who, like others, was moved by the enthusiasm of the American missionaries. Together with Smith, he established a literary society in Beirut in 1847 that delved into then controversial topics, including the education of Arab women. Bustani advocated learning from the West, but not simple imitation of it; he believed firmly in a dialogue between civilizations. "We gave them [the West] knowledge by one route with our left hand, and they are now returning it to us by another route with their right hand," declared Bustani in 1859. "We must put at the first rank in this regard the American missionaries, and the Latin priests and nuns, particularly the Jesuit and Lazarists among them, because their beautiful example and graceful labor through their schools and printing presses are obvious, and can only be denied by those who are ungrateful or who are fanatical and prejudiced."[9] Bustani and other avatars of Arab liberalism in the nineteenth century were a minority; they were elitist, but they seized upon a romanticized and as yet unsullied image of America (among other symbols) to advocate a "modern" nation and to educate their otherwise "ignorant" compatriots.

The missionaries, in turn, served as ethnographers of Arabs to Americans. While they refused seriously to entertain equality between American and Arab, they worked with men such as Bustani and learned from, as well as taught, them. The missionaries themselves changed in the crucible of encounter, especially after it became clear that the proselytizing dimension of their enterprise had failed. Thus an evangelical effort that rejected a current of liberalism growing in early-nineteenth-century New England was transformed—by the labors of missionaries and natives alike—into a major project of essentially secular liberal higher education embodied in institutions such as the 1866 Syrian Protestant College in Beirut and the 1863 Robert College in Istanbul. Nowhere was the fruit of this transformation by actual experience in the Orient more evident than in the words of the famous American missionary-turned-college president Daniel Bliss. When he laid the cornerstone of College Hall at the Syrian Protestant College in 1871, Bliss spoke words as revolutionary in America as they were in the Ottoman Empire:

> This College is for all conditions and classes of men without regard to colour, nationality, race or religion. A man white, black, or yellow; Christian, Jew, Mohammedan or heathen, may enter and enjoy all the advantages of this institution for three, four, or eight years; and go out believing in one God, or

in many Gods, or in no God. But it will be impossible for any one to continue with us long without knowing what we believe to be the truth and our
reasons for that belief.[10]

This conversion from direct proselytization that was openly intoler-
ant of other faiths to more liberal persuasion was fraught with tension.
The secularization of the missionary enterprise coincided with and reflected a dramatic increase in Western ascendancy in the non-Western
world in the late nineteenth century. That ascendancy led to a codifica-
tion of national and racial prejudices—from designations of professors,
to differential pay scales, to the insistence that only the English language
could be a medium of modern instruction—that discriminated against
Arabs even as it offered them educational opportunities that they read-
ily grasped. Students of the Syrian Protestant College—known locally
as the "American college" long before it changed its name to the American University of Beirut in 1920—played a crucial role in building a
thriving late Ottoman Arab print culture, and its medical graduates
greatly contributed to the development of modern health care in
Lebanon and the Arab world. Innovative modern education and the absence of American government imperialism in the late Ottoman Empire
contributed to the benevolent image of the United States in such places
as Beirut, Istanbul, and Tehran. For example, the famous nineteenth-
century Egyptian advocate of women's liberation, Qasim Amin, extolled
American virtues and praised the freedom of women in America. In his
1900 *Al-mar'a al-jadida* (The new woman), he wrote:

> [The] status of women in [Western] societies has reached a level of respect,
> intellectual freedom, and action that is laudable, even though they have not
> yet reached the level that is their just due. American women in the United
> States are completely independent within the private sphere, and govern-
> ment intervention in their private affairs is almost nonexistent. As a conse-
> quence, women's freedom in the United States of America is much greater
> than that of European women. American men and women are equal in the
> realm of personal rights. Women have also gained political equality in some
> states. In the state of Wyoming, for example, women received their voting
> rights in 1869.[11]

Other nineteenth-century Arab subjects of the Ottoman Empire embraced a benevolent idea of America based on the missionary experience—particularly education—and on immigration. In 1893 *al-Hilal*, a
leading Egyptian cultural, literary, and historical journal owned by a former student of the Syrian Protestant College, introduced George Wash-

ington to its readership as "one of the geniuses of the eighteenth century and one of the greatest men of freedom." In the words of the immigrant Mikha'il As'ad Rustum in 1895, America was a bustling "land of cities and civilization" defined by its industry and by its people "from all tribes and races." It was no coincidence that in 1908 the constitutional Persian government invited an American to reorder its finances to stave off British and Russian imperialism. And it was to America that thousands of Arabs emigrated in the late nineteenth century. Philip Hitti, the great scholar of Arab history, the founder of oriental studies at Princeton University, was himself an immigrant to the United States. In a serialized account of life in America that appeared in 1924 in *al-Hilal*, he noted that in America:

> You will feel as though you have arrived in a country whose inhabitants are giants among men. When you enter the city and walk among the people, you will be struck by how eager Americans are to go to their work, how quick their pace is, and how active and energetic they are. You will then realize that you are not in a country like others, and you are not among a people like others, but rather among a people superior in their qualities, distinguished in their vitality, and unique in their abundance of energy. The matchless skyscrapers, the quick pace of life, the ability to focus on one's work, are none other than manifestations of the dynamism of a nation that is full of youth and pulsating with tremendous energy.[12]

Frequently such descriptions contained a notation of cultural difference, more often than not composed of generalizations based on anecdotal experience and ossified notions of gender, culture, spirituality, and materialism. After traveling to America in 1948 Sayyid Qutb, later a famous member of the Muslim Brotherhood, wrote:

> America has a principal role in this world, in the realm of practical matters and scientific research, and in the field of organization, improvement, production, and management. All that requires mind power and muscle are where American genius shines, and all that requires spirit and emotion are where American naiveté and primitiveness become apparent.
> For humanity to be able to benefit from American genius they must add great strength to the American strength.[13]

Like other Arabs in the first half of the twentieth century, neither the Christian Hitti nor the Muslim Qutb initially conceived of America as an enemy. Rather, Hitti emphasized America's youth and dynamism; in particular, he believed that America had a role to play in revitalizing older Eastern cultures. Qutb acknowledged America to be a leader and a teacher in the world of science, but he deplored its materialism and what he considered its startling lack of spirituality; he also noted its discrimination against blacks. Upon his return to Egypt, he began to formulate his ideology of Islam as a viable and necessary political and moral alternative to communism and capitalism at a time when the nature of American involvement in the Arab world, and indeed the Arab world itself, were taking a profoundly different turn.

World War I: America and the Arabs at a Crossroads

The influence of an idea of a benevolent America reached its apex among Arabs during and immediately after World War I. Not only were Americans identified with educational efforts in the region, they were also central to relief efforts amid a terrible wartime famine in Beirut and the surrounding region of Mount Lebanon. Moreover, President Woodrow Wilson's proclamations on self-determination reinforced a notion among nationalist elites in the Arab world that the United States was different from the European powers, which had agreed to partition the postwar Middle East much as they had partitioned Africa in the late nineteenth century, with the notable difference that Africa was partitioned openly while the Arab world was carved up secretly. Most egregious from an Arab perspective was the Balfour Declaration of 1917, which promised British support for the establishment of a Jewish "national home" in Palestine despite the fact that the overwhelming majority of the native inhabitants—90 percent—were Arabs who opposed what they saw as European colonialism bent on dispossessing them of their land. Arthur James Balfour, who as British foreign secretary had committed Great Britain officially to Zionism, stated in 1919 that

> in Palestine we do not propose even to go through the form of consulting the wishes of the present inhabitants of the country, though the American Commission has been going through the form of asking what they are. The four Great Powers are committed to Zionism. And Zionism, be it right or wrong, good or bad, is rooted in age-long traditions, in present needs, in future hopes, of far profounder import than the desires and prejudices of the 700,000 Arabs who now inhabit that ancient land.

In 1919 Howard Bliss, son of Daniel Bliss and then president of the Syrian Protestant College, urged Wilson to form a mission to find out what the Arab peoples wanted, an idea that squarely contradicted the spirit of the Balfour Declaration and the colonial wisdom on which it was based.[14]

The American section of the resultant Inter-Allied Commission on Mandates in Turkey was popularly known as the King-Crane commission, headed as it was by two Americans: Charles Crane, a Chicago industrialist and contributor to Wilson's presidential campaign, and Henry King, president of Oberlin College. The British and the French opposed it from the outset, reluctant to participate in what they regarded as American meddling in their imperial spheres of influence. Zionist leaders regarded it with "deepest disquietude," for travel to Palestine and interviews with natives threatened to expose a fundamental (and still often unacknowledged) problem of the Zionist project in Palestine: Namely, by what right could one create a Jewish state in a land where the vast majority of the indigenous population was not Jewish?[15] The King-Crane commission represented the tension between two strands of nineteenth-century American experience of the Arab world. On the one hand, the commissioners by their own admission began with a "predisposition" to the Zionist perspective: They were well informed about the passionate claims to Palestine made by Jews. At the outset of their mission, therefore, they reflected a dominant nineteenth-century American view of Palestine that overlooked the Arab reality on the ground or dismissed it as marginal to the allegedly true Judeo-Christian heritage of the land or to its modern civilized future. This predisposition was summed up by Capt. William Yale, a member of the commission who ultimately dissented from its final report. Yale insisted that the "national history, national traditions, and a strong national feeling" of Jews worldwide who would bring Western science and civilization outweighed the fact that Zionism in Palestine was "entirely contrary to the wishes of the people in Palestine and those of most of the inhabitants of Syria."[16] On the other hand, the commissioners made a concerted effort to find out what the native inhabitants actually thought.

After conducting interviews with local mayors and municipal councils and professional and trade organizations and making an extensive tour of Palestine and Syria, the King-Crane commission issued a final report that outraged British and French imperial sentiments as well as Zionist aspirations. It recommended an independent unified Arab state in Syria, Palestine, and Lebanon that, if necessary, should be placed under American mandatory control. In recommending an American mandate, the commissioners drew on a discourse of American exceptionalism and a history of American missionary contributions to higher education in the region that, they claimed, had led Arabs to know and trust the United States. The Arab people, noted the final report, "declared that their choice was due to knowledge of America's record: the unselfish aims with which she had come into the war; the faith in her felt by multitudes of Syrians who had been in America; the spirit revealed in American educational institutions in Syria, especially the College in Beirut, . . . their belief that America had no territorial or colonial ambitions"; and finally "her genuinely democratic spirit; and her ample resources."[17]

The King-Crane commission urged a "serious modification of the extreme Zionist program for Palestine of unlimited immigration of Jews, looking finally to making Palestine distinctly a Jewish State." If the Wilsonian principle of self-determination was to be upheld "and so the wishes of Palestine's population are to be decisive as to what is to be done with Palestine, then it is to be remembered that the non-Jewish population of Palestine—nearly nine-tenths of the whole—are emphatically against the entire Zionist program." Presciently, the commission warned that Zionism could be accomplished only through violence.

> That of itself is evidence of a strong sense of the injustice of the Zionist program, on the part of the non-Jewish populations of Palestine and Syria. Decisions, requiring armies to carry out, are sometimes necessary, but they are surely not gratuitously to be taken in the interests of a serious injustice. For the initial claim, often submitted by Zionist representatives, that they have a "right" to Palestine, based on an occupation of two thousand years ago, can hardly be seriously considered.[18]

The King-Crane report fell on deaf ears in Washington, London, and Paris. Wilson, who had already committed himself to the Balfour Declaration and to British imperial interests, did not publish the report officially. The British and the French proceeded with their predetermined partition of the Arab world. In 1920 Palestine became a British mandate formally committed to the terms of the Balfour Declaration, and the French dismantled the fledgling Arab state in Syria, exiling its leader, who became instead king of the newly constituted British-dominated state of Iraq.[19] The King-Crane report notwithstanding, the dissociation of the Holy Land from its native inhabitants was far more entrenched in popular and official American imagination than its association, and Zionism as a nationalist project in Palestine was premised upon that dissociation. Outside of some missionary circles, Arabs existed in popular American imagination in silent films—for example, *The Sheik* (1921) with Rudolph Valentino—and novels and tales such as the

Arabian Nights: They were represented as exotic, outlandish, primitive, romantic desert nomads or medieval city dwellers but not as a modern people deserving political rights and ready for independence.

Modern Politics and the Emergence of Anti-Americanism

The discovery of oil in Saudi Arabia in 1938 pushed the United States into a more direct role in the Middle East. It was in oil, not in mandatory Palestine or Syria, that the United States had a strategic stake. And unlike the largely passive U.S. Middle Eastern policy of the immediate post–World War I decades, post–World War II policy was far more extensive and direct. The result was a symbiotic relationship between American oil companies, the U.S. government, and the emerging Saudi state. The brilliant novel *Cities of Salt* (1984) by Abdelrahman Munif depicts the extraordinary political transformations entailed by the almost overnight conversion of an Arab tribal society into an oil kingdom, the corruption it induced, and the alienation created as rulers became increasingly independent of their subjects and dependent on oil companies and foreign protection. The novel explores the historical tensions between the American racialist paternalism toward Arabs, epitomized in the white American compounds from which natives were barred, and the collaboration between Americans and Arabs to explore for, market, and profit from oil.[20]

The Saudi state became an oil frontier not only for American companies, as the political scientist Robert Vitalis has argued, but also for thousands of Arabs from the Levant and tens of thousands of migrant workers from South Asia.[21] It was from this oil frontier that the Saudi regime emerged in its present form, on the one hand deeply dependent on expatriates and on the government of the United States, and on the other hand constantly emphasizing its Islamic (and hence non-American) heritage and mandate in an effort to maintain its legitimacy with its own people. The autocratic Saudi state has sought to co-opt and outflank domestic opposition both by appearing to uphold a "pure" version of Islam and by using oil profits to build a modern infrastructure of highways, hospitals, airports, schools, and electricity grids for its citizens. The American-Saudi relationship inaugurated a U.S. involvement with the Arab world far more secular in form, strategic in conception, and nationalist in interest than the nineteenth-century spiritual and educational missionary enterprise. Henceforth, while the United States remained a land of opportunity for many Arabs and American oil companies were instrumental in realizing undreamed-of profits for many gulf Arab states (as well as for themselves), the U.S. government saw itself far less as a force for liberal or democratic change than as a guarantor of the status quo.

The Cold War exacerbated the suspicion felt by U.S. policy makers toward any potentially destabilizing force in the Middle East, particularly populist secular Iranian and Arab nationalisms. In Iran, for example, after the parliament nationalized the British-dominated Anglo-Iranian Oil Company in 1951, the Central Intelligence Agency (CIA) organized the overthrow in 1953 of the nationalist prime minister Mohammed Mossadeq. Thereafter, the United States supported the absolutist dictatorship of Mohammed Reza Shah Pahlavi, rationalizing or ignoring the tremendous popular disaffection with Pahlavi rule. As late as New Year's Eve 1978, Jimmy Carter lavishly praised "the great leadership of the Shah," which, he insisted, had turned Iran into "an island of stability in one of the more troubled areas of the world." The United States helped the shah establish (with Israeli advisers) the infamous SAVAK internal security agency that rounded up and tortured political prisoners. The historian Nikki R. Keddie concluded her study of the Iranian revolution of 1979 by noting that it was American policies in Iran that led to a marked increase in anti-American feeling.[22]

A similar process unfolded in the Arab world. American hostility to Mosaddeq paralleled American animosity toward the secular Pan-Arab nationalism of Gamal Abdel Nasser in Egypt. Despite some initial sympathy, American policy makers were ultimately unwilling to interpret his nationalist Pan-Arab rhetoric within the context of the recent history of British and French colonial exploitation of the Arab world. Nasser saw Israel as the greatest threat to the Arabs, whereas the Americans focused on the dangers of alleged Soviet intrusion into the Middle East. Thus they perceived Nasser within a Cold War logic that dismissed his attempt at nonalignment. Although much of the Arab world, indeed, the Third World, saw in Nasser a genuinely charismatic leader and an authentic voice for Arab aspirations, for the Palestinian people, and for Egypt, Americans portrayed him as dangerously ambitious. They regarded his 1955 decision to seek arms from the eastern bloc (after being rebuffed by the West) and his 1956 nationalization of the Suez Canal (after the United States suddenly pulled out of financing the Aswan Dam project) as destabilizing to pro-Western regimes in the region, including Saudi Arabia and Iraq (whose monarchy was indeed overthrown). When the Iraqi monarchy fell in July 1958, 14,000 American troops were immediately dispatched to a Lebanon embroiled in civil conflict. They were sent to shore up the pro-Western regime of Camille Chamoun and also to signal U.S. determination to stave off perceived radical Arab nationalism and Soviet expansionism.[23] This politicization of the United States on the side of conservative autocratic regimes fostered a first round of anti-American sentiment in the Arab world that was similar to the anti-Americanism then evident in Latin America and Asia, where the United States more often than not sided with dictatorships in the name of fighting communism and radical nationalism.

This anti-Americanism was not characterized by hatred of America or things American as much as by a relatively new identification of American power as a force for repression rather than liberation in the Arab world. Nasser expressed this succinctly in a speech he gave in Damascus on July 22, 1958:

> America, brothers, revolted on 4 July. . . . It engaged in a revolution in order to get rid of British colonialism and in order to raise the living standards across the United States. America revolted and won and proclaimed the very same principles that are today proclaimed by your brothers in Iraq.
> But in proclaiming its anger today, America refuses to see the reality of the situation in the Middle East and forgets also its own history and its own revolution and its own logic and the principles invoked by Wilson. They fought colonialism as we fight colonialism. . . . How do they deny us our right to improve our condition just as they did theirs? I don't understand, brothers, why they do not respect the will of the peoples of the Arab East? . . . We all call for positive neutrality. All the peoples of the Arab Middle East are set on non-alignment. Why should these peoples not have their way? And why is their will not respected?[24]

The secular anti-imperialist rhetoric of student movements, leftist intellectuals, and "progressive" governments such as Nasser's now regarded the U.S. government as a representative of the historic force of colonialism and imperialism (and capitalism) and as a power holding the Arab world back from its rightful place at the eagerly anticipated postcolonial "rendezvous of victory." Enormous differences within the secularist camp notwithstanding (Nasser's regime, for example, persecuted Communists), this secular criticism of perceived American imperialism was based ultimately, not on a theory about a clash of civilizations, but on a discourse about a historic clash between the reactionary forces of imperialism and the progressive forces of revolution. It interpreted politics as a struggle between two stages of a single teleological reading of history in which the United States supported allegedly retrograde regimes, be it in the shah's Iran or in Chamoun's Lebanon and Nuri Said's Iraq in 1958 against supposedly more progressive ones. Anti-imperialist mobilization involved anti-American rhetoric, but its characterizations were broad, its criticism tempered by the fact that the United States as a nation remained a promised land for many, a source of admiration for still more, and on occasion—as during the Suez crisis in 1956 when President Dwight D. Eisenhower reversed a British, French, and Israeli invasion of Egypt following Nasser's nationalization of the Suez Canal— a symbol of hope for a new kind of relationship between the Third World and the great powers.

For the most part secular anti-imperialist rhetoric prevailed from Cairo to Baghdad, especially in the 1960s as the secular Arab nationalism represented by Nasser remained ascendant. But there also existed an undercurrent of Islamist dissidence from the autocratic governments of the Arab world and Iran. Unlike secularists, Islamists (who were also split into many ideological factions) framed their politics as a response to the violation of an alleged tradition and envisioned a revival of an ostensibly pure Islamic state and society. Unlike many of the great nineteenth-century Islamist reformers such as Jamal al-Din al-Afghani and Muhammad 'Abdu, who had tried to reconcile Islam and the West, many Islamists now regarded the West as a representative of an antagonistic secular and un-Islamic history, culture, and civilization. They witnessed the Arab inability to prevent the loss of Palestine and the dispersion of the Palestinian people—the first of which was justified, and the second largely ignored, by the West. They also seethed at the corruption of postcolonial Arab regimes. Qutb, who had once awkwardly admired certain facets of the United States, turned away from it in the 1950s because of its materialism and its support for Israel. He was further radicalized following his arrest in 1954 after a failed assassination attempt on Nasser by a member of the Muslim Brotherhood to which Qutb belonged. Qutb suffered, as did many other Egyptians, at the hands of Nasser's secret police, and he ultimately advocated not only delinkage from the West but also a struggle against rulers, including Nasser, mired in what he called an ignorant or *jahili* culture, purposefully deploying the classical Islamic designation of the pre-Islamic age as one of *jahiliyya* or ignorance. Qutb's harsh analysis of Muslims as besieged sustained a rigid yet influential Islamist interpretation of history and politics as an age-old clash of civilizations between "believers" and their "enemies." It was not freedom or temptation per se that Qutb opposed; it was what he saw as the degradation, corruption, injustice, authoritarianism, and materialism imposed on Muslims by their enemies. Qutb was hanged by Nasser's regime in 1966.[25]

A year later Nasser's regime and secular Arab nationalism were shaken by Israel's success in the June 1967 war. The Israeli defeat of Nasser and secular Arab nationalism, which by then had amassed a dismal human rights and economic record, and the Iranian revolution of 1979 sapped secularist rhetoric and galvanized the Islamist alternative. What Qutb, an adherent of the dominant Sunni branch of Islam, advocated in Egypt, Ayatollah Ruhollah Khomeini succeeded in accomplishing in predominantly Shiite Iran. Not surprisingly, when the shah of Iran finally fell in 1979, an intense power struggle between Islamists and secularists and among Islamists themselves began not only in Iran but also in the Arab world. Many self-styled spokesmen for Islam denounced American and Western culture, and some have also criticized and on occasion persecuted those women, minorities, and Muslim men who did not conform to "proper" Islamic codes of conduct. In the Arab world, however, Islamist movements have remained oppositional forces to authoritarian governments. In Iran the Islamists led by Khomeini triumphed and ushered in the "Islamic Revolution" and with it the most sustained challenge to U.S. regional hegemony. Khomeini did not hide his antipathy to the West and the United States in particular for propping up the shah's repressive regime. "With the support of America," Khomeini wrote in 1978, "and with all the infernal means at his disposal, the Shah has fallen on our oppressed people, turning Iran into one vast graveyard."[26]

But unlike Nasser, and unlike Islamists such as Ali Shariati who promoted an Islamic liberation theology, Khomeini mobilized and channeled revolutionary aspirations into a Manichaean theocracy that viewed Islam and America as totally antithetical civilizations. The taking of American hostages in 1980 dramatically illustrated the gulf that separated the revolutionary Iranian sense of an "imperialist" America and the U.S. image of itself as a benevolent nation. Khomeini's fiery denunciation of America in 1980 drew on a history of American overseas politics of which most Americans were ignorant but that Iranians and Arabs encountered on a daily basis. "The most important and painful problem confronting the subjugated nations of the world, both Muslim and non-Muslim," Khomeini said, "is the problem of America." He continued:

America is the number-one enemy of the deprived and oppressed people of the world. There is no crime America will not commit in order to maintain its political, economic, cultural, and military domination of those parts of the world where it predominates. It exploits the oppressed people of the world by means of the large-scale propaganda campaigns that are coordinated for it by international Zionism. By means of its hidden and treacherous agents, it sucks the blood of the defenseless people as if it alone, together with its satellites, had the right to live in this world.

Iran has tried to sever all its relations with this Great Satan and it is for this reason that it now finds wars imposed upon it.[27]

The Islamist anti-American sentiment that came to the fore during the Iranian revolution was ironically and unintentionally exacerbated by covert U.S. and Saudi mobilization, training, and financing of Muslim fighters to repel the Soviet invasion of Afghanistan. Their victory over one "imperialist" superpower turned their attention to another. Indeed, the United States loomed in the 1980s and 1990s ever more clearly as the unequivocal regional hegemon, the largest arms seller to the Middle East (particularly the gulf Arab states), an increasingly staunch supporter of Israel, and the guarantor of the authoritarian status quo in the gulf states (the wealthiest Arabs) and, since Camp David, in Egypt (the most populous Arab nation). And the United States military firmly planted itself in Saudi Arabia following the Gulf War and continues to oversee a stringent sanctions regime against Iraq. It is in this context of Iranian revolutionary upheaval, the defeat of the Soviets in Afghanistan, and the rise of U.S. dominance in the Persian Gulf that some Saudi Islamists, for example, have incorporated a militant anti-Americanism into their opposition to an increasingly obvious dependency of Saudi Arabia and to the "unjust" regional order that the United States has overseen. Their specific political anti-Americanism is inextricably bound up with their religious defensiveness and their more general repudiation of secular culture. Their anti-Americanism is not, however, simply a reaction against the basing of U.S. "infidels" near Mecca and Medina; nor is it simple fury at long-lost Muslim ascendancy. Such Islamists see the United States as a leader of a new crusade, a term that in the Arab world is replete not only with religious connotations of spiritual violation but equally with political ideas of occupation and oppression, in short, of worldly *injustice*.[28]

For all their appeals to a transhistorical Islam, most of the religiously, culturally, and politically diverse Islamist movements in the Middle East took their cue from nationalist struggles and discourses, each with its own nuances, audience, and resonances. Some, such as the Lebanese Hezbollah, which emerged following Israel's 1982 invasion of Lebanon —in which Israel used U.S. weapons and was protected by U.S. diplomatic support as it besieged an Arab capital for three months, killing thousands of civilians—regard the U.S. government as a major political enemy but have accommodated themselves to the multireligious environment of Lebanese politics. Others, such as the Algerian Islamic Salvation Front (FIS), are involved in an altogether different struggle— which does not immediately involve the United States—against the military-dominated government, which in 1992 annulled the results of democratic parliamentary elections the FIS was poised to win, unleashing an extremely bloody civil war. Islamist mobilizations remain, for the most part, firmly rooted in nationalist politics in which they are but one current among many.[29]

Anti-Americanism and Israel

On no issue is Arab anger at the United States more widely and acutely felt than that of Palestine. And on *no* issue, arguably, has there been more misunderstanding and less candor in mainstream commentaries purporting to explain Arab anger to American audiences following September 11. For it is over Palestine that otherwise antithetical Arab secularist and Islamist interpretations of history converge in their common perception of an immense gulf separating official American avowals of support for freedom from actual American policies. No account of anti-Americanism in the Arab world that does not squarely address the Arab understanding of Israel can even begin to convey the nature, the depth, and the sheer intensity of Arab anger at the United States.

Viewed from an exclusively Western perspective, the creation of the state of Israel represented Jewish national redemption, both because of a history of European anti-Semitism (especially the Holocaust) and because of the centrality of the Jewish presence (and the marginality of Islam) in Christian, particularly evangelical, thought about Palestine. But from an Arab perspective, Israel never has been and never could have been so understood. Zionism in Palestine, a land whose overwhelming majority was Arab at the turn of the twentieth century and for over a thousand years before that, caused the destruction of Palestinian society and the dispossession of its Arab inhabitants. As early as 1938 one of the most thoughtful modern Arab historians, George Antonius, warned the West about the implications of its support for Zionism in Palestine.

> The treatment meted out to Jews in Germany and other European countries is a disgrace to its authors and to modern civilisation; but posterity will not exonerate any country that fails to bear its proper share of the sacrifices needed to alleviate Jewish suffering and distress. To place the brunt of the burden upon Arab Palestine is a miserable evasion of the duty that lies upon the whole of the civilised world. It is also morally outrageous. No code of morals can justify the persecution of one people in an attempt to relieve the persecution of another. The cure for the eviction of Jews from Germany is not to be sought in the eviction of Arabs from their homeland; and the relief of Jewish distress may not be accomplished at the cost of inflicting a corresponding distress upon an innocent and peaceful population.

Antonius grasped the importance of Zionism for Jews and realized that blocking it would

> cause intense disillusionment and bitterness. The manifold proofs of public spirit and of capacity to endure hardships and face danger in the building up of the national home are there to testify to the devotion with which a large section of the Jewish people cherish the Zionist ideal. And it would be an act of further cruelty to the Jews to disappoint those hopes if there existed some way of satisfying them, that did not involve cruelty to another people. But the logic of facts is inexorable. It shows that no room can be made in Palestine for a second nation except by dislodging or exterminating the nation in possession.[30]

Compounding the original uprooting of the Palestinians in 1948 from their homes and lands—what Palestinians refer to as the *nakba* (catastrophe)—has been Israel's 1967 military occupation of the West Bank, Gaza, East Jerusalem, and the Golan Heights, an occupation that remains in full force today. Successive Israeli governments, Labor and Likud alike, have steadily confiscated more and more Palestinian land, demolished Palestinian homes, and exiled Palestinians, thus dismantling an Arab reality in Palestine and transforming it into a Jewish one. In the immediate aftermath of the 1948 war, for example, the new state of Israel razed approximately four hundred Palestinian villages; today Jewish settlements continue to be built on expropriated Palestinian land in East Jerusalem and the West Bank.[31] Because of this, Israel represents, for Arabs, a gross injustice. The contradictions and nuances within Israeli society are lost in the fact that Israel's creation and its persistence in its present form came and *continues* to come at the expense of the indigenous inhabitants of the land. From an Arab perspective, the creation of Israel marked the triumph of Western colonialism over native Arabs at a time when India and much of Africa and Asia were freeing themselves from European colonial rule. The specific question of Palestine has always been a broader Arab one as well, both because of the hundreds of thousands of Palestinian refugees in several Arab countries and because of a common history, language, culture, and politics that leads Arabs—Muslim and Christian—to identify with Palestinians.

American support for Israel has several foundations, ranging from the evangelical to the secular, from putative Judeo-Christian affinity to Cold War strategy, from passionate belief in the necessity of a Jewish state to opportunistic appeal to American Jewish voters, and from memory of the Holocaust to a perception of Israel as a small democratic nation surrounded by hostile Arab nations. For those reasons American financial support for Israel currently stands at nearly $3 billion a year, making it by far the single largest recipient of U.S. foreign aid.[32] But as Kathleen Christison, a former CIA analyst, has recently put it, "the singular U.S. focus on Israel's perspective in the conflict renders the United States unable to perform the role it has always set for itself as ultimate mediator and peacemaker."[33] In the United States (unlike most other parts of the world, including Europe) and among most Americans, the cumulative costs borne by Palestinians particularly and Arabs more generally for the violent creation of a Jewish state in the Arab world against the explicit wishes of the indigenous population are rarely acknowledged in public debate. To the extent that Arab hostility to Israel is known, it is often assumed to be based on age-old or irrational hatreds, anti-Semitism, or an intrinsic antidemocratic Arab sensibility. Just as support for Israel has become fundamental to an American imagination of the Middle East, particularly following the 1967 war, it is largely through Israel that most Arabs have come to judge the United States politically (although within often contradictory secular and Islamist narratives and hence with different implications). Satellite television stations such as Al-Jazeera daily beam pictures of Palestinian *suffering* under Israeli *occupation* directly into Arab households at a time when American television represents the Palestinian-Israeli conflict largely as Arab *violence* against Israel and Israeli *retaliation* against this violence.

It is not lost on Arabs that current American government officials describe the United States as an "honest broker." But those officials (and those in administrations before them) have explicitly condemned Palestinian terror against Israeli civilians while remaining largely silent when Palestinian civilians in far greater numbers are killed by Israeli terror.

This American silence is seen in the Arab world as complicity in Israeli occupation—particularly when it is American planes, helicopters, and bombs that enforce the thirty-five-year-old occupation. The dominant view in the Arab world is that American foreign policy regarding the Arab-Israeli conflict is shaped by the pro-Israel lobby, notably the American Israel Public Affairs Committee (AIPAC). Even regimes considered "pro-American" such as those of Saudi Arabia, Jordan, and post–Camp David Egypt are embarrassed by their apparent inability to make any significant impact on this state of affairs. And those who are not tied to the United States, such as Sayyid Muhammad Husayn Fadlallah, the spiritual leader of Hezbollah, declare without hesitation:

> I believe that America bears responsibility for all of Israel, both in its occupation of the lands of [19]48 or in all its settlement policies [in the lands occupied after 1967], despite the occasional utterance of a few timid and embarrassed words which disapprove of the settlements. [America] does not apply any pressure on [Israel] on par with the pressures it applies against the Palestinian Authority. America is a hypocritical nation when it comes to the question of Palestine: for it gives solid support and lethal weapons to the Israelis, but gives the Arabs and the Palestinians [only] words.[34]

Such stark condemnations of an evident U.S. bias toward Israel rarely acknowledge the Arabs' own role in solidifying that affinity, given the lack of democratic governance in the Arab world and the consequent inability of Arab leaders (and recently of Yasir Arafat) to articulate the moral and political nature of the Palestinian struggle for self-determination in terms that will resonate with the American public. Nor is it to deny that many Arab regimes and opposition parties have ruthlessly exploited the Palestinian question or that those regimes treat Palestinians and their own citizens callously. Nor is it to suggest that Arab convergence on the question of Palestine indicates unanimity on how to resolve the Arab-Israeli conflict. On that question, as on so many others, Arabs are deeply divided. Nor is it to deny that the Palestinians' own leadership under Yasir Arafat has successively alienated Arab people after people, beginning in Jordan, going on to Lebanon, and most recently in Kuwait, both tarnishing the image and immensely complicating the meaning of the Palestinian struggle within the Arab world. Nor is it, finally, to deny that criticism of Israel covers up a multitude of Arab sins, from the suppression of democratic opposition, the torture and banishment of dissidents, and the rampant corruption of state institutions to the cultivation of one-party and, indeed, one-family rule in Arab regimes (pro-American or not) from Saudi Arabia to Syria. Yet it *is* testament to the unresolved simplicity of the basic underlying issue that fuels this struggle—Arab natives evicted from their homes by Zionists, languishing stateless in refugee camps, and still suffering under Israeli occupation—that Arabs, from Morocco to Yemen and from all walks of life, still strongly sympathize with the Palestinians as a people for their half century of tribulations and exile from their land.

Whatever good Americans and the United States as a nation do in the region—from food aid to technological assistance to educational outreach to efforts at bilateral Arab-Israeli peacemaking—has been constantly overshadowed and tainted in Arab eyes by the continuation of the Arab-Israeli conflict, in which Arabs do not see the United States as evenhanded. Anti-American sentiment stemming from American support for Israel has been compounded in the past decade by the punitive American-dominated United Nations (UN) sanctions regime against Iraq put in place following the second Gulf War. The sanctions have contributed—according to UN statistics—to the deaths of several hundred thousand Iraqi civilians.[35] In 1996 CBS correspondent Lesley Stahl noted a report that "half a million children" had died in Iraq as a result of sanctions and asked then secretary of state Madeleine Albright, "Is the price worth it?" Albright replied, "I think this is a very hard choice, but the price, we think the price is worth it."[36] Americans see the image of Saddam Hussein and hear about frightening "weapons of mass destruction." Arabs see a flagrant double standard—Iraq punished and humiliated for invading Kuwait; Israel effusively supported despite its far longer occupation of Lebanon (which began in 1978 and ended in April 2000 because of a successful resistance campaign waged by Hezbollah), both occupations in clear defiance of UN resolutions. In the Arab world, therefore, the hope in America evident at the beginning of the twentieth century was transformed by the mid-twentieth century into disillusionment and by the end of the twentieth century into outright anger and hostility.

Conclusion

Most Arabs do not and will not act on this anger at U.S. policy in the region; like other people, most Arabs try to get on with their daily lives and, when they do turn to politics, can and do separate what they think of American culture, of Americans, and of American foreign policy. Yet September 11 is ultimately a mutilated and hijacked expression of immense Arab anger at the United States. Osama bin Laden is no more representative of Arabs than David Koresh or Timothy McVeigh were representative of Americans. But bin Laden *is* a manifestation of a deeply troubled Arab world beset by Arab government authoritarianism, a rise of Islamic fundamentalism, Israeli occupation and settlement of Arab lands, continuing Palestinian exile, and, finally, by American policies toward the region during and after the Cold War that have done little to encourage justice or democracy. Osama bin Laden's anti-American perspective is tied to a profoundly antisecular and illiberal world view; it is fueled by a dangerous self-righteousness that divides the world neatly between believer and infidel, good and evil. But his actions and his vocabulary must be placed in their modern historical and political context if we are to draw any meaningful conclusions from them.

The merest familiarity with modern history, then, would indicate that widespread Arab opposition to America is a sign of the times. It is based, not on *long-standing hatred* of "American" values, but on more *recent anger* at American policies in the region, especially toward Israel. Anti-Americanism is therefore not civilizationally rooted, even if it is at times expressed in civilizational terms. Nor does it stem primarily from Islamic philosophy or exegesis, even if it is sometimes expressed (especially at present) in Islamist idiom. A deep political gulf certainly now separates Arab peoples from the United States. However, a just solution to the Arab-Israeli conflict that recognizes the equality and the humanity of both Israelis *and* Palestinians will go a long way toward healing the very modern rupture in American and Arab relations. But before that can happen, there must be an acknowledgment of both Jewish and Arab histories rather than a consistent subordination of one to the other. What is most important at this juncture is a realization by both Americans and Arabs of the interactive process, the dialectical relationship, that has shaped Arab attitudes toward the United States and vice versa. This essay has attempted to historicize the evolution of Arab attitudes toward the United States, and it is written in the belief that similar attempts must be made to help explain the United States and American society to the Arab world. To do so in any meaningful way, however, requires that both Arabs *and* Americans move away from narratives of innocence and purity—whether of religions or of nations.

Notes

1. U.S. Congress, House of Representatives, Committee on Foreign Affairs, Subcommittee on Europe and the Middle East, *Post-War Policy Issues in the Persian Gulf,* 102 Cong., 1 sess., Feb. 21, 1991, pp. 120, 85. Emphasis added.

2. For a recent interpretation that subscribes to the "clash of civilizations" thesis, see Bernard Lewis, "The Revolt of Islam: A New Turn in a Long War with the West," *New Yorker*, Nov. 19, 2001, pp. 50–60. The most famous pronouncement on this thesis is Samuel P. Huntington, "The Clash of Civilizations?" *Foreign Affairs*, 72 (Summer 1993), 22–49.

3. There was one final outbreak of hostilities during the War of 1812. See Robert J. Allison, *The Crescent Obscured: The United States and the Muslim World, 1776–1815* (New York, 1995), esp. 35–59. In the 1780s John Adams favored negotiations, but Thomas Jefferson staunchly advocated resolving the captivity crisis through war. "1. Justice is in favor of this opinion," he wrote to Adams on July 11, 1786. "2. Honor favors it. 3. It will procure us respect in Europe. 4. It will arm the federal head with the safest of all the instruments of coercion over their delinquent members and prevent them from using what would be less safe. . . . 5. I think it least expensive. 6. Equally effectual." Lester J. Cappon, ed., *The Adams-Jefferson Letters* (Chapel Hill, 1988), 142.

4. Hilton Obenzinger, *American Palestine: Melville, Twain, and the Holy Land Mania* (Princeton, 1999); Mark Twain, *The Innocents Abroad* (1869; New York, 1966).

5. Robert Smythe Hichens, *The Garden of Allah* (New York, 1904); Holly Edwards, ed., *Noble Dreams, Wicked Pleasures: Orientalism in America, 1870–1930* (Princeton, 2000).

6. See Ussama Makdisi, "Reclaiming the Land of the Bible: Missionaries, Secularism, and Evangelical Modernity," *American Historical Review*, 102 (June 1997), 680–713.

7. A. L. Tibawi, *American Interests in Syria, 1800–1901: A Study of Educational, Literary, and Religious Work* (Oxford, Eng., 1966), 36–41.

8. *New York Morning Herald*, May 19, 1840, box 3/2, Eli Smith Family Papers, Record Group 124, Special Collections (Yale Divinity School Library, New Haven, Conn.).

9. Butrus al-Bustani, *Al-Jam'iyya al-suriyya li al-'ulum wa al-funun, 1847–1852* (The Syrian Society for the Sciences and Arts) (Beirut, 1990), 112. Unless otherwise indicated, translations from Arabic are my own.

10. F. J. Bliss, ed., *The Reminiscences of Daniel Bliss* (New York, 1920), 198.

11. Qasim Amin, *The New Woman: A Document in the Early Debate on Egyptian Feminism*, trans. Samiha Sidhom Peterson (1900; Cairo, 1995), 8.

12. "Bab ashhar al-hawadith wa a'zam al-rijal" (Chapter on the most famous of events and the most outstanding of men), *al-Hilal* (Cairo), 1 (1893), 152. Mikha'il As'ad Rustum, *Kitab al-gharib fi al-gharb* (Book of a stranger in the West) (1895; Beirut, 1992), 11; Philip Hitti, "America in the Eyes of an Easterner; or, Eight Years in the United States," in *America in an Arab Mirror: Images of America in Arabic Travel Literature: An Anthology, 1895–1995*, ed. Kamal Abdel-Malek (New York, 2000), 49.

13. Sayyid Qutb, "The America I Have Seen," in *America in an Arab Mirror*, ed. Abdel-Malek, 26.

14. "Memorandum by Mr. Balfour Respecting Syria, Palestine, and Mesopotamia, 1919," in *From Haven to Conquest: Readings in Zionism and the Palestine Problem until 1948*, ed. Walid Khalidi (Washington, 1987), 208. On Howard Bliss and the fact-finding mission, see Harry N. Howard, *The King-Crane Commission: An American Inquiry into the Middle East* (Beirut, 1963), 24–25.

15. Kathleen Christison, *Perceptions of Palestine: Their Influence on U.S. Middle East Policy* (Berkeley, 2000), 33.

16. Howard, *King-Crane Commission*, 205. For an incisive account, see James L. Gelvin, "The Ironic Legacy of the King-Crane Commission," in *The Middle East and the United States: A Historical and Political Reassessment*, ed. David W. Lesch (Boulder, 1999), 13–29.

17. "The Recommendations of the King-Crane Commission," in Howard, *King-Crane Commission*, 353.

18. *Ibid.*, 349–51.

19. Christison, *Perceptions of Palestine*, 27–33.

20. Abdelrahman Munif, *Cities of Salt* (New York, 1989). For a scholarly account, see Rosemarie Said Zahlan, *The Making of the Modern Gulf States* (Reading, 1998).

21. Robert Vitalis, "Black Gold, White Crude: Race and the Making of the World Oil Frontier," in *The United States and the Middle East: Diplomatic and Economic Relations in Historical Perspective*, ed. Abbas Amanat (New Haven, 2000), 187–233.

22. For Jimmy Carter's statement, see William Shawcross, *The Shah's Last Ride* (New York, 1988), 130. Nikki R. Keddie, *Roots of Revolution: An Interpretative History of Modern Iran* (New Haven, 1981), 275–76.

23. On this crisis and how it affected American-Egyptian relations, see Irene L. Gendzier, *Notes from the Minefield: United States Intervention in Lebanon and the Middle East, 1945–1958* (Boulder, 1999).

24. Ahmad Yusuf Ahmad, ed., *Al-majmu'a al-kamila li-khutab wa ahadith wa tasrihat Jamal 'Abd al-Nasir* (The complete collection of the speeches, interviews, and declarations of Gamal Abdel Nasser), vol. III: *1958–1959* (Beirut, 1999), 231–32.

25. See Yvonne Haddad, "Sayyid Qutb: Ideologue of the Islamic Revival," in *Voices of Resurgent Islam*, ed. John L. Esposito (New York, 1983), 67–98.

26. Ruhollah Khomeini, *Islam and Revolution: Writings and Declarations*, trans. and annotated by Hamid Algar (London, 1985), 238.

27. *Ibid.*, 304–5.

28. See Yvonne Haddad, "Islamist Perceptions of U.S. Policy in the Middle East," in *Middle East and the United States*, ed. Lesch, 433–52.

29. For a good overview of U.S. policies and Islamist politics, see Fawaz Gerges, *America and Political Islam: Clash of Cultures or Clash of Interests?* (Cambridge, Eng., 1999).

30. George Antonius, *The Arab Awakening: The Story of the Arab National Movement* (1938; New York, 1968), 411–12.

31. See Walid Khalidi, *Before Their Diaspora: A Photographic History of the Palestinians, 1876–1948* (Washington, 1991). See also the words of Moshe Dayan quoted in Edward W. Said, *The Question of Palestine* (New York, 1992), 14. See also the work of revisionist Israeli historians such as Avi Shlaim, *The Iron Wall: Israel and the Arab World* (New York, 2001); and Eugene L. Rogan and Avi Shlaim, eds., *The War for Palestine: Rewriting the History of 1948* (New York, 2001).

32. On the cultural reasons for U.S. support for Israel, see Melani McAlister, *Epic Encounters: Culture, Media, and U.S. Interests in the Middle East, 1945–2000* (Berkeley, 2001). The aid figure does not include substantial loan guarantees nor U.S. subsidies for the Arrow missile project. Egypt is granted nearly $2 billion an-

nually and has thus been the second-largest recipient of U.S. aid since the signing of the Camp David peace treaty with Israel. Yet on a per capita basis, aid to Israel far surpasses aid to Egypt. For more information on the extent of U.S. aid to Israel, see the *Washington Report on Middle East Affairs* <http://wrmea.com> (June 18, 2002). See also the *Jewish Virtual Library* <http://www.us-israel.org/jsource/US-Israel/U.S._Assistance_to_Israel1.html> (July 30, 2002).

33. Christison, *Perceptions of Palestine*, 293. Christison's book provides an overview of U.S. policy toward Israel and the Palestinians.

34. "Al-muqawama al-musallaha al-filastiniyya: As'ilat al-bu'd al-akhlaqi, Al-sayyid Muhammad Husayn Fadlallah" (Palestinian armed resistance: Questions relating to its moral dimension, Sayyid Muhammad Husayn Fadlallah), *al-Adab* (Beirut), 50 (nos. 1–2, 2002), 19.

35. See a work published by UNICEF and the Iraqi Ministry of Health, *Child and Maternal Mortality Survey, 1999: Preliminary Report* ([Baghdad], 1999), available on-line at <http://www.unicef.org/reseval/iraqr.html> (April 19, 2002). The estimate was based on a pattern of "substantial reduction in the under-five mortality rate during the 1980s" reversed in the 1990s. Two UN humanitarian coordinators for Iraq have resigned in protest against the sanctions regime, one in 1998, the other in 2000. The first said, "We are in the process of destroying an entire society. It is as simple and terrifying as that. It is illegal and immoral." See *Campaign against Sanctions on Iraq* <http://www.cam.ac.uk/societies/casi/halliday/quotes.html> (April 19, 2002); and <http://www.cam.ac.uk/societies/casi/guide/quotes.html> (April 19, 2002).

36. "Punishing Saddam," prod. Catherine Olian (episode of "60 Minutes") (CBS, May 12, 1996).

History in the Fundamentalist Imagination

R. Scott Appleby

R. Scott Appleby compares the ways contemporary radical religious movements in Christianity, Islam, and Judaism have reconstructed the past to create distinctive world views. Such "fundamentalists" share a tortured construction of history that stresses a dispiriting record of humiliation, persecution, and exile of the true believers as a necessary prelude to God's decisive intervention and the final vanquishing of the apostates. To contextualize the historical vision of Muslim fundamentalists, Appleby explores the experience of the Islamic world in the twentieth century as it has been constructed and popularized by Sunni Muslim extremists such as Sayyid Qutb and one of his disciples, Osama bin Laden.

The Fundamentalist Past as Prelude

Historians are not alone in reconstructing the past. Richly imagined and ingeniously documented versions of the past shape and sustain religious, social, and political movements. Such is the case with the antisecular, antimodernist religious movements that are sometimes compared under the term "fundamentalism." In this essay I first examine fundamentalist reconstructions of the past as a way of understanding the distinctive world views such histories reinforce and the appeal they hold for individuals and movements. In the second part of the essay, I explore the experience of the Islamic world in the twentieth century as it has been historicized and popularized by Sunni Muslim extremists such as Sayyid Qutb (1903–1966) and one of his contemporary disciples, Osama bin Laden.

The mentality of fundamentalists is shaped by a tortured vision of the past—a construction of history that casts the long and otherwise dispiriting record of humiliation, persecution, and exile of the true believers (punctuated by an occasional, atypical golden age of faith) as a necessary prelude to the decisive intervention of God and the final vanquishing of the apostates.

157

That sentence deserves several qualifications. First, the blanket use of the term "fundamentalism" may incorrectly suggest that Protestant fundamentalism—an early case of organized, militant religious opposition to secular modernity and its accomplices (pluralism, relativism, feminism)—is the template for all other fundamentalisms. The scriptural inerrancy invented by critics of the higher criticism of the Bible in the late 1880s, however, is hardly the defining mark of all such religious movements that arose in reaction against the modern nation-state with its absolutist pretensions and ever-increasing reach. Almost a generation before U.S. Protestant fundamentalism appeared, the Roman Catholic Church promulgated the *Syllabus of Errors* (1864), in which Pope Pius IX condemned most aspects of modernity, inaugurating an antimodernist campaign on a platform of ecclesial rather than scriptural "inerrancy." (The doctrine of papal infalliblity was defined by the First Vatican Council in 1870.) "Scriptural inerrancy" as a distinctive mark of fundamentalism is redundant when applied to Islam, given all Muslims' traditional—not, that is, antimodern—belief about the Koran. And so on.[1]

Second, some Muslims, Christians, and Jews have objected to the term "fundamentalism" because it implies that their militant co-religionists are the true believers, the righteous defenders of the faith, whereas, they argue, the militants manipulate sacred texts and traditional teachings to serve political ends. Mainstream believers note the irony in the posturing of self-anointed defenders of the faith who have little respect for the integrity of its fundamentals. Fundamentalism, in other words, is best understood as a mode of thought and action, an identifiable configuration of ideology and organizational resources— not as an essence or constitutive trait of any or all of the host religious traditions. And even within the family of fundamentalisms reaching across time zones and religions, the differences between the movements are far greater than their similarities.

Third, to describe fundamentalists' views of the past as "tortured" is to run the outsider's risk of missing the full significance and function of history as they learn, teach, and re-enact it. Each of the subgroups has developed an enduring religious culture by discerning meaning and purpose amid the farrago of its own particular and in some sense incomparable historical experiences.

Yet one ventures to speak of a mentality shared by disparate militant religious movements of self-styled true believers who attempt to arrest the erosion of religious identity, fortify the borders of the religious community, and create viable alternatives to secular institutions and behaviors. Islam in the latter half of the twentieth century produced a particularly formidable and radical expression of the fundamentalist mode, but other major religious traditions have also given birth to movements that can be fruitfully compared to the Islamist movements (what comparativists call Muslim fundamentalism), as well as to the original Christian cases.

A key to that mentality is found in the fundamentalists' appropriation of history. For them history is decidedly not just "one damn thing after another"; it is the arena in which the divine plan is enacted, in which souls gain or lose their salvation, in which God's elect—the *dramatis personae* in the passion play—take center stage. There they may perform in a passive, quiescent mode by building the religious enclave, converting, indoctrinating, and gathering in the true believers, and awaiting the coming of the messiah or renewer. The *haredi*, or ultraorthodox, Jews of Israel occupy this niche prominently, as do Christians of the United States and Europe who anticipate the "rapture," in which true believers are raised directly up to the heavens, followed by the coming of the Antichrist, the great cosmic battle of Armageddon, and the thousand-year rule of Christ. For much of their history, adherents of the Shiite branch of Islam adopted a similar quiescent mode, awaiting deliverance by the divinely guided leader, the Hidden Imam.[2]

Or, conceiving themselves to be active agents of the Almighty, fundamentalists organize for cultural power, political takeover, or military conquest. The "new Christian Right" of the 1980s derived energy from a fundamentalist core who had decided that the United States was becoming so godless that Bible-believing Christians could no longer wait privately for the return of Christ; the elect were required to "take back" the public schools, the Supreme Court, the Congress, and the presidency.[3] Islamic militants in Arab countries, adherents of the Sunni branch of Islam, seek to restore the caliphate, the religious-political office traditionally responsible for guaranteeing that the Islamic state followed and enforced Islamic law.[4] Shiite ayatollahs awoke from their political slumbers in the late 1970s to strive to transform Iran and Lebanon into Islamic republics that would eventually merge into an "all-encompassing Islamic state" embodying the *umma* or worldwide Islamic community.[5]

History has a double edge for many militant antisecular groups. On the one hand, the past is filled with horrible suffering for the believers and apparent victories for the apostates—those who have fallen away from the true faith and succumbed to materialism, the corruptions arising from sexual license and lust for money, and the other spiritually enervating seductions of modernity. The enemy seems to control the centers of power. And yet, to the eyes of the true believer, even now God is bringing this dour history to an unexpected, dramatic, and rewarding culmination. The Jews of Gush Emunim, the Bloc of the Faithful in Israel, combine in their small movement a remarkable balance of the extremes of euphoria and expectation, on the one hand, and disgust with, or despair at, mundane realities, on the other, that are found less expertly blended in many other movements. The establishment of the state of Israel, in Gush historiography, is clearly a sign and instrument of the arrival of the messianic age, as are Israel's military victories over the surrounding Arab populations. Gush Emunim itself is the chosen agent of the divine plan to restore "the whole land of Israel" to its biblical proportions. By aggressively establishing settlements in the occupied territories, the Bloc of the Faithful is coaxing the secular Zionist government to defend the Jewish presence and thus to restore the Jews to their rightful place as sovereigns over the Holy Land. But the confident and often ecstatic behavior of the Gush coexists with bouts of severe depression when what they call other "facts in the field" occur—such as the 1982 bulldozing of the Yamit settlement on the Sinai by the Israeli government in compliance with the Camp David accords or the defection of the late prime minister Yitzhak Rabin, who negotiated the Oslo accords with Yasir Arafat in the early 1990s and presumed to trade "Jewish" land for peace.[6]

Both the near euphoria and the despair are rooted in a supernaturalist reading of history. Professional secular historians typically are reluctant to identify or even search for a transcendent meaning to the narratives they manage to piece together: Ordinary time, with all its humbling ambiguities, is their métier. Fundamentalists seem less bothered by the multivalent and often contradictory testimonies culled from archives and archaeological digs or encountered within their own sacred scriptures and religious traditions.

Seldom, in fact, is the true believer confounded by the multiple motives of historical actors, random occurrences, and unintended consequences—in a providential universe there are no random occurrences and unintended consequences. Details that reinforce the received worldview receive dutiful attention. Like all historians, fundamentalists select from the jumble of facts and events, prioritizing and weighing some few more heavily than all the rest; no attempt at narrative can avoid the sifting process. But fundamentalists often reach beyond the personal inclinations and biases that influence any historian to an external source such as Scripture that provides an inerrant, that is, a trustworthy, foundation for hermeneutics. Indeed, the proprietors of the cottage industry in Christian apocalypticism, including megaselling authors such as Tim LaHaye (author of the wildly popular *Left Behind* series) and Hal Lindsey (of *The Late Great Planet Earth*), endorse—and profit from—the fundamentalist assertion that reading history through the lens of biblical prophecy is a more "objective" method than reading with one's own subjectivity as guide.[7]

Apocalypticism is a defining feature of fundamentalisms. The expectation of a dramatic reversal of history at the hands of God or a messiah, in which the faithful or holy remnant are vindicated and their enemies brutally punished, is not confined to fundamentalists—it is a deep strain within the premodern (and thus prefundamentalist) history of all three major monotheisms. But apocalyptic or millenarian fervor takes on a decidedly therapeutic role in the lives and imagination of the modern antimodernists. The anticipated reversal of ordinary history is a source of great comfort for millions of believers living amid squalor, relative

A bumper sticker in Texas, in the heart of the Bible belt, reads: "In case of rapture this car will be unmanned." It reduces to a popular slogan the premillennialist idea that true believers will be rescued from the punishment and chaos awaiting the masses of sinners at the end of time. (Photograph by Micah Marty. Courtesy of R. Scott Appleby.)

deprivation, or moral decadence. The fundamentalists' present suffering is but a prelude to a profoundly satisfying reward for their perseverance, whether they live in the putrid refugee camps of Gaza or southern Lebanon or the relative affluence but spiritual sterility of the Dallas suburbs.

Thus, the Gulf War of 1990 provoked in the Christian fundamentalists of Dallas and elsewhere a mixture of dread and rapturous joy. To these dispensationalists—who believe God has divided history into several "dispensations," or eras, the last of which, the apocalyptic end times, is imminent—the reports of Saddam Hussein lobbing Scud missiles at Israel seemed to augur the outbreak of Armageddon. The Bible predicts, the dispensationalists believe, that the great and unimaginably bloody final battle between the forces of Christ and antichrist will occur at Megiddo, a hill in Israel not far from where the missiles were falling. True believers found reason to celebrate the approach of the end times in their conviction that they would be taken directly to heaven to escape the chastisement and conflagration awaiting the mass of sinful humanity. In *The New World Order*—a 1991 book that borrowed its title, with intended irony, from President George H. W. Bush—the Pentecostal preacher and erstwhile presidential candidate Pat Robertson detailed the chaos to come for those left behind. Exploiting the military victory over Iraq, Bush, Robertson claimed, was leading a well-organized, well-financed, multigenerational "cabal" in a "conspiracy" to create a one-world socialist state, centered in the United Nations and eventually to be governed by the antichrist of biblical prophecy. To demonstrate this thesis, Robertson took the history of the twentieth century as his text, pointing to events as disparate as loans made to Bolshevik Russia in 1917, the creation of the European Common Market and its plans for a Europe-wide currency, the euro, and the recent scandal involving the Bank of Credit and Commerce International (BCCI) to "prove" that the satanic conspiracy had been building for generations.[8]

Those self-styled true believers whom we are calling fundamentalists hardly fall into lockstep, however, in their methods of relating temporality to eternity. Sensibilities differ. Some attempt entirely to shut out developments occurring apart from, or subsequent to, sacred time. Ultraorthodox rebbes living in contemporary Israel, ensconced in their enclave of Mea Shearim, look longingly at maps of areas of Jewish settlement in Eastern Europe marking villages, regions, and place names that have not existed for more than a century. Others shut out every bit of data but what the sacred text provides. The sociologist Samuel C. Heilman reports that sixth-grade boys in a Lithuanian yeshiva in Jerusalem immediately prior to the Gulf War were unable to sketch the outline of a map of Israel or to tell him the names of the surrounding countries. One youngster, asked what bordered on Israel, confidently answered that Israel was surrounded by *chutz la'aretz*, the Hebrew expression that most Israelis use to refer to the rest of the world. "In this boy's mind the world was neatly divided," Heilman writes. "Just as there were goyim and Jews, so similarly there was Israel and *chutz la'aretz*." None of the boys could identify Jordan, Syria, Lebanon, and Egypt. None had ever heard of Saudi Arabia.[9]

By contrast, members of Gush Emunim are a reliable source for the latest news of Middle East politics; they follow unfolding events closely, using them to buttress their distinctive reading of modern (messianic) history. The radical Jewish settlers are not waiting anxiously for the messiah like their haredi counterparts; they are instead proclaiming a messianic era and forcing Israel's hand by creating new settlements in the occupied territories of "Judea" and "Samaria." History is our currency, said Daniella Weiss, a Gush publicist.[10]

Their different settings, beliefs, and goals notwithstanding, Jewish, Christian, and Islamic fundamentalists interpret the history of the modern period, especially the twentieth century, in remarkably similar ways. It has been a period of dramatic and gut-wrenching decline—they typically use such words as "erosion," "alienation," "isolation," and "exile" to characterize the weakened state of traditional religious observance, family life, parental authority, and patriarchal privilege. In their constructions of history, the atheistic or agnostic modern state is the recurring culprit, whether it be a United States Supreme Court that legalized abortion, an Israeli prime minister who attempted to trade land for peace with the Palestinians, or a Saudi monarchy that entered into military and business alliances with the Western infidels. "*The bottom line*," concluded the influential Christian thinker Francis A. Schaeffer, who could have been speaking for the disgruntled Jews of Israel or the Muslims of Egypt, "is that at a certain point there is not only the right, but the duty, to disobey the state."[11]

The treachery of supposedly orthodox co-religionists is another defining mark of fundamentalist history. Christian ideologues such as Schaeffer and Tim LaHaye point to the Christian foundations of the American republic and lament their erosion at the hands of secularized

Yeshiva students in Israel standing under a redrawn globe, with Israel occupying the area outlined in black. From the Talmud, the Hebrew reads: On three pillars does the world stand: on Torah, on mitzvah, and on kindnesses. (Courtesy of Samuel C. Heilman.)

Christians. Jewish extremists see the peace movement in Israel as expressive of the fragmentation of Orthodox Judaism and the confusion wrought by that crisis. And Muslim extremists, whose reading of history—and plans to alter its course—have captured our attention in dramatic fashion since September 11, 2001, have their own distinctive litany of traitors and of heroes.

Redeeming the History of Humiliation

On Sunday, October 7, 2001, the Al-Jazeera television network, based in Qatar, broadcast a videotaped statement by Osama bin Laden commenting on the events of September 11. "America has been filled with horror from north to south and east to west, and thanks be to God," bin Laden exulted. "What America is tasting now is only a copy of what we have tasted," he continued. "Our Islamic nation has been tasting the same for more [than] eighty years, of humiliation and disgrace, its sons killed and their blood spilled, its sanctities desecrated."[12]

The period of Muslim "humiliation," that is, began with the defeat of the Ottoman Empire in World War I and the subsequent abolishment of the caliphate, in 1924, by the new secular republic of Turkey under the leadership of Mustafa Kemal Atatürk. The caliphate had been recognized by the vast majority of Muslims as the office of the successors of the Prophet Muhammad. Over the centuries, the role of the caliph varied. Under the Umayyad dynasty, established by the caliph Muawiyah I in 661, the caliphate commanded absolute religious and political power. Under the Abbasids (750–1258), its temporal role was usurped by military commanders (the sultans or emirs). In the eighteenth century the Turkish sultans of the Ottoman Empire presented themselves as caliphs —that is, as the paramount spiritual leaders and defenders of Islam. If the caliph did not wield direct political power for much of this history, his supreme spiritual authority was intended to ensure that Muslim states were governed in accordance with the Islamic law, or shari'a.[13]

The abolishment of the caliphate, according to the reading of history favored by bin Laden and perhaps hundreds of thousands of like-minded Islamic fundamentalists, triggered the precipitous decline of Islam as a civilization-shaping force in the Arab world and beyond. Thus, the origins of Islamism (Muslim fundamentalism) are connected with the loss of a transnational and sacralized Muslim political unit. Sunni and Shiite Muslims have different historical experiences of religiously sanctioned politics; accordingly, their reactions to the fall of the Ottoman Empire and the end of the caliphate have differed. Until the ascendancy of Ayatollah Ruhollah Khomeini in 1978, Shiite Muslims, who are concentrated in Iran, Iraq, and Lebanon, had suffered the loss of divinely guided political leadership since the occultation, or disappearance into hiding, of the Twelfth Imam, in 931 C.E. By contrast, for Sunni Muslims, approximately 90 percent of the Muslim world, the loss of the caliphate after World War I was devastating in light of the hitherto continuous historic presence of the caliph, the guardian of Islamic law and the Islamic state. Sunni fundamentalist leaders thereafter emerged in nations such as Egypt and India, where contact with Western political structures provided them with a model awkwardly to imitate (as in the "theo-democracy" of Maulana Sayyid Abdul Ala Maududi, discussed below) as they struggled after 1924 to provide a viable alternative to the caliphate.

In 1928, four years after the abolishment of the caliphate, the Egyptian schoolteacher Hasan al-Banna founded the first Islamic fundamentalist movement in the Sunni world, the Muslim Brotherhood (al-Ikhwan al-Muslimun). Al-Banna was appalled by "the wave of atheism and lewdness [that] engulfed Egypt" following World War I. The victorious Europeans had "imported their half-naked women into these regions, together with their liquors, their theatres, their dance halls, their amusements, their stories, their newspapers, their novels, their whims, their silly games, and their vices." Suddenly the very heart of the Islamic world was penetrated by European "schools and scientific and cultural institutes" that "cast doubt and heresy into the souls of its sons and taught them how to demean themselves, disparage their religion and their fatherland, divest themselves of their traditions and beliefs, and to regard as sacred anything Western."[14] Most distressing to al-Banna and his followers was what they saw as the rapid moral decline of the religious establishment, including the leading sheikhs, or religious scholars, at Al-Azhar, the grand mosque and center of Islamic learning in Cairo. The clerical leaders had become compromised and corrupted by their alliance with the indigenous ruling elites who had succeeded the European colonial masters.

Even as the Ikhwan was gaining momentum in Egypt, in India Maududi was launching the prodigious career as a journalist, editor, and writer that made him the chief ideologue of Islamic fundamentalism. Modern Muslim discourse on the social, political, and economic teachings of Islam owes an enormous debt to Maududi, who coined and systematically defined terms such as "Islamic politics," "Islamic ideology," "the economic system of Islam," and "the Islamic constitution." More systematically than any other author, Maududi recast Islam as an ideological alternative to both Western liberalism and Soviet Marxism. Envisioning Islam as a comprehensive political system as well as a way of life, Maududi advocated *iqamat-i-deen* (the establishment of religion)— the total subordination of civil society and the state to the authority of the shari'a. Islamic law and Islamic governance should extend, Maududi taught, "from the mosque to the parliament, from the home to the school and economy; from art, architecture and science to law, state and international relations."[15]

In August 1941 Maududi founded the Jamaat-i-Islami, which became the major Islamist movement of Pakistan, to give institutional shape to his religiopolitical ideas. But his influence extended far beyond Pakistan and South Asia. He was a major influence on Sayyid Qutb, the ideological founder of the school of Sunni extremism to which Osama bin Laden is heir.[16]

Despite the early virulent Islamic reactions to "Westoxication," as an Iranian intellectual described the cultural colonization of Islam, the "humiliation and disgrace" visited upon "the Islamic nation" only mounted, reaching their apex with the establishment of the state of Israel in 1948 and the first of several demoralizing military defeats at the hands of the Zionists.[17] The Arab and Muslim identities of that imagined, transnational nation clashed violently in the 1950s and 1960s following the ascent to power of Gamal Abdel Nasser in Egypt. Nasser's vision of Pan-Arab unity buttressed by state socialism captured the imagination of the Arab Middle East. But his state-guided, state-dominated plan to build the public sector of the economy suffered from a balance of payments crisis, domestic entanglements (including an alleged plot by the Muslim Brotherhood), and the excessive bureaucratization and overmanagement often associated with central planning. At the same time, Nasser's political leadership of the Arab world suffered a mortal blow when Israel won the Six-Day War of 1967 and occupied the West Bank, Gaza, and the Sinai. Not least, Nasser also made the fateful choice to isolate and then outlaw the Muslim Brotherhood (which had become increasingly violent), arresting more than one thousand of its leaders and eventually executing six, including Qutb.[18]

While in prison, Qutb penned a treatise that his followers disseminated across the Sunni world. *Milestones* (1960, also known as *Signposts on the Road*) became the manifesto of Sunni extremism and the justification for terrorism.[19] In *Milestones* Qutb developed an interpretation of jihad, Islamic holy war, that would become the core doctrine of the Islamic Liberation Organization of Egypt and Jordan, the Jihad Organization and Takfir wal-Hijra of Egypt, and similar cells in Egypt, North Africa, Lebanon, Israel, Saudi Arabia, the West Bank, and the gulf states. Qutb's radical innovation was the application of the concept of *jahiliyyah* (the pre-Islamic condition of ignorance of the guidance of God) to fellow Muslims, including Arab leaders such as Nasser, who had abandoned Islam, he charged, in favor of atheistic philosophies and ideologies. "Our whole environment, people's beliefs and ideas, habits and art, rules and laws is—Jahiliyyah, even to the extent that what we consider to be Islamic culture, Islamic sources, Islamic philosophy and Islamic thought, are also constructs of Jahiliyyah!" As a result, he charged, "the true Islamic values never enter our hearts . . . our minds are never illuminated by Islamic concepts, and no group of people arises among us who are of the calibre of the first generation of Islam."[20]

Maududi's concept of *iqamat-i-deen* echoes in Qutb's exhortations from prison to his fellow Muslim Brothers. Significantly for our purposes, Qutb justifies "the establishment of religion" by positing a golden age or primordial state of purity, resolve, and religious integrity, standards from which subsequent generations departed. People of the caliber of the Prophet and his companions do not arise because the vicissitudes of historical experience have eroded the social and institutional structures within which true belief flourished. True believers of the past have too often let events—the normal course of history—determine the outcome of the perennial struggle between the righteous and the unbelievers. The remedy to historical erosion? "We must return to that pure source from which those people [the earliest followers of the Prophet Muhammad] derived their guidance—the source which is free from any mixing or pollution," Qutb wrote. "From [Islam] we must also derive our concepts of life, our principles of government, politics, economics and all other aspects of life."[21]

Qutb's dour reading of long stretches of the Muslim past informs the elements of fundamentalist ideology in *Milestones:* alarm over the perceived loss of religious integrity; refusal to compromise with outsiders; the sense of apocalyptic crisis; the envy and imitation of secular modernity juxtaposed to revulsion from its immoral excesses; and, finally, the desire to build a comprehensive religious alternative to secularism. For Qutb withdrawal from the existing, compromised Islamic society was a prelude to an offensive jihad against infidels and apostates around the world. The Islamic fundamentalist movement would use the weapons and tactics of the secular world against it.

> Since this movement comes into conflict with the Jahiliyyah which . . . has a practical system of life and a political and material authority behind it, the Islamic movement had to produce parallel resources. . . . This movement uses the methods of preaching and persuasion for reforming ideas and beliefs; and it uses physical power and Jihaad for abolishing the organisations and authorities of the jahili system.[22]

Jihad is not restricted to defense of the homeland, Qutb insists. Rather, it is a command to extend the borders of Islam to the ends of the earth:

> If we insist on calling Islamic Jihaad a defensive movement, then we must change the meaning of the word "defense" and mean by it "the defense of man" against all those elements which limit his freedom. These elements take the form of beliefs and concepts, as well as of political systems, based on economic, racial or class distinctions. . . . When we take this broad meaning of the word "defense," we understand the true character of Islam, and that it is a universal proclamation of the freedom of man from servitude to other men, the establishment of God and His Lordship throughout the world, the end of man's arrogance and selfishness, and the implementation of the rule of the Divine Sharia'ah in human affairs.[23]

Here Qutb broke with contemporary interpreters of Islamic law. Like fundamentalists in other religions, he invoked the doctrines of a sage who had legitimated extremism, in this case Ibn Taymiyya (1268–1328), a scholar of Islamic law who had characterized Mongols as "false Muslims" and blessed those who fought them. Qutb also retrieved the practice of *ijtihad*, the use of independent reasoning when no clear text was available from the Koran or the hadith (sayings) of the Prophet. Finally, he gave an extremist interpretation of a traditional precept—jihad—justifying it by recourse to "exceptionalism," the argument that the onset of crisis (here *jahiliyya*) requires extreme countermeasures.

In *Milestones* Qutb argued that the Prophet's prohibition against fighting was only "a temporary stage in a long journey" during the Meccan period, and he uses inflammatory language easily construed as legitimating lethal violence against Islam's numerous enemies. (It was so construed by Qutb's intellectual disciples, notably the Jihad group that assassinated President Anwar Sadat of Egypt in 1981.) Yet Qutb himself disavowed any intent to harm individuals, claiming that Islamists attack

An Algerian woman, c. 1992, seems to agree with the graffiti behind her: An Islamic State Coming Soon! (Photograph by Micah Marty. Courtesy of R. Scott Appleby.)

only institutions, and a sympathetic scholar described him as "essentially a philosopher who shunned violence."[24]

Be that as it may, Qutb's legacy includes the cadres of radical fundamentalist Muslims who created new forms of violent intolerance and religious resistance to the powers that be. Elements of his ideology have inspired fundamentalist movements and terrorist cells that grew up outside his original sphere of influence, including the Taliban, the Harkat Mujahedeen of Pakistan, and the Armed Islamic Group (GIA) of Algeria, which has waged a terrorist campaign against the "jahili" government of Algeria since 1992. Among the terrorist networks influenced by Qutb's notion of jihad is Al-Qaeda, which bin Laden founded in 1985. Bin Laden envisioned his operations as a step toward expelling the Western presence from Islamic lands, abolishing state boundaries, and creating a transnational Islamic society ruled by a restored caliphate.[25]

Thus we return to bin Laden and his distinctive view of Western and Islamic history over the past eighty years. Like al-Banna and Qutb, bin

Laden charges that mainstream Muslim clerics have been co-opted by dictatorial and compromising rulers such as Egyptian president Hosni Mubarak or by the monarchy of Saudi Arabia, which committed the unforgivable sin of allowing U.S. troops to be stationed near the holy cities of Mecca and Medina ("its sanctities desecrated"). Delegitimated in many circles of the Islamic world, the state-supported religious scholars have yielded popular authority to the religiously unschooled but disgruntled laymen, many with educational backgrounds in engineering, applied science, or business. In the late nineties, for example, the engineer bin Laden began to refer to himself as "Sheikh" Osama Bin-Muhammad Bin-laden, as he did in the *fatwa* he issued on February 23, 1998, announcing his legal "ruling" that every Muslim now has the individual duty to "kill the Americans and their allies—civilians and military."[26]

The justification for this tragic distortion of Islamic law and ethics? U.S. policy toward the Middle East and the broader Islamic world, the Islamists charge, has transparently served the narrow interests of an affluent and comfortable American public, which consumes a grossly disproportionate percentage of natural resources (oil-based products in particular) while the mass of humanity in the countries being exploited for their oil live below the poverty level. Muslim lives and livelihoods are routinely sacrificed to support luxurious American life-styles. The United States is a great hypocrite, espousing democracy and freedom in its rhetoric while providing critical financial and military support to Israel, the Zionist interloper in the Middle East, and to antidemocratic and repressive regimes such as those of Egypt, Algeria, and Saudi Arabia, where the voice of the Muslim people is silenced.

This narrative of humiliation and disgrace at the hands of the United States is all the more compelling to its aggrieved Muslim audiences because it conforms to the dispiriting pattern of ordinary history as narrated by the fundamentalists. The plot is familiar: The virtuous true believers are overwhelmed by a treacherous, invasive, and insidious enemy whose conquest of the abode of Islam is abetted by the successful seduction of fellow Muslims who have relaxed their vigilance. Only the extreme measures and extraordinary heroism of radical religion can provide deliverance. Framing the struggles against external and internal colonization in this way fulfills the apocalyptic expectations of the most revolutionary of the fundamentalists. For they look for final deliverance, not to the world, but to God; not to quotidian political struggle against oppression and injustice, but to the self-sacrificing acts of true believers willing to risk everything to vanquish *jahiliyya* society once and for all.

Conclusion

While it may be perfectly reasonable to dismiss fundamentalist readings of history as transparent manipulations of events and data, as mere projections of religious fanaticism and millenarian enthusiasm, it is important to underscore the fundamentalists' devotion to the narratives they have constructed, and their attention to the details they have embedded in the narrative to reinforce its eschatalogical themes. More than the general public, activist fundamentalists are engrossed in the events of history and spend significant time and resources indoctrinating recruits and educating the devout in its moral and political lessons. Furthermore, the moral and political critiques that emerge from a historiography and historical method fundamentally different from that constructed and practiced by professional historians are hardly incoherent or even unpersuasive. Rather, they shed a revealing light on what many historians consider "the real stuff of history," namely, the experience of suffering, injustice, and alienation, mixed with and tempered by hope for deliverance, that characterizes the human condition.

Notes

1. The term *scriptural inerrancy* was coming into vogue in 1887 when William Hoyt, speaking at a conference on the "Inspired Word," declared that the Bible was in every detail "kept *inerrant*." See George M. Marsden, *Fundamentalism and American Culture: The Shaping of Twentieth-Century Evangelicalism, 1870–1925* (New York, 1980), 56. Pope Pius IX, "'Syllabus' or Collection of Modern Errors," in Henry Denzinger, *The Sources of Catholic Dogma (Enchiridion Symbolorum)*, trans. Roy J. Deferrari (St. Louis, 1957), 433–42. See also Roger Aubert, "The Church and Liberalism," in *The Church in a Secularised Society*, ed. Roger Aubert et al. (Ramsey, N.J., 1978), 34–43.

2. Abdulaziz A. Sachedina, "Activist Shi'ism in Iran, Iraq, and Lebanon," in *Fundamentalisms Observed*, ed. Martin E. Marty and R. Scott Appleby (Chicago, 1991), 432–33. See also Fouad Ajami, *The Vanished Imam: Musa al Sadr and the Shia of Lebanon* (Ithaca, 1986).

3. Jerry Falwell, "An Agenda for the Eighties," in *The Fundamentalist Phenomenon: The Resurgence of Conservative Christianity*, ed. Jerry Falwell with Ed Dobson and Ed Hindson (Garden City, 1981), 205; Michael Lienesch, *Redeeming America: Piety and Politics in the New Christian Right* (Chapel Hill, 1993), 1–22.

4. Hasan al-Banna, *Five Tracts of Hasan al-Banna (1906–1949)*, trans. Charles Wendell (Berkeley, 1978), 1–29; Saad Eddin Ibrahim, "Anatomy of Egypt's Militant

Islamic Groups," *International Journal of Middle East Studies*, 12 (Dec. 1980), 423–53; Olivier Roy, *The Failure of Political Islam*, trans. Carol Volk (Cambridge, Mass., 1994), 39–47.

5. Imam Khomeini, *Islam and Revolution: Writings and Declarations of Imam Khomeini*, trans. and annotated by Hamid Algar (Berkeley, 1981), 27–149. On Iran, see Said Amir Arjomand, *The Turban for the Crown: The Islamic Revolution in Iran* (New York, 1988); and Roy Mottahedeh, *The Mantle of the Prophet: Religion and Politics in Iran* (New York, 1985). On Lebanon, see Ayatollah Muhammed Hussein Fadl Allah, "Islam and Violence in Political Reality," *Middle East Insight*, 4 (nos. 4–5, 1986), 4–13. Fadlallah, Hezbollah's founder, envisioned a global and apocalyptic triumph of Islam. "The divine state of justice realized on part of this earth will not remain confined within its geographic borders," a disciple predicted. It "will lead to the appearance of the Mahdi, who will create the state of Islam on earth." Fadlallah assigned Hezbollah the role of purifying a province of Islam to create "the divine state of justice." To rid Lebanese Shiites of their immediate tormentors, the Maronites and the Israelis, Hezbollah's manifesto called for "a battle with vice at its very roots. And the first root of vice is America." See Martin Kramer, "Hizbullah: The Calculus of Jihad," in *Fundamentalisms and the State: Remaking Polities, Economies, and Militance*, ed. Martin E. Marty and R. Scott Appleby (Chicago, 1993), 545.

6. See Gideon Aran, "Jewish Zionist Fundamentalism: The Bloc of the Faithful in Israel (Gush Emunim)," in *Fundamentalisms Observed*, ed. Marty and Appleby, 265–344.

7. Hal Lindsey with C. C. Carlson, *The Late Great Planet Earth* (Grand Rapids, 1970); Tim LaHaye and Jerry B. Jenkins, *Left Behind: A Novel of the Earth's Last Days* (Wheaton, 1995). On fundamentalist interpretations of Scripture, see Kathleen C. Boone, *The Bible Tells Them So: The Discourse of Protestant Fundamentalism* (Albany, 1989).

8. Pat Robertson, *The New World Order* (Dallas, 1991), 6; Lienesch, *Redeeming America*, 239. On the rapture and the end times, see Timothy P. Weber, *Living in the Shadow of the Second Coming: American Premillennialism, 1875–1925* (New York, 1979), 5–26.

9. Samuel C. Heilman, *Defenders of the Faith: Inside Ultra-Orthodox Jewry* (Berkeley, 1992), 232–33.

10. Daniella Weiss is quoted in a film shown on PBS: *The Power and the Glory: The Land*, dir. Jane Treays (Jersey Productions, 1995).

11. Francis A. Schaeffer, *A Christian Manifesto* (Westchester, Ill., 1981), 93.

12. *New York Times*, Oct. 8, 2001, p. B7. The translation from the Arabic is by Reuters.

13. Bernard Lewis, *The Political Language of Islam* (Chicago, 1988), 32, 34, 43–51.

14. Al-Banna, *Five Tracts of Hasan al-Banna*, trans. Wendell, 27–28.

15. Mumtaz Ahmad, "Islamic Fundamentalism in South Asia: The Jamaat-i-Islami and the Tablighi Jamaat of South Asia," in *Fundamentalisms Observed*, ed. Marty and Appleby, 464. *An Introduction to the Jamaat-i-Islami Pakistan* (Lahore, 1978), 5, quoted *ibid.*, 466.

16. Roy, *Failure of Political Islam*, trans. Volk, 35.

17. Jalal Al-e Ahmad, *Gharbzadegi [Weststruckness]* (Euromania), trans. John Green and Ahmad Alizadeh (Lexington, Ky., 1982), 3.

18. John Waterbury, *The Egypt of Nasser and Sadat: The Political Economy of Two Regimes* (Princeton, 1983), 100, 117; Fouad Ajami, *The Arab Predicament: Arab Political Thought and Practice since 1967* (Cambridge, Eng., 1981), 138–200.

19. Sayyid Qutb, *Milestones*, trans. International Islamic Federation of Student Organizations (Stuttgart, 1978). The treatment of Sayyid Qutb is adapted from R. Scott Appleby, *The Ambivalence of the Sacred: Religion, Violence, and Reconciliation* (Lanham, 2000), 91–95.

20. Amira El-Azhary Sonbol, "Egypt," in *The Politics of Islamic Revivalism*, ed. Shireen T. Hunter (Bloomington, 1988), 30; Qutb, *Milestones*, trans. International Islamic Federation of Student Organizations, 32.

21. Qutb, *Milestones*, trans. International Islamic Federation of Student Organizations, 32–33.

22. *Ibid.*, 38, 117.

23. *Ibid.*, 111.

24. Johannes J. G. Jansen, *The Neglected Duty: The Creed of Sadat's Assassins and Islamic Resurgence in the Middle East* (New York, 1986), 30, 141; Sonbol, "Egypt," 31.

25. Al-Qaeda supported Muslim fighters in Afghanistan, Bosnia, Chechnya, Tajikistan, Somalia, Yemen, and Kosovo and trained members of terrorist organizations from such diverse countries as the Philippines, Algeria, and Eritrea. In February 1998 Osama bin Laden announced the creation of a new alliance of terrorist organizations and Islamic extremist movements, the International Islamic Front for Jihad against the Jews and Crusaders, which included the Egyptian al-Gama'at al-Islamiyya, the Egyptian Islamic Jihad, and the Harkat Mujahedeen of Pakistan. John K. Cooley, *Unholy Wars: Afghanistan, America, and International Terrorism* (Sterling, 2000), 120, 219.

26. World Islamic Front, "Jihad against Jews and Crusaders," Feb. 23, 1998, *Federation of American Scientists* <http://www.fas.org/irp/world/para/docs/980223-fatwa.htm> (June 11, 2002).

Conjuring with Islam, II

Bruce B. Lawrence

How will we remember what happened on September 11, 2001?
Many historians of American foreign policy, Bruce B. Lawrence
predicts, will remember it as the real end of the Cold War, marked
by the onset of a new, very hot war with Arab Muslim enemies.
Lawrence argues that the Arab pilots who flew into the Pentagon
and the World Trade Center towers were not motivated solely by
religion: They protested U.S. political and military might and the
attendant global economic disparities. To address the cause of that
hatred and not just its violent expression, the war on terrorism must
also be a war against poverty, injustice, and dictatorship.

I recall Tuesday September 11, 2001, as "black Tuesday," the
day when commercial airplanes were turned into weapons of mass destruction as suicidal bombers destroyed two major monuments of U.S.
commercial prowess in New York City, damaged a wing of the United
States central military command in Washington, D.C., and took their
own lives as well as those of nearly three thousand persons, many, but
not all, of them American citizens. Black Tuesday was the worst terrorist attack on American soil. Its agents were identified as nineteen Arab
men, all Muslim and all linked to a global terrorist network, Al-Qaeda,
based in Afghanistan but directed by a Saudi dissident in exile, Osama
bin Laden.

Since black Tuesday Islam has been invoked, written about, challenged, and defended in a variety of forums. It is almost as if a new religious tradition had come onto the everyday screen of middle-of-the-
road Americans. On Friday September 14, with the ravages of Tuesday
still fresh in mind, I got a phone call from my former college roommate,
a retired businessman. He was aghast at the carnage, but he was also
eager to get behind the episode and to grapple with its causes. "Look,"
he reasoned, "I am Joe Six-Pack. I'm your average work-hard, play-hard
American. I want to know about Islam. I want to learn the ABCs of the
Arab world, I want to understand why they hate us so much."

Though the question seemed new to Joe Six-Pack, it is in fact a very old question, one confronting Americans at least since the Iranian revolution of 1979–1980. The return of an aging cleric from Paris to Tehran, the toppling of a supposedly invincible American ally, the eighteen-month Iranian hostage crisis—all brought Islam onto the television screens and into the headlines, into the awareness and imagination of average Americans over two decades ago.

What is interesting now, six months after September 11, is the pervasive amnesia about that earlier crisis. Most Americans, including most American scholars and certainly nearly all journalists, do not link the two periods. I think the linkage between the periods is one of the instructive lessons of history, and I will focus on it in the pages that follow.

In the confusion and perplexity that marked first the Iranian revolution, then the Iranian hostage crisis, Clifford Geertz, the distinguished anthropologist from Princeton University, wrote about the variant perspectives that those events evoked from commentators. Although there was a recurrent focus on jihad, then as now the interpretation of its significance depended on the location, the background, and the training of the interpreter. Journalists, scholars, politicians, and apologists do not have similar agendas, and their contrasting views have to be sorted out by the unsuspecting reader, that is, by middle-class, middle-of-the-road Americans such as Joe Six-Pack. The interpreters, noted Geertz,

> tend to come in recognizable sorts. There are the more traditional Orientalists, whom Edward Said and others have recently subjected to wholesale attack as field agents of imperialism. . . . The ideologists grind their various axes to so fine an edge as to wound mainly themselves. The historians attempt to arrange elliptical records from a mythicized past into a plausible story. The journalists cover fires. And then there are the social scientists, who are going to explain it all.[1]

It is not surprising that Geertz is toughest on his own guild of practitioners in the art of interpretation, but that harsh dose of self-criticism should not obscure his great achievement. Unlike almost anyone else writing about Islam in the 1980s, he stressed how difficult, yet crucial, it is to make sense of Islam from variant disciplinary perspectives: whether one writes as an ideologist or as a journalist, as a historian or as a social scientist determines what one sees and what one projects for others to see. At the outset of his far-flung review of seven books on Islam, the media, and Muslim societies, Geertz surmised that there is no Islam apart from the study of Islam, and that almost all studies are divided into two camps, either Third World sociology with an Islamic accent or comparative religion with a Christian one.[2] Ideologists and journalists tend to favor the latter, invariably invoking religion in general but Islam in particular as the problem, while social scientists and historians influenced by a sociological approach tend to think of broad systemic differences within a global profile of economic privilege or scarcity, political power or marginality. Now, in the aftermath of September 11, there is an even greater need both to acknowledge Geertz's point—disciplinary perspectives matter—and to declare my own preference, namely, to interpret religion through a historical, which is always also a comparative, lens.

That double need is made the more urgent by confusion in the academy and mockery in the popular media about what counts as evidence about Islam. We have not moved beyond conjuring with Islam; in 2002 as in 1982, when Geertz wrote his piece of that title, we have the imperative to engage the Muslim world beyond the mere invocation of Islam as a self-evident category. My essay, "Conjuring with Islam, II," is intended to foreground the disciplinary variables we face today and also to underscore why history, despite Geertz's reservations, remains the indispensable vantage point for interpreting September 11 and its aftermath.

Not long ago I participated in a weekend workshop with community college teachers. Our topic was religion and violence. I was attempting to demonstrate that in one part of the Muslim world, South Asia, religion is blamed for violence that also has systemic causes—political, economic, social, and cultural—that have very little to do with religion defined as the individual assent of belief, the collective observance of ritual, and the ceaseless negotiation and renegotiation of identity between this world and the next. One of my co-panelists in the workshop objected. The issue has changed since September 11, she asserted. We are no longer talking about religion viewed through the fine-ground lens of history. We are now confronting a deluge of stereotypes. All of them make us Americans out to be secular, whatever our religious preference, and we therefore belong to an advanced, civilized species of the human race, while all others, especially Muslim Arabs, who make religion their passion, belong to a barbaric, uncivilizable species of the human race. Never shall the twain meet. For the near future, and maybe into the distant future, they will hate us and we will oppose them. The stereotype, dividing the world into two, allows for no peace between good and evil.

I appreciated her accent on the pervasive impact of stereotypes, nowhere more evident than in the mindless reversion to Hindu-Muslim stereotypes in India as if they explained the latest collective bloodletting of late February/early March 2002. But I objected to my colleague's retreat from historical inquiry. To acknowledge the pervasiveness of stereotypes, I rejoined, is not a reason to abandon fine-grained history; on the contrary, it makes our labor as historians even more critical. For what other discipline provides tools to move beyond stereotypes—to interrogate their hard edges, to unravel their seamless classificatory logic, and to make all groups part of a common future that has a shared past as well as a contested present?

Unfortunately, the situation post–September 11 is more precarious than it was for Geertz and other social scientists during the Iranian hostage crisis of the early 1980s. Since September 11 professional historians have been drafted into the ranks of wordsmiths proliferating footage for major journals or TV talk shows. Nearly all of them reinscribe the very stereotypes that do injustice to historical nuance, even while seeming to confirm the patriotic goodwill as well as the intellectual relevance of those same academics.

Indeed, many so-called Middle East experts, including one well-known historian, have abetted the incendiary penchant of journalists, making certain that one stereotype predominates over all others in middle America's reflection on Islam. It is the stereotype of a backward Arab Muslim world counterposed to a progressive secular American world. Rather than as a stereotype, this contrast is presented as the logical development of age-old historical patterns. I will summarize the views of some by name, but first let me be clear about their collective message: (1) Islam is *not* a peaceful religion in practice, (2) Arab Muslims are *not* democratic capitalists in tune with the modern world, and (3) since Islam is not peaceful and since Arab Muslims are not democratic, they hate us. They hate us because we are so different from them. We do love peace, we are tolerant, we are hardworking, and because we are hardworking, we also prosper. Moreover, we elect our leaders and hold them accountable for their policies and actions.

It would be impossible to summarize the many, often sophisticated variants of this response that have appeared since September 11. Thomas L. Friedman, a major columnist for the *New York Times*, sees the issue as Islam versus modernity. We are modern; Muslims are not. His popular book, *The Lexus and the Olive Tree*, posits a clear cleavage between Arab Muslim premoderns and Japanese, as well as other capitalist, moderns. An article of his on January 28, 2000, said it even more succinctly. Visiting Egypt, he noted that an elevator operator prayed before he pushed the button. "To a Westerner," lamented Friedman, "it is unnerving to hear your elevator operator utter a prayer before he closes the door." Piety and globalization require different mind-sets, reasons Friedman, so that "for all of globalization's obvious powers to elevate living standards, it is going to be a tough, tough sell to all those millions who still say a prayer before they ride the elevator."[3]

Reinforcing the arguments Friedman makes has been Bernard Lewis, an emeritus history professor from Princeton University. Lewis wrote about the rage of Islam over a decade ago, but more recently he has decried all Arab polities, noting that in only two Middle Eastern countries are both the governments and the people friendly to the United States: Turkey and Israel. He chides U.S. policy makers for their attitude toward the region's two democracies: "We slight the one (Turkey) and bully the other (Israel)," while he blames Islamic resentment and passivity for the tribal/military dictatorships that dot the region. Lewis's own stance reflects his professional orientation, that of a British and American orientalist bestirred by historical interests but ever attached to their linguistic resonance. In his earlier book, *The Political Language of Islam*, he demonstrated that he sees military urges and nostalgia for past glory as the keynotes to Arab and Islamic history. In dismissing the influence of reformers and modernizers, Lewis admitted that some Arab rulers and Muslim jurists wanted to "transform Muslim government and society," but he pitted them against other jurists and "the mass of the population" who refused such changes. "Clearly," concluded Lewis, "the logical result of such a refusal is to deny the name of Muslim to those who seek to enforce such changes." Absent from the discussion is the influence of European colonial rule, and when he addressed the aftermath of British, French, Dutch, and Russian rule over parts of Asia and Africa with majority-Muslim populations, he dismissed efforts at democracy or constitutional government. "None [of these imported remedies] has worked very well, and increasing numbers of Muslims have begun to look to their own past, or what they perceive as their own past, to find a diagnosis for their present ills and a prescription for their future well-being." To be Arab and Muslim and modern for him is a contradiction in terms. All Muslims (except Turks) are out of step with the modern age. Neither free-marketeers nor democrats, they cannot be, they are not, modern.[4]

While Friedman and Lewis speak about Islam and Arabs with a recurrent negativity, other American academics frame an equal negativity toward Islam and Arabs by accenting Western exceptionality. It is not just that we are modern, market-oriented, liberal democrats, say these other critics, while our enemies are not. The chief problem is that they have not understood how to distance themselves from their own dark past. They continue to obey ancient civilizational reflexes that impel them to hate us. Even were some of them to change their outlook and become more like us, Arab Muslims as a group could not escape the civilizational urge to resent and oppose, to hate and to rage against the secular West but above all against its triumphant flag bearer, the United States of America. The clash of civilizations is as inevitable as it is nasty; we are only in its early stages. It will be with us through the early decades of this century; it will mark our national and international life at least till 2020 but perhaps beyond.

Samuel P. Huntington of Harvard University, borrowing the term without acknowledgment from Bernard Lewis's 1990 article "The Roots of Muslim Rage," first presented his clash-of-civilizations thesis in a 1993 *Foreign Affairs* article, "The Clash of Civilizations?," and then in a book-length sequel, *The Clash of Civilizations and the Remaking of World Order*. Edward Said has etched the flaws of Huntington's thesis.[5] The most evident are its narrow rigidity and unempirical abstraction: Civilizations become fixed containers of norms and values, loyalties and dispositions. No real live people or ground-level issues matter. For Huntington, nation-states are influenced, above all, by civilizational/religious interests. He discounts the significance of pragmatic or ideological considerations that may have little to do either with the long sweep of history or the deep reflex of religion. Instead, Huntington marks entire regions by singular civilizational motivations, ignoring the internal diversity that characterizes Asia and Africa as much as it does Europe and North America. In this sense, Huntington's policy-driven project parallels the scurrilous fiction of the recent Nobel laureate, V. S. Naipaul: on the one hand, to laud the unique benefits conferred by Western civilization and, on the other, to excoriate those who challenge or limit its benefits, especially Muslims.[6]

Scarcely less acerbic than the dire fulminations of Huntington are the spectral projections from Francis Fukuyama, also a professor of political science (at Johns Hopkins University). Fukuyama is best known for his early 1990s book, *The End of History and the Last Man*. In it he discounts the impact of radical Islam, predicting that in the next chapter of world history economic issues and consumer fads will make radical Islam, like Communism post-1989, an ideology with no followers or at least no followers who pose an international threat to those beyond their borders. That prediction proved wrong, yet the special 2002 Davos Edition of *Newsweek International* promises on its cover both Huntington's "The Age of Muslim Wars," which is banal, and Fukuyama's "Today's New Fascists," which is incendiary. (Inside the magazine Fukuyama's essay bears the title "The Real Enemy: Radical Islamists Are the Fascists of the Modern World.") In it Fukuyama highlighted a new breed of Islamo-fascists. Apart from that derogatory, defaming label for Muslim extremists, Fukuyama restates his well-known thesis that capitalist democracy is the inevitable tide of the future, crossing economic, political, and finally cultural boundaries in forging a global society. So strong is "the inner historical logic to political secularism," according to Fukuyama, that it will inevitably produce a more liberal strand of Islam. In the meantime, however, there will be spoilers—the Islamo-fascists. Islamo-fascists? Yes, because they hate the more liberal democratic and secular state for one overriding reason: It is "dedicated to religious tolerance and pluralism, rather than to serving religious truth." They want a hierarchically structured Islamic state that is dedicated to serving Islamic truth under Islamic law. No other truth and no other believers are acceptable. These modern-day Manichaeans see only a struggle between believers and unbelievers. Because they number at most 15 percent of all Muslims, they will be defeated, argues Fukuyama. In the long-term convergence of the West with the rest, they will be outstripped by the liberal democrats who are Muslims, but in the short run the Islamo-fascists will test Western institutions and try to foil the emergence of a new global order.[7]

I have cited but four names: Friedman, Lewis, Huntington, Fukuyama. I could have cited the names of other popular journalists or academic experts who oppose their views. I could have cited newspapers other than the *New York Times*, such as the *Christian Science Monitor*, or periodicals other than *Newsweek*, such as the *Nation*, that carry story lines nuancing the post–September 11 world, but I believe that Joe Six-Pack, along with other average Americans, both male and female, would agree that those names etch the mood and the response of what C. Wright Mills once called the men of knowledge, or the knowledge class, in America.[8] As such, they deserve special attention, and their views stand in need of severe correction.

Friedman, Lewis, Huntington, Fukuyama—all claim the authority of experience and insight, yet none of them except Friedman has visited many countries of the Arab Muslim world. Even Lewis, the oft-cited Middle East expert, is largely an armchair observer, except for Turkey and Israel. The haze of negativity is strongest in the journalist, Friedman, and the historian, Lewis. The cocoon of exceptionalism is most evident in the two political theorists, Huntington and Fukuyama. Yet none of those policy pundits directly tackles the issue: Why do Arab Muslims hate us so much? Fukuyama, to his credit, does look at how poverty, economic stagnation, and authoritarian politics combine to make not just the Arab Muslim world but also a large stretch of the Central and South Asian Muslim world (including Uzbekistan, Afghanistan, and Pakistan) a hotbed for potential terrorists. He shares this concern with the best of the South Asian journalists writing on Central and South Asian Islamist movements, Ahmed Rashid.[9] But unlike Rashid, Fukuyama blames faulty aid policies and corrupt regimes, rather than calling into question current U.S. foreign policy, which, like U.S. policy before the Iranian revolution, unblinkingly accepts the legitimacy of the tyrannical military dictators whom the United States needs as allies in warring against other, equally tyrannical military dictators.

One can escape this conundrum only by reexamining our notion of history. One must expand the media image of Muslims as premodern Arabs by linking religious with cultural history, but one must also refer to the different phases of Islamic civilization and to the continuous interaction of Muslim leaders and organizations with their non-Muslim counterparts in what Marshall G. S. Hodgson termed the Afro-Eurasian *oikumene*. The early, middle, and modern periods require separate skills and caveats for their successful analysis. The most difficult period to analyze is the one closest in time, the modern. Hodgson was the most creative and productive world historian of his generation. He never forgot that he was American and Quaker but, above all, modern. Along with a host of other world historians, Hodgson made clear just how decisive an impact the modern phase of global economic change has had on all Is-

The white man's burden, from the American frontier via the Ku Klux Klan, the Vietnam War, and now the global war on terrorism, as seen by the Syrian cartoonist Fares Garabet in 2002. (Courtesy of Fares Garabet.)

lamic (or, in his terms, Islamicate) civilization. He terms this momentous change the Great Western Transmutation. Though it takes place in the West, it is not limited to the West; it depends on the agency, the creative choices, and the equally creative responses of multiple players in different parts of the *oikumene* from the early sixteenth to the late twentieth century.[10]

Among the most creative responses to the notion that only the West became modern was an Iranian retort, reverberating with special force after the Islamic revolution of 1979. Just as late-twentieth-century Euro-America claimed that only its post-Christian secular world was modern, so, argued Jalal Al-i Ahmad, the renowned Iranian essayist, there persists an Islamic totality that mirrors the hubris of the West and answers it back with its opposite, an anti-Christian, anticolonial, and now anti-Western mind-set that conceives the world only in dyads, or irreconcilable opposites. Islamic totality, like Western triumphalism, refuses any effort at compromise, either in thought or in speech or in practice.[11]

If there is one overriding lesson from Hodgson and other world historians, it is that the battle of dyads must be replaced with a dialectic of accommodation. The first essential step in the effort to achieve accommodation is to go beyond facile categories or simplistic causal explanations. Instead, one must see common issues that face all humankind; one must examine underlying economic patterns and shifting political priorities.

Seen in this light, President George W. Bush's state of the union address at the end of January 2002 raises deep, long-term issues that have yet to be addressed. Mr. Bush signaled that the war on terrorism will be extended into a war on nations that develop weapons of mass destruction. Citing North Korea, Iraq, and Iran as, in his words, the "axis of evil," he followed President Ronald Reagan in moralizing American foreign policy. Just as President Reagan had pledged to fight the Soviet Union as "an evil empire," so President Bush now pledged to fight one Asian rogue state, North Korea, and two Muslim states, Iraq and Iran, lumping them together.[12]

Yet the lessons from the Afghanistan campaign may suggest other options. Even though American bombing in Afghanistan has driven the Taliban from power, reduced Al-Qaeda to a network in shambles, and signaled to the entire world that U.S. military might can exact a fearsome toll on any group that targets, attacks, and kills American citizens, has the war on terrorism succeeded? The war on terrorism has to become more than a military exercise. It also requires a larger war on poverty and injustice and dictatorship. In short, it has to take account of economic issues that have a historical prologue, placing them in a multilateral rather than a bilateral frame of reference.

Neither Islam nor the Arab world, despite Friedman's lapidary alliterations, can be blamed for the current level of global poverty. The North/South divide, the gap between the haves and the have-nots or have-lesses, encompasses broader categories than religious difference or regional exceptionalism. There is a huge deficit in human resources, job opportunities, quality of life, and education throughout much of Africa and Asia, where Muslims predominate, but the deficit is also huge in Latin America and eastern Europe, where Muslims are a minority. A central problem, even before September 11, was: How can we mount a sustained attack on poverty across creedal, national, and geographic boundaries? Since September 11, and in part because of it, the question has become more urgent. Even though the actual terrorists were middle-class moderns in most respects, and Osama bin Laden a member of the richest nonroyal family in Saudi Arabia, it is endemic poverty, and

The ABCs of poverty require more than a literacy tutorial. (Courtesy of Fares Garabet.)

also the gap between the very rich and the masses of poor and destitute Arab and Asian Muslims, that provides the breeding ground for discontent, the elementary school for terrorism.[13]

Alas, American strategists who have waged a successful military campaign against terrorists and terrorist supporters in Afghanistan have scarcely begun to chart the more massive, less defined, but more crucial terrain of poverty. On that score the renowned financier and public policy advocate George Soros has offered a new approach to fighting global poverty that deserves attention. Oppressive or corrupt regimes, according to Soros, are the leading causes of poverty and misery today. It is not enough to devise better means to provide public goods; we must also find ways to encourage (since we cannot compel) sovereign states to make economic and political reforms. Soros proposes an international foreign aid market. Operating under the aegis of the International Monetary Fund (IMF) but not controlled by it, the board of this unit would decide on programs' eligibility for aid and then monitor them. Those who won would have special drawing rights (SDR), a concept long familiar to those who specialize, as does Soros, in currency exchanges and liquidity balances. Three kinds of programs would be prioritized: (1) eliminating health risks (such as AIDS [acquired immune deficiency syndrome] and tuberculosis), (2) government-sponsored programs to eliminate poverty, and (3) nongovernmental development programs. None of the three channels that Soros proposes for SDR is new. Collectively, they amount to the mandate that the advanced industrialized nations (the G-8) have put on their annual agenda for more than two decades, but they have remained distant, elusive goals. As Soros notes, public goods such as peace, health, and relief of poverty are much more difficult to measure than profit, yet we can and must begin to make them more palpable and attainable in the near term, especially in regions of Africa and Asia that have been further devastated by the aftermath of the September 11 attacks on the United States.[14]

Beyond Soros's plan or one like it, in rethinking a post–September 11 world order, we must include political solutions. Contrary to Fukuyama's prediction, it is not inevitable that a new global order will, or should, be modeled on Western institutions nor should it simply extend U.S. commercial and political interests under the guise of a Pax Americana. Ironically, if the war on terrorism is to be won in the long term, the other major point of Bush's speech on January 29 needs far more attention than military strategies. His other major point was the strong commitment to base U.S. foreign policy on nonnegotiable demands for compliance with basic human values. What are those values?

> "The rule of law. . . . respect for women. . . . private property. . . . free speech. . . . equal justice. . . . religious tolerance." The aim is admirable. The application will be harder. It will be harder because so many countries around the world do disagree with it, including many that now play host to American bases or are acting as allies: Saudi Arabia, Pakistan, Kuwait, Uzbekistan, to name but a few. It will be harder also, though, if the list comes to be a rigid indicator of who must be an ally and who an enemy. Alas, democracies that follow these values are also capable, on occasion, of being in the wrong and even of committing atrocities. The danger that President Bush might take too rigid an approach, with a ruinous effect on his other foreign-policy goals, is particularly acute in the Middle East.[15]

The analysis and the warning are not mine, but those of the anonymous editorial writer for a recent issue of the *Economist*. What seems clear is that President Bush, and by extension the American people, in the aftermath of September 11 want contradictory outcomes: on the one hand, a world free of further terrorist attacks on Americans, either at home or abroad, and, on the other hand, a world where the values of American society can be exported and enhanced in societies very different from our own. The challenge has been etched by Jean Bethke

The Syrian cartoonist Fares Garabet's 2002 view of the Israeli and Palestinian combatants. The Arabic reads: Terrorist! (Courtesy of Fares Garabet.)

Elshtain: to find coalitions of values and not just coalitions of interest. Coalitions of interest, as Fukuyama makes clear, project only one model of power, political, economic, and cultural, but coalitions of value require dialogue and compromise.[16] That means, among other things, that the United States cannot retain the Kingdom of Saudi Arabia as a major ally unless the kingdom changes both its form of governance and the current distribution of benefits within its single-commodity economy. It also means that we cannot continue with Gen. Pervez Musharraf of Pakistan as an ally unless he takes a page from his neighbor, India, and provides for fair presidential elections, even if they result in his exit from power. Though we cannot compel either King Fahd of Saudi Arabia or General Musharraf to change his ways, we can find better methods of inducing each to undertake needed political and economic reforms. Furthermore, that challenge means that we cannot remain quiet, or capitulate to Israeli interests, when Gen. Ariel Sharon repeats his mantra that there must be an end to all Palestinian violence yet does everything in his power to provoke still further, and more extreme, acts of violence.

It is not clear how the United States or its allies or the rest of the world, including the Arab Muslim world, will view September 11, 2001, once time softens the worst images and most vivid memories of that day. Neither Joe Six-Pack nor his American counterparts will soon accept Islam as a religion of peace. Their lingering fear will be that certain Muslims, especially Arab Muslims, will commit further acts of violent protest against an imposed and alien world order. Still, the likelihood of such violent protest can be reduced if our foreign policy goals and our cultural values are more closely aligned. Not only can we advocate our fundamental values evenhandedly, to both allies and opponents of American political and economic interests, but we can also press for major initiatives—cooperative and long-term—to address large-scale poverty and its dire consequences. In the immediate aftermath of September 11, many Americans showed—as numerous bumper stickers attested— "power of pride." Faced with deep-seated inequities at home and abroad, all Americans must now demonstrate a different resolve: to curtail pride of power. It is not us against them; it is us with them, the United States leading the way to collective acknowledgment and active engagement with global problems. In his state of the union speech, President Bush urged his fellow countrymen to be "humble, but strong." The greater need, however, is to recognize the burdens of being a moral as well as a military superpower. We need to be "strong, but humble." If we are, the lessons of September 11 might yet be transformative. Though the victims of that horror can never be brought back to life, the hate that provoked the attack that ended their lives can be stemmed, not by proud acts of war but by humble deeds of creativity, courage, and persistence. Our collective future, if it is to be marked by peace and security, will require an axis of good that is much stronger, but also more flexible, than any axis of evil.

In a perfect world, one would like to go beyond Manichaean thinking, to drop moralizing from foreign policy rhetoric and to focus instead on the tough pragmatic choices that a post–Cold War and post-colonial world pose for the rich and the poor alike. But as September 11 demonstrated, the next turns in our collective future are uncharted. We have as our top elected official a president who is determined to moralize collective options, and so the only way forward may be to appeal to the moral register of Abrahamic goodwill and exemplary behavior. Accepting that constraint, we must invoke humility with strength and exercise restraint with pride. We must project all four traits as the true American vision for a sustainable collective future. If history provides any lessons, this may be the hardest, and most important, lesson of all.

Notes

1. Clifford Geertz, "Conjuring with Islam," *New York Review of Books*, May 27, 1982, pp. 25–28.

2. *Ibid.*, 26. Emphasis added. Almost all efforts to come to terms with representations of Islam since September 11 miss this point. The absence of critical insight into knowledge production about religion is not limited to Islam; the same could be said of *every* religion: There is no Christianity apart from the study of Christianity, etc. To invoke any religious tradition as unitary, seamless, and self-evident is to ignore the context, the motives, and the assumptions of the speaker, the believer, or—as has happened again and again since September 11—the reporter!

3. *New York Times*, Jan. 28, 2000, p. A23. Thomas L. Friedman was in Egypt promoting the Arabic translation of his book, Thomas L. Friedman, *The Lexus and the Olive Tree* (New York, 2000).

4. Bernard Lewis, "The Roots of Muslim Rage," *Atlantic Monthly*, 266 (Sept. 1990), 52–60. For Bernard Lewis's statement, see George F. Will, "Afghans Can Be Candid and Laugh at Themselves," *International Herald Tribune*, Oct. 26, 2001, p. 18. On violence and nostalgia as characteristic of Muslims, see Bernard Lewis, *The Political Language of Islam* (Chicago, 1988), esp. chap. 4, 88–89, 115. For a different read of the last century of colonial and postcolonial government in the Muslim world, see Bruce B. Lawrence, *Shattering the Myth: Islam beyond Violence* (Princeton, 1998), esp. 40–56.

5. Lewis, "Roots of Muslim Rage," esp. 60. Lewis wrote his essay after the international uproar that followed the publication of Salman Rushdie, *The Satanic Verses* (London, 1988). The novel was deemed to insult the prophet Muhammad and his wives and the religious leadership of the Muslim world. Reactions became still more intense when the then spiritual leader of Iran, Ayatollah Ruhollah Khomeini, issued a juridical decree, or *fatwa*, on February 14, 1989, condemning the author to death on charges of blasphemy. Against this background Lewis declared, "We are facing a mood and a movement far transcending the level of issues and policies and the governments that pursue them. This is no less than a clash of civilizations—the perhaps irrational but surely historic reaction of an ancient rival against our Judeo-Christian heritage, our secular present, and the worldwide expansion of both." To his credit, Lewis went on to say, "we on our side should not be provoked into an equally historic but equally irrational reaction against that rival." *Ibid.* That cautionary note has been lost in Lewis's subsequent reflections and even more in Samuel P. Huntington's polemical, simplistic invocation of the "clash of civilizations" as a post–Cold War mantra. See Samuel P. Huntington, "The Clash of Civilizations?" *Foreign Affairs*, 72 (Summer 1993), 22–49; and Samuel P. Huntington, *The Clash of Civilizations and the Remaking of World Order* (New York, 1996). Edward Said, "The Clash of Definitions," in *The New Crusades: Constructing the Muslim Enemy*, ed. Michael Sells and Emran Qureishi (forthcoming, New York, 2003).

6. V. S. Naipaul lampoons all his Muslim subjects in the two books he has written on Islam, attributes to Islam both nihilism and neurosis, and caricatures—some would say, cannibalizes—the very Muslim sources who hosted and helped him in writing his fictive travelogues of Pakistan, Iran, Indonesia, and Malaysia. See V. S.

Naipaul, *Among the Believers: An Islamic Journey* (New York, 1981); and V. S. Naipaul, *Beyond Belief: Islamic Excursions among the Converted Peoples* (New York, 1998). Note the critique of Naipaul in Eqbal Ahmad, *Confronting Empire* (Boston, 2000), 107–11.

7. Fareed Zakaria, "The End of the End of History," *Newsweek*, Sept. 24, 2001, p. 70. Zakaria is criticizing Francis Fukuyama, *The End of History and the Last Man* (New York, 1992). See Samuel P. Huntington, "The Age of Muslim Wars," *Newsweek International*, Special Davos Edition (Dec. 2001–Feb. 2002), 6–15; and Francis Fukuyama, "The Real Enemy: Radical Islamists Are the Fascists of the Modern World," *ibid.*, 58–63.

8. C. Wright Mills, *The Sociological Imagination* (New York, 1967), 179.

9. Ahmed Rashid's most famous book appeared before September 11 but was widely read only later. See Ahmed Rashid, *Taliban: Militant Islam, Oil, and Fundamentalism in Central Asia* (New Haven, 2000). His more recent book examines the newly created, desperately poor, and brutally repressive regimes of Central Asia—Kazakhstan, Uzbekistan, Turkmenistan, Kyrgyzstan, and Tajikistan—with special attention to the largest and potentially most disruptive of them, Uzbekistan. See Ahmed Rashid, *Jihad: The Rise of Militant Islam in Central Asia* (New Haven, 2002).

10. Marshall G. S. Hodgson, *The Venture of Islam: Conscience and History in a World Civilization* (3 vols., Chicago, 1977), I, 110; III, 176–208. A similar emphasis on the global scope of economic change and its import and an assessment of Hodgson's influence appear in Marshall G. S. Hodgson and Edmund Burke III, eds., *Rethinking World History: Essays on Europe, Islam, and World History* (New York, 1993).

11. For contrasting Muslim responses to the Euro-American challenge, see Lawrence, *Shattering the Myth*, 19–20.

12. "George Bush and the Axis of Evil: America Is Set on a Brave but Hazardous Course," *Economist*, Feb. 2, 2002, pp. 13–14. The citations from President George W. Bush's speech appear in this editorial. Ronald Reagan, "Remarks at the Annual Convention of the National Association of Evangelicals in Orlando, Florida," March 8, 1983, *Ronald Reagan Presidential Library* <http://www.reagan.utexas.edu/resource/speeches/1983/83mar.htm> (June 10, 2002).

13. As the *Washington Post* observed in a March 2002 editorial, "Poverty and violence are not directly linked, to be sure, but poverty does breed the alienation and despair that foster violence. Sometimes, as in Sierra Leone or East Timor, the violence affects rich countries by sucking in peacekeepers; sometimes, as we found in Afghanistan, the violence affects rich countries because terrorists export it." Reprinted, *International Herald Tribune*, March 13, 2002, p. 6.

14. George Soros proposes something akin to a new, multinational Marshall Plan. See George Soros, "The Free Market for Hope," *Soros Foundations Network* <http://www.soros.org/911/GSNewsweekOct30.html> (Nov. 1, 2001).

15. "George Bush and the Axis of Evil," 13–14.

16. Jean Bethke Elshtain used this phrase on November 1, 2001, at the National Humanities Center in a question-and-answer session following my presentation, "Making Sense of Islam and the Muslim World after 11 September."

9/11, the Great Game, and the Vision Thing

The Need for (and Elements of) a More Comprehensive Bush Doctrine

Bruce R. Kuniholm

The "great game" of imperial rivalry in the Middle East and South-west Asia has fundamentally changed since September 11, 2001, Bruce R. Kuniholm contends. The zero-sum contest between great powers has been superseded by a clash of values that cuts across traditional boundaries and cultures. Relating the war on terrorism to earlier U.S. presidential doctrines concerning the region, Kuniholm calls for a broader definition of international interests and a shared, transnational vision of how to protect them. President George W. Bush should, he argues, make clear the elements of cooperation, underscore the costs of violating the new rules of the game, and address the political and economic realities that create support for terrorism in the region.

Developments in the Middle East and Southwest Asia after the events of September 11, 2001, suggest that the historical geopolitical imperatives driving U.S. policy in the region since World War II continue to be salient. The context in which the United States is now operating, however, is fundamentally different from the zero-sum rivalry between great powers that characterized the Cold War. In the post–Cold War/post-9/11 world, the "great game" of imperial rivalry has been transformed.[1] On one hand, regional powers (states capable of projecting themselves regionally) that possess or seek to possess weapons of mass destruction have become the most serious threat both to stability and to vital U.S. interests in the region.[2] Among international, or great, powers, on the other hand, the threat of nuclear war has receded; common threats such as regional wars and international terrorism are facilitating a recognition of common interests; old rivals have become allies of a sort; and the great game is morphing into a clash of values and prin-

191

ciples that cuts across traditional borders and cultures, posing serious problems but also providing opportunities for enlightened leadership.

The new great game is not a conflict *between* civilizations, as some would have it; rather, it is a conflict *within* states, *within* cultures, and *within* an increasingly global community over the values and ideas that underpin modernization and the norms and direction of modern civilization—a conflict being played out on a *global* playing field under new rules not yet clearly articulated or accepted.[3] The enemy now is international terrorism—an elusive enemy that can be targeted only through massive international cooperation coupled with the will to go after terrorists and the states that harbor them. The nature of the remedy is dictated by the nature of the threat. If terrorists are willing to die for a cause, and if states support or harbor them, rooting out terrorism requires aggressive action not only against the terrorists but also against states that flout the norms of civilized behavior.[4] If they are not contained, civilization as we know it is at risk.

Such an apocalyptic statement, coming as it does after an attack by a few people and following a "war" with relatively few combatants, may seem excessive. But Al-Qaeda's penetration of as many as sixty countries, the world's vulnerability to the dictates of Osama bin Laden and the many organizations under Al-Qaeda's umbrella, and the serious threat that increasingly accessible weapons of mass destruction pose to civilization itself—all meant that the attack on the United States served as a wake-up call, putting the world on notice that an almost tectonic shift is required in the way people think about threats to their security and that a vast increase is required in the resources they mobilize to counter those threats.

The Historical Context

A brief history of regional geopolitics may help put this sea change in perspective and offer some instructive cautionary observations to U.S. officials. In the nineteenth century, the expansion of British sea power in the Indian Ocean and Persian Gulf and the expansion of Russian troops into Transcaucasia and Central Asia eventuated in a struggle for power across a region that stretched from the Balkans to Afghanistan. Each great power—driven by the dictates of empire, motivated by fears of dangers both imagined and real, or trying to "contain" a rival by defensive action—sought to serve its perceived interests and clashed with the other.

In the twentieth century, the players in this great game of imperial rivalry, as it came to be called, were transformed: In 1917 the Soviet empire replaced the Russian Empire; and after World War II the United States, guided by rationales outlined in a series of presidential doctrines, gradually replaced a declining British Empire and, thanks to a policy most popularly articulated by George F. Kennan, assumed Britain's role of containing Soviet expansion in the region.[5]

Over time, the great game of advancing and protecting great power interests, which initially involved trade but which increasingly revolved around oil, resulted in *modi vivendi* resting on the implicit assumptions that there should be an equilibrium of forces in the region and that the vital interests of both powers would not be threatened. When observed, such arrangements maintained the balance of power in the region. If they were deficient in addressing the needs of the region's emerging nationalist forces, they mitigated tensions between the great powers, whose post–World War II nuclear arsenals magnified the risks of brinkmanship at the international level.

The emerging nations in the buffer zone that separated the imperial powers, which were subject to whatever understandings the great powers chose to reach, meanwhile did what they could to survive. Between World War I and World War II, for example, since the threat to them came from outside the region, they allied among themselves against threats from without. The Balkan Pact of 1934 between Greece, Romania, Yugoslavia, and Turkey and the Sa'adabad Pact of 1937 between Turkey, Iraq, Iran, and Afghanistan constituted attempts to escape from traditional rivalries to which these emerging states were being subjected. The alternatives to forming alliances with each other were playing one power off against the other, balancing one against the other, or looking to third powers (for example, Germany between the wars) for assistance. After World War II, as their survival was threatened by the relative disparity between Soviet and British power, Iran and Turkey turned to the United States for assistance.

In 1947, as Britain contemplated withdrawing from its empire, including Burma, India, and Palestine, both the decision of the British Foreign Office to cease supporting Greece and Turkey and the Soviet threat to Iran and Turkey led President Harry S. Truman to enunciate the Truman Doctrine. In doing so, he made the first in a series of postwar U.S. commitments to contain the Soviet threat and maintain the balance of power in a region that the United States had previously regarded as within the British Empire's sphere of influence. That Joseph Stalin did not expand his sphere of influence in the Near East as he did in Europe and the Far East following World War II does not mean, as some revisionists would suggest, that U.S. concerns were overdrawn. Firm U.S. policies put Stalin on notice that expansion to the south could be carried out only at the risk of confrontation. In the end, he was not prepared to take that risk (nor was any Soviet government until the invasion of Afghanistan in 1979).[6]

In the early 1950s, as Britain continued to contemplate withdrawal from the region—this time from Suez—Secretary of State John Foster Dulles encouraged development of a broader regional defense arrangement in the Middle East's "northern tier" states. Following Britain's departure and the debacle over Suez, President Dwight D. Eisenhower in 1957 promulgated the Eisenhower Doctrine to serve notice that the United States would defend the Middle East against a perceived Soviet threat. The Eisenhower Doctrine extended the containment policy from the northern tier states to the Middle East in general; it was institutionalized in both the Baghdad Pact and, following the 1958 revolution in Iraq and that country's withdrawal from the pact, the Central Treaty Organization (CENTO). However one criticizes the Eisenhower Doctrine and the concept of the northern tier, and however fashionable it is to discuss the ease with which the Kremlin leapfrogged over it, the lack of contiguity between the Soviet Union and the Arab world and the barrier between them formalized in CENTO posed serious logistical impediments to Soviet intervention in subsequent Middle East crises, particularly those involving Arabs and Israelis.

U.S. problems in the Middle East under the Eisenhower Doctrine were minor relative to those presented by the 1968 British decision to leave (by 1971) the area "east of Suez," including the Persian Gulf, which had been within Britain's sphere of influence for over a century. Britain's impending departure from the gulf created what was perceived as a power vacuum at a time when the Soviet Union was becoming much more active in the region. Global commitments and the war in Vietnam, however, precluded a U.S. effort to fill the vacuum and resulted instead in the application of the Nixon Doctrine (initially, the Guam Doctrine, by which the United States relied on regional states to assume primary responsibility for their own defense). In accordance with President Richard M. Nixon's endorsement in 1970 of what became the "twin-pillar" policy, the United States sought to ensure stability in the gulf through cooperation with Iran, which American officials recognized as the region's predominant power, and Saudi Arabia.

Inept application of the Nixon Doctrine to the Middle East eventually created problems that were as serious as those it was intended to resolve. The failure of the United States to abide by the rules of the great game in Iran may well have encouraged the Soviets to break them in Afghanistan, where the Soviets had to learn, as the Americans did in Iran, the limits of their capacity to dominate the region. The Iranian revolution, which undermined the premise of the Nixon Doctrine, with the subsequent hostage crisis, the burning of the American embassy in Pakistan, and the Soviet invasion of Afghanistan in 1979—all made clear that the twin-pillar policy was in ruins and U.S. policy along the northern tier in disarray. The response of President Jimmy Carter in 1980 was the Carter Doctrine, under which the president publicly emphasized the vital U.S. stake in the Persian Gulf and, in a departure from the Nixon Doctrine, assumed ultimate responsibility for regional defense. The Carter administration subsequently began construction of a security framework for the Persian Gulf and Southwest Asia, complete with improved regional defense capabilities and facilities that would be accessible to the Rapid Deployment Force (subsequently the Central Command).

After the promulgation of the Carter Doctrine, the foremost challenge to U.S. interests came from the Soviet Union's occupation of Afghanistan and from two regional states seeking hegemony in the Persian Gulf: revolutionary Iran and, especially, Iraq, from which Saddam Hussein launched wars against Iran (1980) and Kuwait (1990). The Reagan administration, meanwhile, had consolidated the security framework begun under President Carter, supporting what the former assistant for national security affairs Zbigniew Brzezinski referred to as "regional influentials." Turkey and Pakistan received improved assistance packages, and the United States continued to develop a close relationship with Saudi Arabia, which initially became a reluctant beneficiary of the Reagan "corollary" to the Carter Doctrine (the United States would not permit Saudi Arabia "to be an Iran"). With Saudi and Pakistani assistance, U.S. support for Afghan resistance to the Soviet occupation resulted, by the late 1980s, in the withdrawal of Soviet troops and contributed to the subsequent collapse of the Soviet Union (not to mention the subsequent influence of Saudi Arabia and Pakistan in Afghanistan, which, in turn, contributed to the subsequent rise of the Taliban).

When Saddam Hussein invaded Kuwait in 1990, the impending transformation of the Soviet Union made it possible for the Bush administration to enlist Soviet cooperation and coordinate a multinational military coalition that, thanks to the security framework set up by previous administrations, deterred Saddam from intimidating Saudi Arabia and eventually expelled him from Kuwait. Saddam's defiance of the conditions of the cease-fire, his persecution of Iraq's Shiite and Kurdish minorities, and his ongoing secret chemical, biological, and nuclear weapons programs resulted in a continuing embargo on Iraq's oil, restrictions on his military activities, and, for a time, United Nations (UN) inspections of Iraqi weapons sites. Under President Bill Clinton, the United States continued to pursue a dual containment policy directed, not toward the Soviet Union, but rather toward Iran and Iraq, the two regional states bent on hegemony in the gulf. Due to an erosion of coalition solidarity, this policy was only partially effective. Developments in Iran that accompanied the election of President Muhammad Khatami in 1997 offered some reason for hope, but Saddam eventually reconstituted the core of his army, reimposed his authoritarian control over the country, expelled the UN inspectors (in 1998), and continued his efforts to develop weapons of mass destruction.[7]

The attack of September 11, 2001, took place while the Bush administration was still looking for a more effective way to contain the threats to vital U.S. interests in the region posed by Saddam Hussein and the hard-line clerics who controlled the Iranian government. The attack made clear that it is not just the United States with its superpower status and its open society, but the whole international community that faces a threat. An increasingly interdependent world is vulnerable to small groups that are able to find or recruit motivated adherents, channel their rage, and, with relatively modest financing and safe harbor from regimes that share their views (such as the Taliban), utilize global networks and modern technology to wreak havoc on their enemies. 9/11 began to bring home to many historical allies and adversaries alike an awareness that the common threat posed by terrorism might be more real than the threat they pose to each other and that, given ongoing globalization and the collapse of communism, their increasingly common interests and goals might be more important than their differences (even those involving the 1972 Antiballistic Missile [ABM] Treaty).[8] While vital oil interests in the Caspian Sea region, for example, had previously been the subject of contention between Russia and the United States, the oil itself could increasingly be seen as a resource that could be shared by those willing to abide by international norms and that could play an important role in the reconstruction of Afghanistan.[9]

The United States lost more lives in the 9/11 attacks than it lost in implementing its containment policy in the Middle East and Southwest Asia throughout the entire Cold War. The unanticipated magnitude of death and destruction at the World Trade Center and the Pentagon galvanized the will of the administration, made possible an international coalition against an international threat, and prompted determined U.S. and allied action that, in its military phase in Afghanistan, appears to have been a great success. But as the United States continues the war in Afghanistan and, with its allies, begins to address the difficult challenge of Afghanistan's political and economic development, the world awaits a more articulate pronouncement from President George W. Bush than the desire "to rid the world of the evil-doers" or the notion that "either you are with us, or you are with the terrorists."[10]

The "Vision Thing": The Need for a More Comprehensive Bush Doctrine

The history of U.S. policy in the region since World War II suggests that only when interests are vital are they likely to elicit commitments. What is vital? The concept constantly evolves. In July 2000 the bipartisan Commission on America's National Interests, concerned that the United States was "in danger of losing its way" in the post–Cold War era and believing that "American foreign policy should be guided by reasoned, systematic thinking about national interests," identified five interests as genuinely vital and deserving of commitment, including protecting the United States from attack, preventing or reducing threats posed by weapons of mass destruction, and maintaining the viability of the world economy. Commitments to protect such interests, when they are made, are more credible if they are clear and have the support of the American people, because only then will the government have the means to honor its commitments, deter its adversaries, and give its allies the incentives necessary for achieving its goals.[11] Such clarity was characteristic of most of the post–World War II presidential doctrines, all of which applied to the containment of threats to U.S. interests in the Middle East. What is different now from the Cold War era, and what has been recognized after 9/11, is that the balance of power is no longer the key dynamic in the region. The terrorist threat that we are trying to contain, if largely based in the region, is everywhere. Regional powers, less restrained by great power rivalry and hence more adventurous than in the past, possess or seek weapons of mass destruction and together with terrorists threaten vital U.S. interests worldwide. Not all of those adversaries, moreover, respond to deterrence. Only some of those the United States seeks to deter, such as Saddam Hussein in Iraq and the clerics in Iran, represent states in the traditional sense of the word. Other entities that harbor terrorists, such as Yemen, are weak, or "failing," states that may not be able to control their own territory even if they want to. Still others, such as Afghanistan under the Taliban, clearly are "failed" states whose government systems have collapsed, rendering them incapable of providing their citizens with basic resources or protection. Networks such as Al-Qaeda, in contrast, are not states at all, but terrorist organizations that, because of the concept of jihad that they espouse and their willingness to conduct suicide attacks, may be impeded but not necessarily deterred.

Although conventional means can be used to contain or deter some of those adversaries, extraordinary means need to be developed to counter or, if necessary, eliminate others. In developing such means, lessons from the policy of containment in the region are relevant. During the Cold War, conflicting interests and the dictates of necessity created continuing difficulties in developing our allies and containing our adversaries in the region. Our support for Israel clashed with our attempts to work with Arab states. Collaboration with the British, necessitated by limited resources in containing Moscow, not only impeded better relations with the region's emerging nations but also threatened to undermine the security of the region that Anglo-American ties were designed to protect.

There is no reason to believe that the future will be any easier. It is true that the old rules of the great game no longer apply and that the great powers that once threatened the region have learned about the constraints under which they must operate. But conflicting interests are unavoidable, particularly when it comes to choosing among adventurous regional actors whose perceptions are often of a zero-sum variety, as they are for many Israelis and Palestinians or Indians and Pakistanis. Compromises that result in contradictions and accusations of hypocrisy will inevitably create difficulties. During the early years of the Cold War, U.S. officials accepted the risk of association with the vestiges of colonialism because they saw failure to contain the Soviet Union as a much greater threat to U.S. interests. So, today, the occasional necessity of collaborating with repressive states in the fight against terrorism will risk fueling the fire that such a policy is designed to put out.

It is important to be clear about our priorities in the region and to confront such dilemmas head on, particularly since the main threats to peace now come not only from terrorists but also from regional states, many of which have or seek to acquire weapons of mass destruction. The risks of brinkmanship were raised in the last decade by Iraq, then by Afghanistan, followed soon after by Pakistan and India, and most recently by the Palestinians and Israelis. The United States cannot afford to let events in the region escalate out of control, any more than it could in the Persian Gulf in 1990 or in Afghanistan in 2001, where the prohibition on direct U.S. involvement evaporated overnight on September 11. Indeed, Afghans (with the exception of the Taliban), Indians, Pakistanis, Palestinians, and Israelis have all requested a larger, not a smaller, U.S. role in helping to resolve their differences. The inevitability of such a role (and this is part of the message delivered by 9/11) makes it imperative that the United States and President Bush, in developing a doctrine in the long tradition of statements of American policy in the region, carefully consider the rules of the new games being played lest we be sucked into a whirlpool of commitments and fall victim to what might loosely be called messianic globaloney.

The United States is the only country with the capability and will to lead such efforts, which is not to denigrate the role of the United Nations. Secretary General Kofi Annan has underscored the importance of the UN role, asserting that the fight against terrorism is "a moral struggle to fight an evil that is anathema to all faiths," insisting that the global response to terrorism be "truly universal," and calling on states to use political, legal, diplomatic, and financial means to combat terrorism. While Annan and other Nobel laureates have attempted to lay down principles to which the human community can aspire (individual rights and international action legitimized by democracy and the rule of law), such principles will not by themselves advance the war against terrorism or combat aggression in the region.[12] The failure to abide by rules of acceptable international conduct must have clear consequences, mechanisms must be developed to counter serious breaches of those rules, and elements within the region must have an incentive to cooperate in enforcing them.

The threat posed by Saddam Hussein, for example, cries out for a plan of action, based first on a serious effort to reinsert UN arms control inspectors with full powers to search for evidence of Iraq's efforts to develop weapons of mass destruction. Richard Butler, the former executive chairman of the UN Special Commission on Iraq, has made a strong case for doing so. Like Butler, Iraqi defectors have drawn attention to Saddam Hussein's determination to acquire such weapons, while still others (including a well-informed scientist who was the first deputy chief of research and production for the Soviet biological weapons program) have detailed the magnitude of the damage such weapons could do. History, moreover, has illustrated Saddam's willingness to use them, and 9/11 has laid bare the vulnerability of the United States to those with such intentions. Those who reject the Bush administration's conflation of the problems posed by terrorism and by Saddam Hussein ignore the import of these facts.[13]

According to the former director of Iraq's nuclear weapons program, inspections in Iraq will have little effect because Saddam moves his laboratories around. Perhaps for that reason or because of Saddam's previous ability to obstruct inspectors who are homing in on a vulnerable site, the demand for inspections is apparently out of fashion in the U.S. government, although there are occasional rhetorical flourishes (from both the Bush administration and Iraqi officials) that pay lip service to the possibility of examining the question.[14] If there is an international will to impose them, however, and the inspections have teeth, we will find out sooner rather than later whether Saddam takes recent developments to heart and is willing to play by any rules other than his own. It is important now to develop a plan to require inspections—UN inspectors must have immediate and unfettered access to sites they want to inspect—or to use Saddam's refusal to acquiesce in them as a reason to take more aggressive action. A clear statement of what Iraq's failure to comply with UN demands would entail, especially if the Bush administration is able to regain the support of the Security Council, would force the issue and place the blame where it belongs: on Saddam Hussein. In November 2001 President Bush, asked what he would do if Saddam Hussein refused to allow arms inspectors back into Iraq, stated,

"He'll find out."[15] The proper groundwork needs to be laid for such an initiative and a clear policy articulated. The crackdown on militant groups in several countries has already suggested the value of a principled stand on the question of terror. The same could be said for a principled stand on inspections in Iraq unless Saddam responds positively to a united Security Council's insistence on meaningful inspections.

Elements of a More Comprehensive Bush Doctrine

The history of U.S. policy in the Middle East and Southwest Asia since World War II suggests that, while U.S. military capabilities in the region remain essential, what is missing is a comprehensive presidential doctrine that not only clearly defines U.S. interests in the region but also provides a shared vision of how to protect them. President Bush's remarks to the nation on September 11, 2001, enunciated what has come to be called the Bush Doctrine: "We will make no distinction between the terrorists who committed these acts and those who harbor them." The Bush Doctrine was elaborated upon in the president's state of the union address to Congress on January 29, 2002, which committed the nation to the steadfast, patient, and persistent pursuit of "two great objectives": (1) shutting down terrorist camps and bringing terrorists to justice; and (2) preventing terrorists and regimes who seek weapons of mass destruction from threatening the United States and the world. In seeking to contain not just terrorists but also regimes that sponsor terror, which together with their terrorist allies he described as "an axis of evil," President Bush took an important first step in articulating a vision for what he characterized in his speech as "a nation at war."[16]

What was missing in the president's resolute statement was a greater public recognition of the international community's role in this war and a carrot to go along with the stick that he wielded. The president must take the lead but, like the secretary general of the United Nations, he must also speak on behalf of a much larger and broader community, acknowledging that without the close cooperation of that community, U.S. efforts cannot succeed. To be successful, those efforts must *first* draw on an internationally accepted code that lays out norms of behavior for states in the region, enumerates the elements of cooperation, and underscores the costs (which the United States and its allies must be prepared to exact) of failing to abide by the new rules of the game. U.S. efforts must *also* address the needs of individuals in the region who, burdened with hardships (whether poverty, a lack of education, state-lessness, or doctrinaire or authoritarian rule) and lacking incentives to acquiesce, find violence or terrorism their only recourse.

A Code of Conduct and the Costs of Failing to Abide by the New Rules of the Game

On the first set of issues, Security Council Resolution 1373 has already laid out the elements of cooperation required of UN member states in the campaign against terrorism, "from suppressing the financing of terrorism to providing early warning, cooperating in criminal investigations, and exchanging information on possible terrorist acts." The UN secretary general has also urged the General Assembly to ratify a comprehensive convention providing "a common legal framework for international cooperation in the fight against terrorism," and he has called for collaboration in such areas as customs, regulation of immigration, extradition, financial law and practice, police and law enforcement work, and suppression of illegal arms trafficking. This will not be easy. In spite of the secretary general's recognition of a need for moral clarity, a stalemate has developed between the United States, the European Union, and others, on the one hand, and the fifty-six members of the Organization of the Islamic Conference, on the other. Differences over what constitutes a terrorist and whether national liberation movements and resistance to foreign occupation should be exempted from that definition have prevented agreement on a comprehensive treaty. Nonetheless, the United States and the international community must persevere. The UN's legal committee, the Sixth Committee, will have a chance to reconcile these differences in fall 2002.[17]

Also lacking, and what U.S. leadership can help provide even without a consensus on a common legal framework, is a clear sense of potential costs to states in the region that do not fulfill their international obligations. The United States, meanwhile, should do everything in its power to restore consensus in the UN Security Council on the resumption of international inspections in Iraq under UN Security Council Resolutions 687 and 715 and then develop mechanisms to ensure that Iraq fulfills its obligations. In the absence of an agreement on what constitutes terrorism, the United States of necessity has taken the lead in the war on terrorism, and Kofi Annan has legitimized U.S. initiatives insofar as he has noted the council's reaffirmation of the inherent right of individual or collective self-defense in accordance with the Charter of the United Nations.[18]

Incentives to Cooperate

What made the policy of containment effective during the Cold War was not just the political/military commitment articulated in the Truman and subsequent presidential doctrines; equally important in obtaining the confidence of our allies was the economic component—the vision elaborated in the Marshall Plan, which was directed not at any country, but against hunger, poverty, desperation, and chaos. Its goal was "to permit the emergence of political and social conditions in which free institutions can exist." The Marshall Plan spoke to those who needed hope. So did Point Four of President Truman's inaugural address in 1949, a program of assistance for underdeveloped areas that addressed issues of social welfare, education, and health but that, because the program it engendered was poorly funded, never had the impact of the Marshall Plan. Such hope is precisely what is being sought today by those living under dangerous dictators such as Saddam Hussein and by those living on the dark side of globalization who are responsive to extremist ideologies. In the latter case, as Mike Moore, the director general of the World Bank, has pointed out, poverty is a "time bomb lodged against the heart of liberty." In short, with the benefits of globalization come costs. As those costs, too, have been globalized, so has terror.[19]

To address this problem and, ultimately, to eliminate it, the essential task of U.S. policy in the Middle East and Southwest Asia must be not only to contain terrorism and aggression by states within the region but also to work with our allies and with countries in the region to help the region develop:

plans for economic growth that are consistent with the capabilities and aspirations of the region, that foster civil societies, and that encourage constructive discourse over common problems;

safety nets for the hungry, the dispossessed, and those in need of health care;

better educational systems that provide alternatives to the doctrinaire and regressive teachings of the madrasahs; and

a recourse to solutions other than violence, such as mechanisms for the arbitration of major conflicts, the peaceful resolution of disputes, and peaceful change.

A comprehensive U.S. energy policy, which should be part of such efforts, should not be seen as an alternative to reliance on the oil fields of

204 Bruce R. Kuniholm

the Caspian Sea and Persian Gulf or involvement in the affairs of the region.[20] Even if we were free of our reliance on oil in the region, we would still be vulnerable to the terrorism rooted there and the weapons of mass destruction that terrorists or regimes that sponsor terror could use. If the president is to contain these scourges, he must articulate a vision comparable to the Marshall Plan in scope, even if it is different in detail and tailored to particular needs of the region. There are serious problems in trying to develop habits of cooperation or to create from whole cloth the infrastructural prerequisites of modern societies and economies where none currently exist, and the United States has not been very good at nation building. There are also problems of legitimacy affecting many regional governments, whose leaders, unless assistance is channeled through nongovernmental and other international agencies, might deflect it from its intended purposes. But the premise of the Marshall Plan is still relevant today, and international collaboration on the political and economic reconstruction of Afghanistan is a start. A major U.S. commitment to work toward a just and equitable settlement of the Palestinian-Israeli dispute that satisfies both Israel's legitimate right to security (but does not condone the building of settlements in the occupied territories or lethal collective punishment) and the Palestinians' legitimate right to self-determination (but does not condone terrorist acts in behalf of a war of national liberation) would be a further step in the right direction.[21] It would also constitute a clear recognition by the administration that terrorism, although it cannot be condoned, does not exist independent of its causes and that in this case the United States has a special responsibility to support a just outcome. Moreover, failure to make such a commitment and continued escalation of the conflict could undermine the war on terrorism throughout the region. A new presidential doctrine, sensitive to the fact that to contain aggression requires a positive dynamic that can give people hope because it acknowledges their needs as well as ours, should speak to the aspirations of all individuals in the region, where the entire world has a stake in the development of stable, responsible, and more democratic governments.[22]

Postscript: The National Security Strategy of the United States, released by the Bush administration on September 17, 2002,[23] resonates with many of the arguments and addresses many of the concerns that I attempted to articulate in this article when it was written in the spring of 2002. For the administration, the events of September 11, 2001, made clear the vulnerability of open, democratic societies to terrorists, to those who harbor them, and to tyrants or "rogue states" who seek weapons of mass destruction (WMD). Such tyrants, or the states that they lead, the administration argues, seek WMD not as weapons of last resort but as "weapons of choice." The events of September 11, coupled with the overlap between such adversaries of open, democratic societies, have transformed the international security environment into one that is more complex than that of the Cold War—one in which former Cold War foes are increasingly seen as allies in a common cause. What the administration now supports is "a balance of power that favors freedom." From the Bush administration's point of view, this new environment requires a shift away from deterrence (a Cold War concept that is less likely to work against rogue states that seek WMD and that won't work against terrorists).[24] What is now required is a strategy of preemption,[25] particularly if the threat the United States is trying to preempt is "imminent"— a concept drawn from international law that the administration believes must be adapted to the capabilities and objectives of today's adversaries.

The National Security Strategy elaborates on what can appropriately be called an expanded Bush Doctrine (even though others would now characterize that doctrine more simply as the articulation of a preemptive strategy), defining U.S. interests in the region and providing a shared vision of how to protect them. The Bush Doctrine recognizes that if terrorism is to be defeated, close cooperation between the United States and the international community is important, but the administration does not shy away from its leadership responsibilities and from the prospect, if necessary, of acting alone (not for unilateral advantage, but to "create the balance of power that favors human freedom"). In spite of rhetorical posturing, meanwhile, the administration did pursue multilateral approaches in combating terror and the impending threat posed by Saddam Hussein, and its resort to the UN made it possible to place the blame for Iraq's behavior where it belongs—on Saddam Hussein—even though, in the end, the United States went to war against Iraq without the blessing of the Security Council.[26] Such cooperation, it should be noted, even if desirable, is not sufficient. The underlying conditions that spawn terrorism (which are manifest in the clash *within* Islam over the norms and direction of modern civilization) must also be addressed. As a means to this end, the administration, clearly, seeks to promote market economies and to nurture those who promote democratic freedoms.[27] Poverty, while not the cause of terrorism, makes weak states vulnerable to terrorism and must also be combated. The administration has proposed a major increase in development assistance (the Millennium Challenge Account) that can serve as a carrot to nations that "govern justly," with an emphasis on health, education and an increase in productivity growth—assistance that will, in effect, help build "the infrastructure of democracy." In conjunction with this proposal, the administration also recognizes the necessity of addressing the Israeli-Palestinian problem in a balanced approach consistent with its core principles. It also makes one of its top priorities the moral imperative of "including all of the world's poor in an expanding circle of development," and it declares that the United States, with other developing countries, should double the size of the world's poorest economies within a decade. Whether the administration will be able to implement this ambitious agenda is open to question, but the vision is there.

Notes

1. For background, see Peter Hopkirk, *The Great Game: The Struggle for Empire in Central Asia* (New York, 1992); and Karl Meyer and Shareen Blair Brysac, *Tournament of Shadows: The Great Game and the Race for Empire in Central Asia* (Washington, 1999).

2. Vital interests are those seen as essential to a state's well-being and survival, those for which states will go to war, as exemplified by the Carter Doctrine: "Let our position be absolutely clear: An attempt by any outside force to gain control of the Persian Gulf region will be regarded as an assault on the vital interests of the United States of America, and such an assault will be repelled by any means necessary, including military force." Jimmy Carter, "State of the Union Address," 1980 <http://www.jimmycarterlibrary.org/documents/speeches/su80jec.phtml> (May 8, 2002). See also n. 11, below.

3. For an argument that culture is the most likely source of conflict in the coming years, see Samuel P. Huntington, *The Clash of Civilizations and the Remaking of World Order* (New York, 1996). For an argument "that increasing connections among civilizations simultaneously sustain a contrary trend toward global cosmopolitanism" that offers the best hope for the future, see William H. McNeill, "Decline of the West?" *New York Review of Books*, Jan. 9, 1997, pp. 18–22, esp. p. 22. Others highlight conflicts within civilizations. On a struggle within Islam between secular modernizers seeking to create legitimacy for nonobservant forms of Islam and extremists such as Osama bin Laden, see Richard W. Bulliet, "The Crisis within Islam," *Wilson Quarterly*, 26 (Winter 2002), 11–19. On a split within Islam between those who advocate a return to a real or imagined Islamic past and those who support secular democracy, see Bernard Lewis, *What Went Wrong? Western Impact and Middle Eastern Response* (New York, 2002).

4. The term "terrorism" requires careful attention such as that given by "Proposal for a Council Framework Decision on Combating Terrorism," Commission

of the European Communities, Brussels, 19.9.2001 COM (2001) 521 final, 2001/0217 (CNS) <http://europa.eu.int/comm/external_relations/cfsp/doc/com_01_521.pdf> (March 9, 2002). For the difficulties of defining terrorism, see "EU Definition of 'Terrorism' Could Still Embrace Protests," *Statewatch News Online* <http://www. statewatch.org/news/2001/dec/07terrdef.htm> (May 8, 2002). For the U.S. Defense Department's efforts, see *The Terrorism Research Center* <http://www.terrorism.com/ terrorism/bpart1.html> (May 8, 2002). For the difficulty of achieving consensus on any definition, see a discussion of the U.S. State Department's annual review of global terrorism: Brian Whitaker, "The Definition of Terrorism," *Guardian Unlimited*, May 7, 2001 <http://www.guardian.co.uk/elsewhere/journalist/story/ 0,7792,487098,00.html> (May 8, 2002); and n. 17, below. On the need for such a definition, see *International Herald Tribune*, Jan. 4, 2002, p. 6. The norms of civilized behavior are discussed later.

5. [George F. Kennan], "The Sources of Soviet Conduct," *Foreign Affairs*, 25 (July 1947), 566–82. Portions of this and the following discussion draw on Bruce R. Kuniholm, "U.S. Policy in the Near East: The Triumphs and Tribulations of the Truman Administration," in *The Truman Presidency*, ed. Michael J. Lacey (Cambridge, Eng., 1989), 299–338; Bruce R. Kuniholm, "Retrospect and Prospect: Forty Years of U.S. Middle East Policy," *Middle East Journal*, 41 (Winter 1987), 7–25; Bruce R. Kuniholm, "The Carter Doctrine, the Reagan Corollary, and Prospects for United States Policy in Southwest Asia," *International Journal*, 41 (Spring 1986), 342–61; Bruce R. Kuniholm, "The U.S. Experience in the Persian Gulf," in *The Persian Gulf Crisis: Power in the Post–Cold War World*, ed. Robert Helms and Robin Dorff (Westport, 1993), 57–69; and Bruce R. Kuniholm, "U.S. Responses to the Persian Gulf Crisis: Grappling for a Policy," *ibid.*, 95–105.

6. The revisionist argument is made by Melvyn P. Leffler. See Melvyn P. Leffler, "The American Conception of National Security and the Beginnings of the Cold War, 1945–48," *American Historical Review*, 89 (April 1984), 346–81; John Lewis Gaddis, "Comments," *ibid.*, 382–85; Bruce Kuniholm, "Comments," *ibid.*, 385–90; Melvyn P. Leffler, "Reply," *ibid.*, 391–400; Melvyn P. Leffler, "Strategy, Diplomacy, and the Cold War: The United States, Turkey, and NATO, 1945–1952," *Journal of American History*, 71 (March 1985), 807–25; and Melvyn P. Leffler, *A Preponderance of Power: National Security, the Truman Administration, and the Cold War* (Stanford, 1992). For a counter to the revisionist argument, see Bruce Kuniholm, *The Origins of the Cold War in the Near East: Great Power Conflict and Diplomacy in Iran, Turkey, and Greece* (Princeton, 1994). See also Eduard Mark, "The War Scare of 1946 and Its Consequences," *Diplomatic History*, 21 (Summer 1997), 383–415; and the debate between Mark and Melvyn P. Leffler on H-Diplo <http://www2. h-net.msu.edu/~diplo> (May 8, 2002). (Click on Discussion Logs, choose July 1997, and look for Leffler's comments posted on July 18, 1997, and Mark's response posted on July 22, 1997.)

7. On Muhammad Khatami, see Shaul Bakhash, "Iran's Unlikely President," *New York Review of Books*, Nov. 5, 1998, pp. 47–51.

8. See a special issue on globalization and its critics, *Economist*, Sept. 29, 2001. On interests common to Russia and the West, see Thom Shanker, "Rumsfeld Sees More Involvement for Russia in NATO," *New York Times*, Dec. 18, 2001 <http://www.

nytimes.com/2001/12/18/international/europe/18RUMS.html> (March 9, 2002); Michael Wines, "Putin Sees Continued Alliance despite the End of ABM Pact," *ibid.* <http://college4.nytimes.com/guests/articles/2001/12/18/891575.xml> (May 8, 2002); and Ahto Lobjakas, "Russia: Analysts Ponder Integration into Euro-Atlantic Community," Jan. 16, 2002, *Radio Free Europe/Radio Liberty* <http://www.rferl.org/nca/features/2002/01/16012002080353.asp> (May 8, 2002).

9.   See Bruce R. Kuniholm, "The Geopolitics of the Caspian Basin," *Middle East Journal,* 54 (Fall 2000), 546–51; and Ahmed Rashid, *The Taliban* (New Haven, 2000), chaps. 11, 12. But for a skeptical account, see Michael Lelyveld, "Caspian: Doubts Raised over U.S.-Russian Cooperation," Oct. 23, 2001, *Radio Free Europe/Radio Liberty* <http://www.rferl.org/nca/features/2001/10/23102001090005.asp> (May 8, 2002).

10.   For President George W. Bush's comments, see "The Terrorist Attack Investigation," Sept. 16, 2001, in *Online NewsHour* <http://www.pbs.org/newshour/terrorism/ata/investigation>, Sept. 20, 2001 <http://www.pbs. org/newshour/bb/military/terroristattack/bush_speech_9-20.html> (May 8, 2002).

11.   The five vital interests defined by the commission as "essential to our survival and well being," were to: "prevent, deter, and reduce the threat of nuclear, biological, and chemical weapons attacks on the United States or its military forces abroad; ensure U.S. allies' survival and their active cooperation with the United States in shaping an international system in which we can thrive; prevent the emergence of hostile major powers or failed states on U.S. borders; ensure the viability and stability of major global systems (trade, financial markets, supplies of energy, and the environment); and establish productive relations, consistent with American national interests, with nations that could become strategic adversaries, China and Russia." (Condoleezza Rice, now the president's national security adviser, was a member of the Commission on America's National Interests.) See "Prioritizing America's National Interests," July 7, 2000, BCSIA: *America's National Interests* <http://ksgnotes1.harvard.edu/BCSIA/BCSIA.nsf/media/PR7-7-00> (April 4, 2002). The lack of systematic thinking about national interests, or what President George H. W. Bush referred to as "the vision thing," was used by the press to caricature him as too pragmatic to have a long-term vision. See Marlin Fitzwater, *Call the Briefing! Bush and Reagan, Sam and Helen: A Decade with Presidents and the Press* (New York, 1995), 245. President George W. Bush has been similarly caricatured. See Patricia Ireland, "George W. Bush: What Does the 'W' Stand For?" <http://www.now.org/nnt/spring-2000/georgewp.html> (May 8, 2002).

12.   On the United Nations' (UN) role, see "Annan to Warsaw Conference on Combating Terrorism," U.S. Department of State International Information Programs, Nov. 7, 2001 <http://usinfo.state.gov/topical/pol/terror/01110714.htm> (May 8, 2002). For principles to which the human community can aspire, see Kofi Annan, Nobel Lecture, Dec. 10, 2001, *Nobel e-Museum* <http://www.nobel.se/peace/laureates/2001/annan-lecture.html> (May 8, 2002). A statement signed by more than one hundred Nobel laureates, including Francis Crick, Nadine Gordimer, and José Saramago, makes the case that the most profound danger to world peace stems from the legitimate demands of the world's dispossessed. See *International Herald Tribune,* Dec. 11, 2001, p. 8. A recent report by the Institute for Energy and Environ-

mental Research and the Lawyer's Committee on Nuclear Policy, ironically, makes the case that U.S. policy on a number of issues undercuts efforts worldwide to strengthen the rule of law. See *ibid.*, April 4, 2002, p. 3.

13. Richard Butler, *The Greatest Threat: Iraq, Weapons of Mass Destruction, and the Crisis of Global Security* (New York, 2001). See also Khidir Hamza, *Saddam's Bombmaker* (New York, 2000); Ken Alibek, *Biohazard* (New York, 1999); Richard Preston, "The Bioweaponeers," *New Yorker*, March 9, 1998, pp. 52–65; and the U.S. government white paper, "Iraq Weapons of Mass Destruction Programs," Feb. 13, 1998 <http://www.state.gov/www/regions/nea/iraq_white_paper.html> (May 8, 2002). For Saddam Hussein's reward of $25,000 to the relatives of each suicide bomber in Israel, see *International Herald Tribune*, April 4, 2002, p. 3.

14. See *International Herald Tribune*, Dec. 18, 2001, p. 6; and Seymour M. Hersh, "The Iraq Hawks," *New Yorker*, Dec. 24 and 31, 2001, pp. 58–63.

15. Bob Kemper and Steve Hedges, "Bush Turns Up Heat on Iraq," *Chicago Tribune*, Nov. 27, 2001 <http://www.chicagotribune.com/news/specials/chi-0111270224nov27.story?coll> (May 8, 2002).

16. See Dan Balz and Bob Woodward, "America's Chaotic Road to War," *Washington Post*, Jan. 27, 2002 <www.washingtonpost.com/wp-dyn/articles/A42754-2002Jan26.html> (May 8, 2002). For the text of the state of the union address, see <www.whitehouse.gov/news/releases/2002/01/20020129-11.html> (March 9, 2002).

17. For UN Security Council Resolution 1373, see <http://www.un.org/News/Press/docs/2001/sc7158.doc.htm> (May 8, 2002). "Annan to Warsaw Conference on Combating Terrorism." On the differences that have prevented a comprehensive anti-terrorism treaty, see Michael J. Jordan, "Terrorism's Slippery Definition Eludes UN Diplomats," *Christian Science Monitor*, Feb. 4, 2002 <www.csmonitor.com/2002/0204/p07s02-wogi.htm> (May 8, 2002).

18. On international inspections in Iraq, see Butler, *Greatest Threat*. On difficulties in implementing UN resolutions, see documents related to the United Nations Special Commission, at <http://www.un.org/Depts/unscom/unscmdoc.htm> (May 8, 2002); and Center for Nonproliferation Studies, "Iraq Special Collection" <http://cns.miis.edu/research/iraq/> (May 8, 2002). On the right to individual or collective self-defense, see "Annan to Warsaw Conference on Combating Terrorism."

19. George C. Marshall, "Commencement Address at Harvard University, Cambridge, Massachusetts, June 5, 1947," USAID <http://www.usaid.gov/multimedia/video/marshall/marshallspeech.html> (May 8, 2002); Truman Presidential Museum and Library, "Point Four Program of Technical Assistance to Developing Nations" <http://www.trumanlibrary.org/hstpaper/point4.htm> (March 9, 2002). For Mike Moore's statement, see *International Herald Tribune*, March 22, 2002, p. 4.

20. Many have advocated this step. See, for example, *International Herald Tribune*, Jan. 4, 2002, p. 7.

21. A useful place to start is the report of the Sharm el-Sheikh Fact-Finding Committee (or the Mitchell Report), April 30, 2001, at <http://usinfo.state.gov/regional/nea/mitchell.htm> (May 8, 2002).

22. For expressions of the need for such hope, see *International Herald Tribune*, Dec. 8–9, 2001, p. 8; and *ibid.*, Dec. 21, 2001, p. 5.

23. See National Security Strategy, Sept. 17, 2002 <http://www.whitehouse.gov/nsc/nss.pdf > (Dec. 10, 2002).

24. See also the arguments by Kenneth M. Pollock, *The Threatening Storm: The Case for Invading Iraq* (New York, 2002), 249 ff.

25. This was first articulated by President Bush in his commencement speech at West Point on June 1, 2002. See <http://www.whitehouse.gov/news/releases/2002/06/20020601-3.html> (Dec. 10, 2002).

26. See <http://www.un.int/usa/sres-iraq.htm> (Dec. 10, 2002). At this writing, the world awaits the outcome of Saddam Hussein's response to UN Security Council Resolution 1441, adopted on November 8, 2002, and the UN's assessment of that response.

27. For the Arab world's "deficit" when it comes to freedom and democracy, see the *Arab Human Development Report: Creating Opportunities for Future Generations* (New York, 2002), available at <http://www.undp.org/rbas/ahdr/CompleteEnglish.pdf> (Dec. 10, 2002).

Afterword

The War Room

Marilyn Blatt Young

In this closing essay, Marilyn Blatt Young looks at U.S. foreign policy one year after the September 11 attacks. She warns that the Bush administration has embarked on a dangerous course away from the older strategies of deterrence and containment and toward preemptive action. Young worries that the Bush administration has resurrected "a fantasy of total control established by military fiat." That vision, she argues, is leading policy makers to defy the accumulated rules of international conduct and to turn instead to unilateral actions and imperialist policies.

Bush on Economy: "Saddam Must Be Overthrown"
—Headline in the humor journal *The Onion*, October 16, 2002

And we, alone again under an oblivious sky, were quick to learn how our best construals of divinity, our "Do unto, Love, Don't kill," could be easily garbled to canticles of vengeance and battle prayers.
—C. K. Williams, "War," *New Yorker*, November 5, 2001

The canticles of vengeance, the battle prayers, have filled the press, the television news and the movie theaters for over a year. Whatever the case may be for American citizens, the government seems to have freed itself from what C. K. Williams calls the "fearful burdens to be borne, complicity, contrition, grief."[1] Historians, political scientists, sociologists, artists, journalists, and philosophers have, one way and another, taken on that burden. In November 2002 Amazon.com listed 182 titles dealing with September 11; Barnes and Noble offered 1,042 titles with the keywords "September 11."[2]

This explosion of writing is hardly surprising. There is a visceral need to understand what happened; to contain the shock; to restore a sense of the familiar, whether a familiar enemy, a familiar sense of having an

211

all-pervasive enemy (a felt absence since the end of the Cold War), or the familiar relief of engaging in the intellectual effort to analyze the world. Academics, used to a slower tempo of reflection and publication, nevertheless responded in great numbers to the sense of crisis.[3]

The national government, on the other hand, has appropriated September 11 for purposes of national mobilization, urging the country to remember the day and remember it again. Melani McAlister points out in this volume that within days of the attack, "September 11 had taken on the folkloric status of the assassination of John F. Kennedy." Any discussion of earlier debates about terrorism and the appropriate response to it, even, as McAlister writes, the "public acknowledgment that there had been a debate," were entirely absent, closing down "the possibility for an expanded political discussion." Instead, it simply "became time for Americans to win the thirty years' war—by pretending it had just begun."[4] The response the government wanted, and got, was best captured by a report in the weekly humor journal, *The Onion*. The lead story in the September 25, 2002, issue was "The Sept. 11 Anniversary Two Weeks Later." "It seems hard to believe," the article began, "but this Wednesday the nation will come together to commemorate the two-week anniversary of the one-year anniversary of the Sept. 11 attacks." Meredith Engelberger, a homemaker and mother of three, was one of those allegedly interviewed for the article: "This past June 11, the three-quarters-of-a-year anniversary of the attacks, I was starting to think I'd never feel whole again. But then, at seven days before the one-year anniversary, it hit me: I'm not alone. Three weeks later, that's still true. If I can just get through the week before, the day of, and the day after the two-week anniversary of the one-year anniversary of Sept. 11, I know I'll be okay."[5]

It is the task of historians, however, to make sure that Engelberger does not feel okay or "whole." In the face of the varieties of political violence that now dominate the world, feeling okay is not an option. Or rather, feeling okay requires determined acts of denial and amnesia, which are the grounds for policies of war making. The essays in this volume all insist that it is urgent not only to remember the near past, but to know its history. Each locates the present moment in longer histories of American nationalism, Islamic religious movements, gendered fantasies, covert operations, overt competitive Cold War modernization schemes, and American policy in the Middle East. It is necessary to know that the U.S. war against terrorism began over three decades ago, that

Afghanistan was enmeshed in U.S./Soviet rivalry long before Zbigniew Brzezinski turned his attention to the Great Game, that for over five decades anger at the United States came from secular anti-imperialists in the Middle East rather than religious fundamentalists. Each lifting of the veil of the present makes possible a better understanding of the present and hints at the future. Yet this would be a more reassuring thought if one were convinced policy makers in Washington shared it. The essays in this volume are filled with irony, unpredictability, the failure of the powerful to control the effects of their own policies, and the risks and damage done to ordinary human beings by the armed and arrogant of the world.

The most immediate effect of September 11 on the Bush administration has been to allow policies contemplated since the administrations of Ronald Reagan and Bush père to be implemented with little or no opposition. International conventions of every variety have either been "unsigned" or never signed, so that the world's only superpower stands unconstrained on issues of the environment, discrimination against women, protection of children, nuclear and other weapons of mass destruction, and the punishment of war criminals. Some elements of recent policy were foreshadowed in the preceding administration. The Nuclear Non-Proliferation Treaty had been eroded by successive Democratic administrations. It was Clinton's secretary of state, Madeline Albright, who thought the United States particularly entitled to use force because it is the "indispensable nation," standing taller and seeing further into the future than the rest of the world, and Clinton's secretary of defense, Les Aspin, who argued for the U.S. right to wage preemptive war.[6] Indeed, Secretary of Defense Donald Rumsfeld's vision of the world has something in common with Robert McNamara's 1960s sense of American imperatives. "We have our view of the way the U.S. should be moving and of the need for the majority of the rest of the world to be moving in the same direction if we are to achieve our national objectives," McNamara told President Lyndon Johnson in 1967. "Our ends cannot be achieved and our leadership role cannot be played if some powerful and virulent nation—whether Germany, Japan, Russia or China—is allowed to organize their part of the world according to a philosophy contrary to ours."[7]

The stakes are higher now and there is no place that is not part of America's world. More specifically, as an administration aide remarked after the midterm elections: "It's W's world and everybody else is living in it. This will change the calculation anybody will have to make before crossing George Bush."[8] The difference between the Bush administration and its predecessors recalls the early Cold War debate between those who saw containment as the best way to control and ultimately bring down the Soviet empire and those who demanded that Communist governments be overthrown. In the event, containment was militarized and rollback restricted to thundering speeches, but not before the effort was made to achieve what would be called, in the new aseptic jargon, "regime change" in North Korea, a failed endeavor that cost millions of lives.

The most disturbing and dangerous aspect of the current policy is the conviction of many of its most important spokesmen that the United States stands alone. Robert Kagan, a senior fellow at the Carnegie Endowment for Peace, has articulated the notion succinctly: "It is time to stop pretending that Europeans and Americans share a common view of the world, or even that they occupy the same world." In a twist on the standard view that the United States operates in a transcendent ahistoric realm, Kagan argues that this country is "mired in history," while an Edenic Europe inhabits a world of "laws and rules and transnational negotiation and cooperation." America labors in the Hobbesian jungle so that Europeans can enjoy their "Kantian paradise." To the extent that law regulates international behavior, it is because "a power like the United States defends it by force of arms." However, in order to do this, the United States "must refuse to abide by certain international conventions that may constrain its ability to fight." This is not a contradiction if one believes that America's double standard "may be the best means of advancing human progress—and perhaps the only means."[9] With this, Kagan arrives at the same conclusion American exceptionalists have always reached: The national history is an apotheosis of all histories, a myth for all time; the United States is Atlas holding up the world or, closer to the religious bent of the Bush administration, it is Christ the Redeemer. After watching the film *Black Hawk Down*, the journalist George Monbiot wrote that the United States had cast itself "simultaneously as the world's savior and the world's victim, a sacrificial messiah on a mission to deliver the world from evil."[10] Monbiot called it a "new myth of nationhood," and whether new or only radically refurbished, it is the governing myth of the current administration.

Kagan does not comment on the propensity of the king of the Hobbesian jungle to engage in promulgating doctrines. As historian Walter

LaFeber has observed, post-World War II American presidents have been given to doctrinal utterances.[11] The interesting thing about American doctrines, which are, after all, only statements of an administration's foreign policy, is that there is an expectation that the rest of the world will live by them. In this volume, Bruce Kuniholm, seeing the current conflict as a clash of "values and ideas that underpin modernization and the norms and directions of modern civilization," suggests the possibility of a new presidential doctrine.[12] The Comprehensive Bush Doctrine would be one that "not only clearly defines U.S. interests in the [Middle East and Southwest Asia] but also provides a shared vision of how to protect them." The assumption is that other countries will indeed wish to protect U.S. interests in the region, and since Kuniholm's version of the doctrine includes many good things—economic growth, safety nets for the destitute, better educational systems, solutions short of violence—perhaps they will. The recently released National Security Strategy of the United States would seem to fulfill Kuniholm's call for a more substantial Bush Doctrine.

It opens with a bold assertion. The twentieth century ended in a decisive victory for the forces of freedom and "a single sustainable model for national success: freedom, democracy, and free enterprise."[13] There is only one model for national success and all other sorts of struggles are definitively done: "The militant visions of class, nation, and race which promised utopia and delivered misery have been defeated and discredited."[14] Thus the American domestic economic order, American prescriptions for the world, and American military supremacy are joined. The notion of deterrence is consigned to the dustbin of history, for the enemies the United States now faces are either risk-taking rogue states or stateless terrorists. In neither case will the old-fashioned strategy of deterrence and containment work. Instead, in this new situation, the United States "will, if necessary, act preemptively." Finally, U.S. forces will be such as to "dissuade potential adversaries from pursuing a military build-up in hopes of surpassing, or equaling, the power of the United States."[15] Hendrik Hertzberg, executive editor of the *New Yorker*, offered a succinct summary of the meaning of the National Security Strategy: "The vision laid out in the Bush document is a vision of what used to be called, when we believed it to be the Soviet ambition, world domination. This goes much further than the notion of America as the policeman of the world. It's the notion of America as both the policeman and the legislator of the world."[16]

What this will mean in practice, Condoleezza Rice told an interviewer, is that another power will never again be allowed to "reach military parity with the United States in the way that the Soviet Union did." Why? Because "when that happens, there will not be a balance of power that favors freedom; there will be a balance of power that keeps part of the world in tyranny the way that the Soviet Union did."[17] The possibility that other freedom-favoring countries might wish to challenge U.S. power is precluded by definition. After September 11, Walter LaFeber wrote, American exceptionalism, "combined with the immensity of American power, hinted at the dangers of being a nation so strong that others could not check it, and so self-righteous that it could not check itself." LaFeber asks whether "American democracy is sufficient to control American unilateralism."[18] The answer is not self-evident.

At any rate, democracy will need to constrain more than unilateralism. For the first time since Thomas Jefferson's metaphorical invocation of an "empire for liberty," commentators regularly refer to the country as an empire, to America as "imperial," as the director of policy planning for the State Department, Richard Haass, put it, if not "imperialist."[19] In the past, a *New York Times* reporter noted, "Americans [were] used to being told—typically by resentful foreigners—that they're imperialists. But lately some of the nation's own eminent thinkers are embracing the idea. Astonishingly, they are using the term with approval."[20] Stephen Peter Rosen, director of the Olin Institute for Strategic Studies and a professor in the government department at Harvard University, is an example of the trend. "A political unit that has overwhelming superiority in military power, and uses that power to influence the internal behavior of other states, is called an empire. . . . We are an informal empire, to be sure, but an empire nonetheless. If this is correct, our goal is not combating a rival, but maintaining our imperial position, and maintaining imperial order." Imperial wars, Rosen observes, are different from conventional wars, which end with the troops' coming home. "Imperial wars end, but imperial garrisons must be left in place for decades to ensure order and stability." And not just garrisons: The United States now employs mercenaries and private contractors to carry out military tasks abroad outside of the public eye and without the need for congressional approval.[21] Moreover, Rosen, like the Bush administration, believes that imperial strategy requires preventing the emergence "of powerful, hostile challengers to the empire: by war if necessary, but by imperial assimilation if possible."[22]

This assumption of the mantle of Rome and the trumpeting of America's military prowess in the name of a realistic response to the post–Cold War order, has frightened even many conservatives. Christopher Layne, writing in what he calls the tradition of Taft Republicans, worries about "a policy of imperial aspirations—[which] undermines important domestic political values that we conservatives hold dear." Surveying the field of defeated empires of the past, Layne believes the Bush administration thinks itself exempt from history. "Flushed with triumph in Afghanistan, and the awesome display of American power, they talk of 'a new American empire.'" Ringing a fire bell in the night, Layne predicts a "geopolitical backlash" against an administration that believes it can "use its muscle to bring about regime changes, and . . . compel others to embrace American-style democracy and free markets."[23]

The Bush administration seems bent on destroying the slow accumulation of the rules of international conduct, the fragile structure of a negotiated world order of mutual respect, in favor of a fantasy of total control established by military fiat. The historian Paul Schroeder put it bluntly in a recent essay: the Bush administration "declares that there is one law for the United States and other states of which it approves, and another law for all the rest. It is Orwellian: all states are equal, but some, especially the United States, are vastly more equal than others."[24] Any state, whether ally, neutral, or enemy will fear the implications.

Empire, J. M. Coetzee has written, "dooms itself to live in history and plot against history." And he goes on:

> One thought alone preoccupies the submerged mind of Empire: how not to end, how not to die, how to prolong its era. By day it pursues its enemies. It is cunning and ruthless, it sends its bloodhounds everywhere. By night it feeds on images of disaster: the sack of cities, the rape of populations, pyramids of bones, acres of desolation. A mad vision yet a virulent one.[25]

The authors of this volume do not share that mad vision, and the history they seek to illuminate demonstrates why it is both mad and doomed.

Notes

1. C. K. Williams, "War," *New Yorker*, Nov. 5, 2001, pp. 80–81.

2. Some of these books are no more than battle prayers, in which September 11 features, literally and opportunistically, as cover art. See, for example, Colonels Qiao Liang and Wang Xiangsui, *Unrestricted Warfare: China's Master Plan to Destroy America* (West Palm Beach, 2002), which can be purchased at a bargain price if you also

buy a book by the same publisher that pictures Bill Clinton against a background of the disintegrating towers (Christopher Ruddy and Carl Limbacher Jr., eds., *Catastrophe: Clinton's Role in America's Worst Disaster*, West Palm Beach, 2002). People who bought those two also ordered Gordon Thomas, *Seeds of Fire: China and the Story Behind the Attack on America* (Tempe, Ariz., 2001); and Patrick Buchanan, *The Death of the West: How Dying Populations and Immigrant Invasions Imperil Our Country and Civilization* (New York, 2001). Rather unnervingly, six people who bought the Buchanan volume suggest that *Mein Kampf* would be a good read.

3. The Social Science Research Council set up an online forum, inviting a wide variety of academics to join in a collective analysis of the event, its causes, and American and world reactions. This effort yielded two volumes of short essays: Craig Calhoun, Paul Price, and Ashley Timmer, eds., *Understanding September 11* (New York, 2002); and Eric Hershberg and Kevin W. Moore, eds., *Critical Views of September 11: Analyses from around the World* (New York, 2002). Several journals, including *SAQ: South Atlantic Quarterly, Diplomatic History, Radical History Review*, and *Public Culture*, put out special issues that may, like this revised edition of the *Journal of American History* special issue, become books as well. No one need fear a dearth of reading matter for future college courses.

4. Melani McAlister, "A Cultural History of the War without End," in this volume, pp. 94–116.

5. "The Sept. 11 Anniversary Two Weeks Later" <http://www.theonion.com> (Sept. 25, 2002).

6. "The Today Show" (NBC, Feb. 1998); "60 Minutes" (CBS, May 11, 1996).

7. Lloyd Gardner, review of *Foreign Relations of the United States, 1964–1968*, in *Diplomatic History*, 22 (Spring 1998), 321.

8. Mike Allen, "Bush Urges Bipartisan Relations: Democrats See Disconnect between Rhetoric and GOP Actions," *Washington Post*, Nov. 8, 2002, p. A12.

9. Robert Kagan, "Power and Weakness," *Policy Review* (no. 113, June–July 2002). It is true that the United States and Europe live in different worlds. But these worlds are distinguished not, as Kagan would have it, by European military weakness and American military strength, but rather by a sharp difference in values and in the way people live. Tony Judt has pointed out in a recent essay that rates of poverty are consistently and considerably higher in the United States than in Europe, as are infant mortality rates and income disparities. European economies are more productive, the economic security and health of their populations greater by far. There is little to attract Europeans to the American model, which, Judt concludes, "is unique and not for export." See Tony Judt, "Its Own Worst Enemy," *New York Review of Books*, Aug. 15, 2002 <http://www.nybooks.com>.

10. George Monbiot, "Both Saviour and Victim," *Guardian Weekly*, Jan. 29, 2002, p. 13.

11. Walter LaFeber, "The Bush Doctrine," *Diplomatic History*, 26 (Fall 2002), 543–58.

12. Bruce Kuniholm, "9/11, the Great Game, and the Vision Thing: The Need for (and Elements of) a More Comprehensive Bush Doctrine," in this volume, pp. 191–210.

13. "The National Security Strategy of the United States of America" <http://www.whitehouse.gov/nsc> (Sept. 17, 2002). For an interesting account of this doc-

ument in comparison to earlier versions under discussion since 1992, see David Armstrong, "Dick Cheney's Song of America," *Harpers*, 305 (Oct. 2002), 76–83.

14. "National Security Strategy," 3.

15. *Ibid.*, 11, 20.

16. Hendrik Hertzberg, "Talk of the Town," *New Yorker*, Oct. 14–21, 2002, p. 65.

17. Condoleezza Rice interview with Margaret Warner, "The NewsHour with Jim Lehrer" (PBS, Sept. 26, 2002).

18. LaFeber, "Bush Doctrine," 558.

19. Nicholas Lemann, "The Next World Order," *New Yorker*, April 1, 2002, p. 46.

20. Emily Eakin, "All Roads Lead to D.C.," *New York Times Magazine*, April 1, 2002 <www.nytimes.com>. For an especially militant and hardy embrace of empire, see Stephen Peter Rosen, "The Future of War and the American Military," *Harvard Magazine*, 104 (May–June 2002), 29.

21. Leslie Wayne, "America's For-Profit Secret Army," *New York Times*, Oct. 13, 2002, sec. 3, p. 1.

22. Rosen, "Future of War and the American Military," 30–31.

23. Christopher Layne, "The Right Peace: Conservatives against a War with Iraq," *LA Weekly*, Oct. 25–31, 2002 <http://www.laweekly.com>.

24. Paul Schroeder, "Iraq: The Case against Preemptive War," *American Conservative*, Oct. 21, 2002 <http://www.amconmag.com>.

25. J. M. Coetzee, *Waiting for the Barbarians* (New York, 1982), 133.

Appendix:
Primary Source Documents

*In the essays in this collection, several historians criticize Samuel P. Hunt-
ington's vision of a longstanding "clash of civilizations" between the Western
and Islamic worlds. (See, for example, the essays by Michael H. Hunt and
Bruce B. Lawrence.) In this excerpt from his 1993 article in the journal*
Foreign Affairs, *Huntington presents his argument. Are current conflicts
the result of particular historical and political developments, as our essayists
write, or do they represent, as Huntington suggests, an age-old clash of cultures? Why do many historians find the latter view troubling?*

The Clash of Civilizations? (1993)

Samuel P. Huntington

World politics is entering a new phase, and intellectuals have not hesitated
to proliferate visions of what it will be—the end of history, the return of traditional rivalries between nation states, and the decline of the nation state
from the conflicting pulls of tribalism and globalism, among others. Each
of these visions catches aspects of the emerging reality. Yet they all miss a
crucial, indeed a central, aspect of what global politics is likely to be in the
coming years.

It is my hypothesis that the fundamental source of conflict in this new
world will not be primarily ideological or primarily economic. The great divisions among humankind and the dominating source of conflict will be cultural. Nation states will remain the most powerful actors in world affairs,
but the principal conflicts of global politics will occur between nations and
groups of different civilizations. The clash of civilizations will dominate
global politics. The fault lines between civilizations will be the battle lines
of the future.

Conflict between civilizations will be the latest phase in the evolution of
conflict in the modern world. For a century and a half after the emergence
of the modern international system with the Peace of Westphalia, the conflicts of the Western world were largely among princes—emperors, absolute
monarchs and constitutional monarchs attempting to expand their bureauc-
racies, their armies, their mercantilist economic strength and, most important, the territory they ruled. In the process they created nation states, and
beginning with the French Revolution the principal lines of conflict were
between nations rather than princes. In 1793, as R. R. Palmer put it, "The

wars of kings were over; the wars of peoples had begun." This nineteenth-century pattern lasted until the end of World War I. Then, as a result of the Russian Revolution and the reaction against it, the conflict of nations yielded to the conflict of ideologies, first among communism, fascism-Nazism and liberal democracy, and then between communism and liberal democracy. During the Cold War, this latter conflict became embodied in the struggle between the two superpowers, neither of which was a nation state in the classical European sense and each of which defined its identity in terms of its ideology.

These conflicts between princes, nation states and ideologies were primarily conflicts within Western civilization, "Western civil wars," as William Lind has labeled them. This was as true of the Cold War as it was of the world wars and the earlier wars of the seventeenth, eighteenth and nineteenth centuries. With the end of the Cold War, international politics moves out of its Western phase, and its centerpiece becomes the interaction between the West and non-Western civilizations and among non-Western civilizations. In the politics of civilizations, the peoples and governments of non-Western civilizations no longer remain the objects of history as targets of Western colonialism but join the West as movers and shapers of history. . . .

During the Cold War the world was divided into the First, Second and Third Worlds. Those divisions are no longer relevant. It is far more meaningful now to group countries not in terms of their political or economic systems or in terms of their level of economic development but rather in terms of their culture and civilization. . . .

Conflict along the fault line between Western and Islamic civilizations has been going on for 1,300 years. After the founding of Islam, the Arab and Moorish surge west and north only ended at Tours in 732. From the eleventh to the thirteenth century the Crusaders attempted with temporary success to bring Christianity and Christian rule to the Holy Land. From the fourteenth to the seventeenth century, the Ottoman Turks reversed the balance, extended their sway over the Middle East and the Balkans, captured Constantinople, and twice laid siege to Vienna. In the nineteenth and early twentieth centuries as Ottoman power declined Britain, France, and Italy established Western control over most of North Africa and the Middle East.

After World War II, the West, in turn, began to retreat; the colonial empires disappeared; first Arab nationalism and then Islamic fundamentalism manifested themselves; the West became heavily dependent on the Persian Gulf countries for its energy; the oil-rich Muslim countries became money-rich and, when they wished to, weapons-rich. Several wars occurred between Arabs and Israel (created by the West). France fought a bloody and ruthless war in Algeria for most of the 1950s; British and French forces invaded Egypt in 1956; American forces went into Lebanon in 1958; subsequently American forces returned to Lebanon, attacked Libya, and engaged in various military encounters with Iran; Arab and Islamic terrorists, supported by at least three Middle Eastern governments, employed the weapon of the weak and bombed Western planes and installations and seized Western hostages. This warfare between Arabs and the West culminated in 1990, when the United States sent a massive army to the Persian Gulf to defend some Arab countries against aggression by another. In its aftermath NATO planning is increasingly directed to potential threats and instability along its "southern tier."

This centuries-old military interaction between the West and Islam is unlikely to decline. It could become more virulent. The Gulf War left some Arabs feeling proud that Saddam Hussein had attacked Israel and stood up to the West. It also left many feeling humiliated and resentful of the West's military presence in the Persian Gulf, the West's overwhelming military dominance, and their apparent inability to shape their own destiny. Many Arab countries, in addition to the oil exporters, are reaching levels of economic and social development where autocratic forms of government become inappropriate and efforts to introduce democracy become stronger. Some openings in Arab political systems have already occurred. The principal beneficiaries of these openings have been Islamist movements. In the Arab world, in short, Western democracy strengthens anti-Western political forces. This may be a passing phenomenon, but it surely complicates relations between Islamic countries and the West.

Those relations are also complicated by demography. The spectacular population growth in Arab countries, particularly in North Africa, has led to increased migration to Western Europe. The movement within Western Europe toward minimizing internal boundaries has sharpened political sensitivities with respect to this development. In Italy, France and Germany, racism is increasingly open, and political reactions and violence against Arab and Turkish migrants have become more intense and more widespread since 1990. On both sides the interaction between Islam and the West is seen as a clash of civilizations. The West's "next confrontation," observes M. J. Akbar, an Indian Muslim author, "is definitely going to come from the Muslim world. It is in the sweep of the Islamic nations from the Maghreb to Pakistan that the struggle for a new world order will begin." Bernard Lewis comes to a similar conclusion:

> We are facing a mood and a movement far transcending the level of issues and policies and the governments that pursue them. This is no less than a

clash of civilizations—the perhaps irrational but surely historic reaction of an ancient rival against our Judeo-Christian heritage, our secular present, and the worldwide expansion of both.[1]

Note

1. Bernard Lewis, "The Roots of Muslim Rage," *Atlantic Monthly*, 266 (Sept. 1990), 60; *Time*, June 15, 1992, pp. 24–28.

*In his essay in this volume, Ussama Makdisi finds that anti-American senti-
ment in the Arab world is a relatively recent development. Makdisi uses the
King-Crane Commission Report, excerpted below, to illustrate a more con-
genial moment in the history of U.S. relations with the Arab world. After
World War I, Henry Churchill King and Charles R. Crane headed the
American Section of a projected Inter-Allied Commission on Mandates in
Turkey. The question they addressed was what would become of various territories formerly part of the Ottoman Empire. In the section of their report addressing the Middle East, they cited the concerns of Arabs, recognized the
rights of Palestinians to the land on which they lived, and warned of the conflicts that would result from creating a Jewish state. The report also provided
evidence that Arabs preferred American "assistance" to British or French
mandate. In the wake of World War I and before the founding (in 1948) of
the state of Israel, what historical developments would explain why Arabs
might have trusted American leadership more than British or French?*

The King-Crane Commission Report
(August 28, 1919)

The American Commissioners of the projected International Commission
on Mandates in Turkey, herewith submit their final report upon the Syrian
portion of their task.

The Commission's conception of its mission was defined in the following statement, which was given to the press wherever the Commission went:

> The American Section of the International Commission on Mandates in
> Turkey, in order that their mission may be clearly understood are furnishing
> to the press the following statement, which is intended to define as accurately
> as possible the nature of their task, as given to them by President Wilson.
>
> The American people—having no political ambitions in Europe or the
> Near East; preferring, if that were possible, to keep clear of all European,
> Asian, or African entanglements but nevertheless sincerely desiring that the
> most permanent peace and the largest results for humanity shall come out of
> this war—recognize that they cannot altogether avoid responsibility for just
> settlements among the nations following the war, and under the League of
> Nations. In that spirit they approach the problems of the Near East.
>
> An International Commission was projected by the Council of Four of the
> Peace Conference to study conditions in the Turkish Empire with reference
> to possible mandates. The American Section of that Commission is in the

Excerpted from <http://www.cc.ukans.edu/~kansite/ww_one/docs/kncr.htm>, originally published in *Editor & Publisher*, Dec. 2, 1922.

Near East simply and solely to get as accurate and definite information as possible concerning the conditions, the relations, and the desires of all the peoples and classes concerned in order that President Wilson and the American people may act with full knowledge of the facts in any policy they may be called upon hereafter to adopt concerning the problems of the Near East whether in the Peace Conference or in the later League of Nations.

This statement of the mission of the Commission is in complete harmony with the following paragraph from the Covenant of the League of Nations, particularly referring to portions of the former Turkish Empire:

"Certain communities formerly belonging to the Turkish Empire have reached a stage of development where their existence as independent nations can be provisionally recognized subject to the rendering of administrative advice and assistance by a Mandatory until such time as they are able to stand alone. The wishes of these communities must be a principal consideration in the selection of the Mandatory." . . .

In his address of July 4, 1918, President Wilson laid down the following principle as one of the four great "ends for which the associated peoples of the world were fighting"; "The settlement of every question, whether of territory, of sovereignty, of economic arrangement, or of political relationship upon the basis of the free acceptance of that settlement by the people immediately concerned and not upon the basis of the material interest or advantage of any other nation or people which may desire a different settlement for the sake of its own exterior influence or mastery." If that principle is to rule, and so the wishes of Palestine's population are to be decisive as to what is to be done with Palestine, then it is to be remembered that the non-Jewish population of Palestine—nearly nine tenths of the whole— are emphatically against the entire Zionist program. The tables show that there was no one thing upon which the population of Palestine were more agreed than upon this. To subject a people so minded to unlimited Jewish immigration, and to steady financial and social pressure to surrender the land, would be a gross violation of the principle just quoted, and of the people's rights, though it kept within the forms of law

It is to be noted also that the feeling against the Zionist program is not confined to Palestine, but shared very generally by the people throughout Syria as our conferences clearly showed. More than 72 per cent—1,350 in all—of all the petitions in the whole of Syria were directed against the Zionist program. Only two requests—those for a united Syria and for independence—had a larger support.

The Peace Conference should not shut its eyes to the fact that the antiZionist feeling in Palestine and Syria is intense and not lightly to be flouted. No British officer, consulted by the Commissioners, believed that the Zionist program could be carried out except by force of arms. The officers generally thought that a force of not less than 50,000 soldiers would be required even to initiate the program. That of itself is evidence of a strong sense of the injustice of the Zionist program, on the part of the non-Jewish populations of Palestine and Syria. Decisions, requiring armies to carry out, are sometimes necessary, but they are surely not gratuitously to be taken in the interests of a serious injustice. For the initial claim, often submitted by Zionist representatives, that they have a "right" to Palestine, based on an occupation of 2,000 years ago, can hardly be seriously considered.

There is a further consideration that cannot justly be ignored, if the world is to look forward to Palestine becoming a definitely Jewish state, however gradually that may take place. That consideration grows out of the fact that Palestine is "the Holy Land" for Jews, Christians, and Moslems alike. Millions of Christians and Moslems all over the world are quite as much concerned as the Jews with conditions in Palestine especially with those conditions which touch upon religious feeling and rights. The relations in these matters in Palestine are most delicate and difficult. With the best possible intentions, it may be doubted whether the Jews could possibly seem to either Christians or Moslems proper guardians of the holy places, or custodians of the Holy Land as a whole.

The reason is this: The places which are most sacred to Christians—those having to do with Jesus—and which are also sacred to Moslems, are not only not sacred to Jews, but abhorrent to them. It is simply impossible, under those circumstances, for Moslems and Christians to feel satisfied to have these places in Jewish hands, or under the custody of Jews. There are still other places about which Moslems must have the same feeling. In fact, from this point of view, the Moslems, just because the sacred places of all three religions are sacred to them have made very naturally much more satisfactory custodians of the holy places than the Jews could be. It must be believed that the precise meaning, in this respect, of the complete Jewish occupation of Palestine has not been fully sensed by those who urge the extreme Zionist program. For it would intensify, with a certainty like fate, the anti-Jewish feeling both in Palestine and in all other portions of the world which look to Palestine as "the Holy Land."

In view of all these considerations, and with a deep sense of sympathy for the Jewish cause, the Commissioners feel bound to recommend that only a greatly reduced Zionist program be attempted by the Peace Conference, and even that, only very gradually initiated. This would have to mean that Jewish immigration should be definitely limited, and that the project for making Palestine distinctly a Jewish commonwealth should be given up.

There would then be no reason why Palestine could not be included in a united Syrian State, just as other portions of the country, the holy places being cared for by an International and Inter-religious Commission, somewhat as at present under the oversight and approval of the Mandatary and of the League of Nations. The Jews, of course, would have representation upon this Commission. . . .

The recommendations now made lead naturally to the necessity of recommending what power shall undertake the single Mandate for all Syria. . . .

The Resolutions of the Peace Conference of January 30, 1919, quoted in our instructions, expressly state for regions to be "completely severed from the Turkish Empire," that "the wishes of these communities must be a principal consideration in the selection of the Mandatory Power." Our survey left no room for doubt of the choice of the majority of the Syrian people. Although it was not known whether America would take a mandate at all; and although the Commission could not only give no assurances upon that point, but had rather to discourage expectation; nevertheless, upon the face of the returns, America was the first choice of 1,152 of the petitions presented—more than 60 per cent—while no other Power had as much as 15 per cent for first choice.

And the conferences showed that the people knew the grounds upon which they registered their choice for America. They declared that their choice was due to knowledge of America's record, the unselfish aims with which she had come into the war, the faith in her felt by multitudes of Syrians who had been in America; the spirit revealed in American educational institutions in Syria, especially the College in Beirut, with its well known and constant encouragement of Syrian national sentiment, their belief that America had no territorial or colonial ambitions, and would willingly withdraw when the Syrian state was well established as her treatment both of Cuba and the Philippines seemed to them to illustrate; her genuinely democratic spirit, and her ample resources.

From the point of view of the desires of the "people concerned," the Mandate should clearly go to America.

In his essay "History in the Fundamentalist Imagination," R. Scott Appleby traces the genealogy of recent Islamic fundamentalism to a group of intellectual leaders of the early and mid-twentieth century. One such leader was Sayyid Qutb, an Egyptian who rejected communism, capitalism, and Arab nationalism and called instead for a revolutionary vanguard to establish an Islamic state. This excerpt from Qutb's influential treatise Milestones, *written in 1960, presents his call for Islamic world leadership. Why does Qutb reject "Western civilization"?*

Milestones (1960)

Sayyid Qutb

Mankind today is on the brink of a precipice, not because of the danger of complete annihilation which is hanging over its head, this being just a symptom and not the real disease, but because humanity is devoid of those vital values which are necessary not for its healthy development but also for its real progress. Even the Western world realises that Western civilization is unable to present any healthy values for the guidance of mankind. It knows that it does not possess anything which will satisfy its own conscience and justify its existence.

Democracy in the West has become infertile to such an extent that it is borrowing from the systems of the Eastern bloc especially in the economic system, under the name of socialism. It is the same with the Eastern bloc. Its social theories, foremost among which is Marxism, in the beginning attracted not only a large number of people from the East but also from the West, as it was a way of life based on a creed. But now Marxism is defeated on the plane of thought, and if it is stated that not a single nation in the world is truly Marxist, it will not be an exaggeration. On the whole this theory conflicts with man's nature and its needs. This ideology prospers only in a degenerate society or in a society which has become cowed as a result of some form of prolonged dictatorship. But now, even under these circumstances, its materialistic economic system is failing, although this was the only foundation on which its structure was based. Russia, which is the leader of the communist countries, is itself suffering from shortages of food. Although during the times of the Tsars Russia used to produce surplus food, it now has to import food from abroad and has to sell its reserves of gold for this purpose. The main reason for this is the failure of the system of collective

Excerpted from <http://www.islamworld.net/qutb/mint.txt>.

farming, or, one can say, the failure of a system which is against human nature.

It is essential for mankind to have new leadership!

The leadership of mankind by Western man is now on the decline, not because Western culture has become poor materially or because its economic and military power has become weak. The period of the Western system has come to an end primarily because it is deprived of those life-giving values which enabled it to be the leader of mankind.

It is necessary for the new leadership to preserve and develop the material fruits of the creative genius of Europe, and also to provide mankind with such high ideals and values as have so far remained undiscovered by mankind, and which will also acquaint humanity with a way of life which is harmonious with human nature, which is positive and constructive, and which is practicable.

Islam is the only system which possesses these values and this way of life.

The period of the resurgence of science has also come to an end. This period, which began with the Renaissance in the sixteenth century after Christ and reached its zenith in the eighteenth and nineteenth centuries, does not possess a reviving spirit.

All nationalistic and chauvinistic ideologies which have appeared in modern times, and all the movements and theories derived from them, have also lost their vitality. In short, all man-made individual or collective theories have proved to be failures.

At this crucial and bewildering juncture, the turn of Islam and the Muslim community has arrived—the turn of Islam, which does not prohibit material inventions. Indeed, it counts it as an obligation on man from the very beginning of time, when God granted him the vicegerent on earth, and regards it under certain conditions as worship of God and one of the purposes of man's creation. . . .

Islam cannot fulfill its role except by taking concrete form in a society, rather, in a nation; for man does not listen especially in this age, to an abstract-theory which is not seen materialized in a living society. From this point of view, we can say that the Muslim community has been, extinct for a few centuries, for this Muslim community does not denote the name of a land in which Islam resides, nor is it a people whose forefathers lived under the Islamic system at some earlier time. It is the name of a group of people whose manners, ideas and concepts, rules and regulations, values, and criteria, are all derived from the Islamic source. The Muslim community with these characteristics vanished at the moment the laws of God became suspended on earth.

If Islam is again to play the role of the leader of mankind, then it is necessary that the Muslim community be restored to its original form.

It is necessary to revive that Muslim community which is buried under the debris of the man-made traditions of several generations, and which is crushed under the weight of those false laws and customs which are not even remotely related to the Islamic teachings, and which, in spite of all this, calls itself the "world of Islam."

I am aware that between the attempt at "revival" and the attainment of "leadership" there is a great distance, as the Muslim community has long ago vanished from existence and from observation, and the leadership of mankind has long since passed to other ideologies and other nations, other concepts and other systems. This was the era during which Europe's genius created its marvelous works in science, culture, law and material production, due to which mankind has progressed to great heights of creativity and material comfort. It is not easy to find fault with the inventors of such marvellous things, especially since what we call the "world of Islam" is completely devoid of all this beauty.

But in spite of all this, it is necessary to revive Islam. The distance between the revival of Islam and the attainment of world leadership may be vast, and there may be great difficulties on the way; but the first step must be taken for the revival of Islam. . . .

To attain the leadership of mankind, we must have something to offer besides material progress, and this other quality can only be a faith and a way of life which on the one hand conserves the benefits of modern science and technology, and on the other fulfills the basic human needs on the same level of excellence as technology has fulfilled them in the sphere of material comfort. And then this faith and way of life must take concrete form in a human society—in other words in a Muslim society. . . .

As Melani McAlister writes in her essay in this volume, the U.S. war on terrorism is not entirely new. From the 1970s on, the American mass media presented and debated terrorism and responses to it, and since the 1980s, U.S. presidents have called for wars against it. In his 1980 state of the union address, President Jimmy Carter denounced "international terrorism" and "military aggression" in Iran and Afghanistan. Notice how the Cold War shaped his view of Afghanistan. (On U.S. involvement in Afghanistan during the Cold War era, see the essays by Nick Cullather and John Prados.) Compare President Carter's address with President George W. Bush's 2002 state of the union address. How do their concerns and approaches differ?

State of the Union Address (January 21, 1980)

President Jimmy Carter

This last few months has not been an easy time for us. As we meet tonight, it has never been more clear that the state of our Union depends on the state of the world. And tonight, as throughout our own generation, freedom and peace in the world depend on the state of our Union.

The 1980's have been born in turmoil, strife, and change. This is a time of challenge to our interests and our values and it's a time that tests our wisdom and our skills.

At this time in Iran, 50 Americans are still held captive, innocent victims of terrorism and anarchy. Also at this moment, massive Soviet troops are attempting to subjugate the fiercely independent and deeply religious people in Afghanistan. These two acts—one of international terrorism and one of military aggression—present a serious challenge to the United States of America and indeed to all the nations of the world. Together, we will meet these threats to peace.

I'm determined that the United States will remain the strongest of all nations, but our power will never be used to initiate a threat to the security of any nation or to the rights of any human being. We seek to be and to remain secure—a nation at peace in a stable world. But to be secure we must face the world as it is.

Three basic developments have helped to shape our challenges: the steady growth and increased projective of Soviet military power beyond its own borders; the overwhelming dependence of the Western democracies on

Excerpted from <http://www.jimmycarterlibrary.org/documents/speeches/su80jec.phtml>.

oil supplies from the Middle East; and the press and social and religious and economic and political change in the many nations of the developing world, exemplified by the revolution in Iran.

Each of these factors is important in its own right. Each interacts with the others. All must be faced together, squarely and courageously. We will face these challenges, and we will meet them with the best that is in us. And we will not fail. . . .

We superpowers also have the responsibility to exercise restraint in the use of our great military force. The integrity and the independence of weaker nations must not be threatened. They must know that in our presence they are secure.

But now the Soviet Union has taken a radical and aggressive new step. It's using its great military power against a relatively defenseless nation. The implications of the Soviet invasion of Afghanistan could pose the most serious threat to peace since the Second World War.

The vast majority of nations on Earth have condemned this latest Soviet attempt to extend its colonial domination of others and have demanded the immediate withdrawal of Soviet troops. The Moslem world is especially and justifiably outraged by this aggression against an Islamic people. No action of a world power has ever been so quickly and so overwhelmingly condemned. But verbal condemnation is not enough. The Soviet Union must pay a concrete price for their aggression. . . .

The Soviet Union is going to have to answer some basic questions: Will it help promote a more stable international environment in which its own legitimate, peaceful concerns can be pursued? Or will it continue to expand its military power far beyond its genuine security needs, and use that power for colonial conquest? The Soviet Union must realize that its decision to use military force in Afghanistan will be costly to every political and economic relationship it values.

The region which is now threatened by Soviet troops in Afghanistan is of great strategic importance: It contains more than two-thirds of the world's exportable oil. The Soviet effort to dominate Afghanistan has brought Soviet military forces to within 300 miles of the Indian Ocean and close to the Straits of Hormuz, a waterway through which most of the world's oil must flow. The Soviet Union is now attempting to consolidate a strategic position, therefore, that poses a grave threat to the free movement of Middle East oil.

This situation demands careful thought, steady nerves, and resolute action, not only for this year but for many years to come. It demands collective efforts to meet this new threat to security in the Perian Gulf and in Southwest Asia. It demands the participation of all those who rely on oil from the Middle East and who are concerned with global peace and stability. And it demands consultation and close cooperation with countries in the area which might be threatened.

Meeting this challenge will take national will, diplomatic and political wisdom, economic sacrifice, and, of course, military capability. We must call on the best that is in us to preserve the security of this crucial region.

Let our position be absolutely clear: An attempt by any outside force to gain control of the Persian Gulf region will be regarded as an assault on the vital interests of the United States of America, and such an assault will be repelled by any means necessary, including military force. . . .

The crises in Iran and Afghanistan have dramatized a very important lesson: Our excessive dependence on foreign oil is a clear and present danger to our Nation's security. The need has never been more urgent. At long last, we must have a clear, comprehensive energy policy for the United States.

Like the war on terrorism, the word "terrorism" itself has a history. In her essay on anti-Americanism and terrorism in Turkey, Nur Bilge Criss provides a simple and sensible definition: Terrorism is "the political use of violence to provoke fear." But which specific historical events qualify as terrorism and which specific historical actors qualify as terrorists? As Bruce R. Kuniholm notes, world leaders cannot agree on the answer. In this article from the Guardian, a British newspaper, Brian Whitaker looks at the U.S. State Department's definition of terrorism, which was published just a few months before September 11. Is it possible to construct an impartial definition or an impartial history of terrorism and terrorists?

The Definition of Terrorism (May 7, 2001)

Brian Whitaker

Decide for yourself whether to believe this, but according to a new report there were only 16 cases of international terrorism in the Middle East last year.

That is the lowest number for any region in the world apart from North America (where there were none at all). Europe had 30 cases—almost twice as many as the Middle East—and Latin America came top with 193.

The figures come from the US state department's annual review of global terrorism, which has just been published on the internet. Worldwide, the report says confidently, "there were 423 international terrorist attacks in 2000, an increase of 8% from the 392 attacks recorded during 1999."

No doubt a lot of painstaking effort went into counting them, but the statistics are fundamentally meaningless because, as the report points out, "no one definition of terrorism has gained universal acceptance."

That is an understatement. While most people agree that terrorism exists, few can agree on what it is. A recent book discussing attempts by the UN and other international bodies to define terrorism runs to three volumes and 1,866 pages without reaching any firm conclusion.

Using the definition preferred by the state department, terrorism is: "Premeditated, politically motivated violence perpetrated against noncombatant* targets by subnational groups or clandestine agents, usually intended to influence an audience." (The asterisk is important, as we shall see later.)

"International" terrorism—the subject of the American report—is defined as "terrorism involving citizens or the territory of more than one country."

The key point about terrorism, on which almost everyone agrees, is that it's politically motivated. This is what distinguishes it from, say, murder or football hooliganism. But this also causes a problem for those who compile statistics because the motive is not always clear—especially if no one has claimed responsibility.

So the American report states—correctly—that there were no confirmed terrorist incidents in Saudi Arabia last year. There were, nevertheless, three unexplained bombings and one shooting incident, all directed against foreigners.

Another essential ingredient (you might think) is that terrorism is calculated to terrorise the public or a particular section of it. The American definition does not mention spreading terror at all, because that would exclude attacks against property. It is, after all, impossible to frighten an inanimate object.

Among last year's attacks, 152 were directed against a pipeline in Colombia which is owned by multinational oil companies. Such attacks are of concern to the United States and so a definition is required which allows them to be counted. For those who accept that terrorism is about terrorising people, other questions arise. Does it include threats, as well as actual violence? A few years ago, for example, the Islamic Army in Yemen warned foreigners to leave the country if they valued their lives but did not actually carry out its threat.

More recently, a group of Israeli peace activists were arrested for driving around in a loudspeaker van, announcing a curfew of the kind that is imposed on Palestinians. Terrifying for any Israelis who believed it, but was it terrorism?

Another characteristic of terrorism, according to some people, is that targets must be random—the intention being to make everyone fear they might be the next victim. Some of the Hamas suicide bombings appear to follow this principle but when attacks are aimed at predictable targets (such as the military) they are less likely to terrorise the public at large.

Definitions usually try to distinguish between terrorism and warfare. In general this means that attacks on soldiers are warfare and those against civilians are terrorism, but the dividing lines quickly become blurred.

The state department regards attacks against "noncombatant* targets" as terrorism. But follow the asterisk to the small print and you find that "noncombatants" includes both civilians and military personnel who are unarmed or off duty at the time. Several examples are given, such as the 1986 disco bombing in Berlin, which killed two servicemen.

The most lethal bombing in the Middle East last year was the suicide attack on USS Cole in Aden harbour which killed 17 American sailors and injured 39 more.

As the ship was armed and its crew on duty at the time, why is this classified as terrorism? Look again at the small print, which adds: "We also consider as acts of terrorism attacks on military installations or on armed military personnel when a state of military hostilities does not exist at the site, such as bombings against US bases."

A similar question arises with Palestinian attacks on quasi-military targets such as Israeli settlements. Many settlers are armed (with weapons supplied by the army) and the settlements themselves—though they contain civilians—might be considered military targets because they are there to consolidate a military occupation.

If, under the state department rules, Palestinian mortar attacks on settlements count as terrorism, it would be reasonable to expect Israeli rocket attacks on Palestinian communities to be treated in the same way—but they are not. In the American definition, terrorism can never be inflicted by a state.

Israeli treatment of the Palestinians is classified as a human rights issue (for which the Israelis get a rap over the knuckles) in a separate state department report.

Denying that states can commit terrorism is generally useful, because it gets the US and its allies off the hook in a variety of situations. The disadvantage is that it might also get hostile states off the hook—which is why there has to be a list of states that are said to "sponsor" terrorism while not actually committing it themselves.

Interestingly, the American definition of terrorism is a reversal of the word's original meaning, given in the Oxford English Dictionary as "government by intimidation." Today it usually refers to intimidation of governments.

The first recorded use of "terrorism" and "terrorist" was in 1795, relating to the Reign of Terror instituted by the French government. Of course, the Jacobins, who led the government at the time, were also revolutionaries and gradually "terrorism" came to be applied to violent revolutionary activity in general. But the use of "terrorist" in an anti-government sense is not recorded until 1866 (referring to Ireland) and 1883 (referring to Russia).

In the absence of an agreed meaning, making laws against terrorism is especially difficult. The latest British anti-terrorism law gets round the problem by listing 21 international terrorist organisations by name. Membership of these is illegal in the UK.

There are six Islamic groups, four anti-Israel groups, eight separatist groups and three opposition groups. The list includes Hizbullah, which though armed, is a legal political party in Lebanon, with elected members of parliament.

Among the separatist groups, the Kurdistan Workers Party—active in Turkey—is banned, but not the KDP or PUK, which are Kurdish organisations active in Iraq. Among opposition groups, the Iranian People's Mujahedeen is banned, but not its Iraqi equivalent, the INC, which happens to be financed by the United States.

Issuing such a list does at least highlight the anomalies and inconsistencies behind anti-terrorism laws. It also points towards a simpler—and perhaps more honest—definition: terrorism is violence committed by those we disapprove of.

In the immediate aftermath of the attacks of September 11, commentators from around the world issued statements concerning it. In a speech before Congress, President George W. Bush called for a war on terrorism and also threatened action against any nations harboring or supporting terrorists. Not surprisingly, President Bush's address differed markedly from that of Al-Qaeda leader Osama bin Laden. What audiences do you think they were imagining for their speeches? How do their language, concerns, and visions of history differ? How might each speech be used as a document by future historians?

Address to a Joint Session of Congress and the American People (September 20, 2001)

President George W. Bush

On September the 11th, enemies of freedom committed an act of war against our country. Americans have known wars—but for the past 136 years, there have been wars on foreign soil, except for one Sunday in 1941. Americans have known the casualties of war—but not at the center of a great city on a peaceful morning. Americans have known surprise attacks—but never before on thousands of civilians. All of this was brought upon us in a single day—and night fell on a different world, a world where freedom itself is under attack. . . .

I also want to speak directly to Muslims throughout the world. We respect your faith. It's practiced freely by many millions of Americans, and by millions more in countries that America counts as friends. Its teachings are good and peaceful, and those who commit evil in the name of Allah blaspheme the name of Allah. (Applause.) The terrorists are traitors to their own faith, trying, in effect, to hijack Islam itself. The enemy of America is not our many Muslim friends; it is not our many Arab friends. Our enemy is a radical network of terrorists, and every government that supports them. (Applause.)

Our war on terror begins with al Qaeda, but it does not end there. It will not end until every terrorist group of global reach has been found, stopped and defeated. (Applause.)

Americans are asking, why do they hate us? They hate what we see right here in this chamber—a democratically elected government. Their leaders are self-appointed. They hate our freedoms—our freedom of religion, our

Excerpted from <http://www.whitehouse.gov/news/releases/2001/09/20010920-8.html>.

freedom of speech, our freedom to vote and assemble and disagree with each other. . . .

We are not deceived by their pretences to piety. We have seen their kind before. They are the heirs of all murderous ideologies of the 20th century. By sacrificing human life to serve their radical visions—by abandoning every value except the will to power—they follow in the path of fascism, and Nazism, and totalitarianism. And they will follow that path all the way, to where it ends: in history's unmarked grave of discarded lies. (Applause.) . . .

This war will not be like the war against Iraq a decade ago, with a decisive liberation of territory and a swift conclusion. It will not look like the air war above Kosovo two years ago, where no ground troops were used and not a single American was lost in combat. Our response involves far more than instant retaliation and isolated strikes. Americans should not expect one battle, but a lengthy campaign, unlike any other we have ever seen. It may include dramatic strikes, visible on TV, and covert operations, secret even in success. We will starve terrorists of funding, turn them one against another, drive them from place to place, until there is no refuge or no rest. And we will pursue nations that provide aide or safe haven to terrorism. Every nation, in every region, now has a decision to make. Either you are with us, or you are with the terrorists. (Applause.) From this day forward, any nation that continues to harbor or support terrorism will be regarded by the United States as a hostile regime.

Our nation has been put on notice: We are not immune from attack. . . .

This is not, however, just America's fight. And what is at stake is not just America's freedom. This is the world's fight. This is civilization's fight. This is the fight of all who believe in progress and pluralism, tolerance and freedom.

We ask every nation to join us. We will ask, and we will need, the help of police forces, intelligence services, and banking systems around the world. The United States is grateful that many nations and many international organizations have already responded—with sympathy and with support. Nations from Latin America, to Asia, to Africa, to the Islamic world. Perhaps the NATO Charter reflects best the attitude of the world: An attack on one is an attack on all. . . .

Americans are asking: What is expected of us? I ask you to live your lives, and hug your children. I know many citizens have fears tonight, and I ask you to be calm and resolute, even in the face of a continuing threat. . . .

Great harm has been done to us. We have suffered great loss. And in our grief and anger we have found our mission and our moment. Freedom and fear are at war. That advance of human freedom—the great achievement of our time, and the great hope of every time—now depends on us. Our nation—this generation—will lift a dark threat of violence from our people and our future. We will rally the world to this cause by our efforts, by our courage. We will not tire, we will not falter, and we will not fail. (Applause.)

Less than a month after the attacks of September 11, Osama bin Laden, the founder and leader of Al-Qaeda terrorist network, gave a speech celebrating the destruction. How does he justify the terrorist acts? Bin Laden was directly influenced by the writings of Sayyid Qutb. In what ways does bin Laden's speech build on the themes in Qutb's 1960 treatise Milestones?

Speech on September 11 Attacks
(October 7, 2001)

Osama bin Laden

I bear witness that there is no God but Allah and that Mohammed is his messenger. There is America, hit by God in one of its softest spots. Its greatest buildings were destroyed, thank God for that.

There is America, full of fear from its north to its south, from its west to its east. Thank God for that. What America is tasting now is something insignificant compared to what we have tasted for scores of years. Our nation (the Islamic world) has been tasting this humiliation and this degradation for more than 80 years. Its sons are killed, its blood is shed, its sanctuaries are attacked, and no one hears and no one heeds.

When God blessed one of the groups of Islam, vanguards of Islam, they destroyed America. I pray to God to elevate their status and bless them. Millions of innocent children are being killed as I speak. They are being killed in Iraq without committing any sins and we don't hear condemnation or a fatwa from the rulers.

In these days, Israeli tanks infest Palestine—in Jenin, Ramallah, Rafah, Beit Jalla, and other places in the land of Islam, and we don't hear anyone raising his voice or moving a limb. When the sword comes down (on America), after 80 years, hypocrisy rears its ugly head. They deplore and they lament for those killers, who have abused the blood, honour, and sanctuaries of Muslims. The least that can be said about those people is that they are debauched. They have followed injustice. They supported the butcher over the victim, the oppressor over the innocent child. May God show them his wrath and give them what they deserve.

I say that the situation is clear and obvious. After this event, after the senior officials have spoken in America, starting with the head of infidels worldwide, Bush, and those with him, they have come out in force with their men and have turned even the countries that belong to Islam to this treachery, and they want to wag their tail at God, to fight Islam, to suppress people in the name of terrorism.

When people at the ends of the earth, Japan, were killed by their hundreds of thousands, young and old, it was not considered a war crime, it is something that has justification. Millions of children in Iraq, is something that has justification. But when they lose dozens of people in Nairobi and Dar es Salaam [capitals of Kenya and Tanzania, where US embassies were bombed in 1998], Iraq was struck and Afghanistan was struck. Hypocrisy stood in force behind the head of infidels worldwide, behind the cowards of this age, America and those who are with it.

These events have divided the whole world into two sides. The side of believers and the side of infidels, may God keep you away from them. Every Muslim has to rush to make his religion victorious. The winds of faith have come. The winds of change have come to eradicate oppression from the island of Muhammad, peace be upon him.

To America, I say only a few words to it and its people. I swear by God, who has elevated the skies without pillars, neither America nor the people who live in it will dream of security before we live it in Palestine, and not before all the infidel armies leave the land of Muhammad, peace be upon him. God is great, may pride be with Islam. May peace and God's mercy be upon you.

In the fall of 2001, the Pew Global Attitudes Project inaugurated "a series of worldwide public-opinion surveys" to "measure the impact of globalization, modernization, rapid technological and cultural change and recent terrorist events on the values and attitudes of 30,000 people in 25 countries worldwide." In its first report, the Pew project interviewed "influentials," or people it identified as public opinion leaders, about September 11, the United States, and the war on terrorism. Notice how the "influentials" outside the United States differ in their views from American public opinion leaders.

Opinion Leaders on America
(December 19, 2001)

Pew Global Attitudes Project

Opinion leaders around the world believe that the events of Sept. 11 opened a new chapter in world history, but their views about the United States and its struggle with terrorism reflect a more familiar love-hate relationship with America. Influentials in much of the world, except for Western Europe, see mixed public attitudes toward the war on terrorism. For example, while popular support is reported in most regions of the world, the U.S. is seen as overreacting to the terrorist attacks. Most important, a huge gulf of disagreement exists between American elites and opinion leaders in other parts of the world about the causes of terrorism and the sources of resentment and respect for the U.S.

Commenting on public sentiment in their countries, opinion leaders in most regions say U.S. policies are believed to be a principal cause of the Sept. 11 attack. And majorities in all parts of the world, including Western Europe, say that many or most of the people in their countries think it is good that Americans now know what it is like to be vulnerable.

Asked for their own view, most opinion leaders say they think the U.S. is conducting the war on terrorism without taking into account its allies' interests. There also is little backing among the 275 political, media, cultural, business and government leaders in 24 countries surveyed by the Pew Research Center and the International Herald Tribune for extending the war to Iraq or Somalia, even if it is shown that these countries have supported terrorism. While half of U.S. opinion leaders would favor expanding the conflict, large majorities in most parts of the world say the war should be confined to Afghanistan.

Reprinted courtesy of the Pew Research Center for the People and the Press, at www.people-press.org. Excerpted from <http://people-press.org/reports/display.php3?ReportID=145>.

But reflecting a broad ambivalence toward the United States, a majority of non-U.S. opinion leaders, including nearly half of influentials in Islamic countries, say many or most people in their countries think the U.S. is doing the right thing in fighting terrorism. Moreover, when speaking for themselves, even opinion leaders in Islamic nations say the war against terrorism is worth the risk of destabilizing Muslim states that support the anti-terror coalition.

Few opinion leaders, even in Muslim countries, see popular support for the al Qaeda position and most report at least a moderate degree of public backing for the U.S. More generally, two-thirds of opinion leaders outside the U.S. say ordinary people in their countries have a favorable view of the U.S. The notable exception is the Middle East/conflict area, where roughly half say ordinary people have a negative impression of the U.S.

It should be noted that these are observations that opinion leaders around the world make about people in their countries. A principal objective of the forthcoming Pew Global Attitudes Project will be to test these findings by conducting public opinion surveys in 25 countries over the course of the next year.

American elites see the world image of the U.S. through a different lens than do their counterparts overseas. While they recognize that U.S. power is resented, opinion leaders in the United States believe America's support of Israel is also a big problem. Not so, say opinion leaders in most other parts of the world, except for those in Islamic nations. Even among leaders in the Middle East conflict area (Egypt, Turkey, Pakistan and Uzbekistan), U.S. support for Israel is not a bigger factor than are criticisms of the American role in the world.

Along with resentment of U.S. power, the other leading reason that people around the world dislike the United States, according to foreign opinion leaders, is the perception that U.S. policies contribute to the growing gap between rich and poor nations. While acknowledged by some American opinion leaders as well, influentials in most other regions see this as a bigger problem. Similarly, while American opinion leaders think the U.S. is liked for its good works around the world, fewer than one-in-four leaders in all other regions agree. What U.S. influentials underestimate is the importance of the nation's role as a technological and scientific leader in bolstering America's image overseas. Two-thirds of foreign opinion leaders rate this as a major reason why people like the U.S.

The perception of the United States as the land of opportunity is what most opinion leaders—both in the United States and overseas—see as America's strong suit. American democratic ideals also are thought to be appealing by majorities of leaders in most parts of the world, with Muslim countries not far behind.

While U.S. support for Israel is not seen as a major factor in why ordinary people dislike the United States, except in Muslim states, a 73% majority of opinion leaders around the world believe the U.S. has been too supportive of Israel. Just 35% of American elites concur. And there is broad consensus among influentials that if the U.S. pressured Israel to create a Palestinian state, terrorism would be reduced—67% of American leaders subscribe to that view, as do 74% of those overseas.

There is little indication that criticisms of the United States by anti-globalization activists hold much sway with people around the world. The growing power of U.S. multinational corporations is not seen as a leading factor in why the U.S. is disliked, except in Western Europe. The spread of American culture through movies, TV and music is at most a minor reason for animosity toward the U.S., according to foreign influentials. Looking forward, few see the sale of American products and the popularity of American entertainment being hurt by the war on terrorism.

When asked directly whether globalization has been a cause of terrorism, pluralities of opinion leaders viewed it as a minor factor at best. Nor is globalization likely to become a casualty of the war. The consensus is that the pace of globalization has barely slowed—and even this is seen as a temporary phenomenon by most opinion leaders, in the United States and abroad. This despite the fact that strong majorities see migration, travel and tourism being hurt by the war.

These findings are based on 275 interviews with influential people in politics, media, business, culture and government conducted by the Pew Research Center, Princeton Survey Research Associates and the International Herald Tribune, Nov. 12 to Dec. 13. Almost all interviewing was conducted after the fall of Kabul as the Taliban was in full retreat. Of the 275 interviews, 40 were conducted in the U.S. and approximately 10 were conducted in each of the countries listed. [The countries included in the survey were Argentina, Bangladesh, Brazil, Egypt, France, Germany, India, Indonesia, Japan, Korea, Mexico, Pakistan, Philippines, Poland, Russia, Spain, Turkey, Ukraine, United Kingdom, Uzbekistan, and Venezuela.]

On November 17, 2001, First Lady Laura Bush gave a radio address on the oppression of women under the Taliban regime in Afghanistan. For years, feminists worldwide had protested the situation of women in Afghanistan. But it was only after the attacks of September 11 that the Bush administration began to show significant concern. In her essay in this volume, Emily S. Rosenberg places Laura Bush's radio address at the crossroads of two competing traditions: transnational networks that challenge the subordination of women, and a patriarchal nationalism that promises to rescue women and children "from the grasp of barbaric, premodern men." Why, she asks, do "the equality of and well-being of women become highly visible on foreign policy agendas in particular times and places and invisible in others"?

Radio Address on Women in Afghanistan
(November 17, 2001)

Laura Bush

Good morning. I'm Laura Bush, and I'm delivering this week's radio address to kick off a world-wide effort to focus on the brutality against women and children by the al-Qaida terrorist network and the regime it supports in Afghanistan, the Taliban. That regime is now in retreat across much of the country, and the people of Afghanistan—especially women—are rejoicing. Afghan women know, through hard experience, what the rest of the world is discovering: The brutal oppression of women is a central goal of the terrorists. Long before the current war began, the Taliban and its terrorist allies were making the lives of children and women in Afghanistan miserable. Seventy percent of the Afghan people are malnourished. One in every four children won't live past the age of five because health care is not available. Women have been denied access to doctors when they're sick. Life under the Taliban is so hard and repressive, even small displays of joy are outlawed—children aren't allowed to fly kites; their mothers face beatings for laughing out loud. Women cannot work outside the home, or even leave their homes by themselves.

The severe repression and brutality against women in Afghanistan is not a matter of legitimate religious practice. Muslims around the world have condemned the brutal degradation of women and children by the Taliban regime. The poverty, poor health, and illiteracy that the terrorists and the Taliban have imposed on women in Afghanistan do not conform with the treatment of women in most of the Islamic world, where women make important contributions in their societies. Only the terrorists and the Taliban forbid education to women. Only the terrorists and the Taliban threaten to pull out women's fingernails for wearing nail polish. The plight of women and children in Afghanistan is a matter of deliberate human cruelty, carried out by those who seek to intimidate and control.

Civilized people throughout the world are speaking out in horror—not only because our hearts break for the women and children in Afghanistan, but also because in Afghanistan, we see the world the terrorists would like to impose on the rest of us.

All of us have an obligation to speak out. We may come from different backgrounds and faiths—but parents the world over love our children. We respect our mothers, our sisters and daughters. Fighting brutality against women and children is not the expression of a specific culture; it is the acceptance of our common humanity—a commitment shared by people of good will on every continent. Because of our recent military gains in much of Afghanistan, women are no longer imprisoned in their homes. They can listen to music and teach their daughters without fear of punishment. Yet the terrorists who helped rule that country now plot and plan in many countries. And they must be stopped. The fight against terrorism is also a fight for the rights and dignity of women.

In America, next week brings Thanksgiving. After the events of the last few months, we'll be holding our families even closer. And we will be especially thankful for all the blessings of American life. I hope Americans will join our family in working to insure that dignity and opportunity will be secured for all the women and children of Afghanistan.

Have a wonderful holiday, and thank you for listening.

By early 2002, President Bush had expanded his vision of the war against terrorism. How does this state of the union address differ from the speech he gave on September 20, 2001? How does it differ from President Carter's 1980 state of the union address? Notice the new emphasis on an "axis of evil" outside of Afghanistan, and notice especially the concern with Iraq. In her essay in this collection, Marilyn Blatt Young warns against the kinds of unilateral action and preemptive military strikes that Bush seems to threaten in this address.

State of the Union Address (January 29, 2002)

President George W. Bush

What we have found in Afghanistan confirms that, far from ending there, our war against terror is only beginning. Most of the 19 men who hijacked planes on September the 11th were trained in Afghanistan's camps, and so were tens of thousands of others. Thousands of dangerous killers, schooled in the methods of murder, often supported by outlaw regimes, are now spread throughout the world like ticking time bombs, set to go off without warning. . . .

Our nation will continue to be steadfast and patient and persistent in the pursuit of two great objectives. First, we will shut down terrorist camps, disrupt terrorist plans, and bring terrorists to justice. And, second, we must prevent the terrorists and regimes who seek chemical, biological, or nuclear weapons from threatening the United States and the world. (Applause.) . . .

But some governments will be timid in the face of terror. And make no mistake about it: If they do not act, America will. (Applause.)

Our second goal is to prevent regimes that sponsor terror from threatening America or our friends and allies with weapons of mass destruction. Some of these regimes have been pretty quiet since September 11th. But we know their true nature. North Korea is a regime arming with missiles and weapons of mass destruction, while starving its citizens.

Iran aggressively pursues these weapons and exports terror, while an unelected few repress the Iranian people's hopes of freedom.

Iraq continues to flaunt its hostility toward America and to support terror. The Iraqi regime has plotted to develop anthrax, and nerve gas, and nuclear weapons for over a decade. This is a regime that has already used poison gas to murder thousands of its own citizens—leaving the bodies of

Excerpted from <http://www.whitehouse.gov/news/releases/2002/01/20020129-11.html>.

251

mothers huddled over their dead children. This is a regime that agreed to international inspections—then kicked out the inspectors. This is a regime that has something to hide from the civilized world.

States like these, and their terrorist allies, constitute an axis of evil, arming to threaten the peace of the world. By seeking weapons of mass destruction, these regimes pose a grave and growing danger. They could provide these arms to terrorists, giving them the means to match their hatred. They could attack our allies or attempt to blackmail the United States. In any of these cases, the price of indifference would be catastrophic. . . .

As President Bush threatened war against Iraq's dictator Saddam Hussein, human rights activists worried about the consequences for Iraqi civilians. After 1990, when the United Nations Security Council voted for economic sanctions against Iraq, the standards of living and health care in Iraq deteriorated dramatically, as the document below attests. Like the sanctions, the threat of war posed the ethical question: Should the people of Iraq be punished for the deeds of their autocratic ruler?

Campaign against Sanctions on Iraq

On 6 August 1990, the United Nations Security Council imposed economic sanctions on Iraq in response to its invasion of Kuwait. Under these sanctions, all imports into Iraq (except medical supplies) and all exports from Iraq were prohibited, unless the Security Council permitted exceptions. A spokesman from the US State Department later referred to these sanctions as "the toughest, most comprehensive sanctions in history." Similarly, a Select Committee of the UK House of Commons said that the Iraqi sanctions regime "is unprecedented in terms of longevity and its comprehensive nature" (§28).

Since 1990, there has been a severe and prolonged deterioration in the standards of living of the vast majority of the inhabitants of Iraq. These problems have been detailed most clearly in two reports of the highest integrity, written in 1999.

Firstly, the Security Council itself set up a "Humanitarian Panel" to investigate the effects of sanctions. This Panel produced a report on 30 March 1999. This is a summary of its findings:

> In marked contrast to the prevailing situation prior to the events of 1990–91, the infant mortality rates in Iraq today are among the highest in the world, low infant birth weight affects at least 23% of all births, chronic malnutrition affects every fourth child under five years of age, only 41% of the population have regular access to clean water, 83% of all schools need substantial repairs. . . .

The second report was produced by the United Nations Children's Fund (UNICEF) in August 1999. This was the summary produced by UNICEF of their findings:

> The first surveys since 1991 of child and maternal mortality in Iraq reveal that in the heavily-populated southern and central parts of the country, children under five are dying at more than twice the rate they were ten years

Excerpted from <http://www.cam.ac.uk/societies/casi/guide/problem.html>.

ago. UNICEF Executive Director Carol Bellamy said the findings reveal an ongoing humanitarian emergency. . . .

The surveys reveal that in the south and center of Iraq—home to 85 per cent of the country's population—under-5 mortality more than doubled from 56 deaths per 1000 live births (1984–1989) to 131 deaths per 1000 live births (1994–1999). Likewise infant mortality—defined as the death of children in their first year—increased from 47 per 1000 live births to 108 per 1000 live births within the same time frame. The surveys indicate a maternal mortality ratio in the south and center of 294 deaths per 100,000 live births over the ten-year period 1989 to 1999.

Ms. Bellamy noted that if the substantial reduction in child mortality throughout Iraq during the 1980s had continued through the 1990s, there would have been half a million fewer deaths of children under-five in the country as a whole during the eight year period 1991 to 1998.

UNICEF also reported that approximately one in every three Iraqi women who die while of child bearing age (15–49 years old) die due to complications surrounding maternity (pp. 15–16).

In summary, as Denis Halliday, the former United Nations Humanitarian Co-ordinator in Iraq said after resigning his post in protest at the sanctions regime, we "are in the process of destroying an entire society. It is as simple and terrifying as that. It is illegal and immoral."

Soon after September 11, Americans began to memorialize the attacks on the World Trade Center and the Pentagon. The mass media may have dominated, and even orchestrated, the national moments of remembrance, but hundreds of local memorials on street corners, on the Web, and in churches, synagogues, and mosques conveyed the outpouring of concern among ordinary Americans. In her essay in this collection, Mary Marshall Clark describes Columbia University's project to collect and preserve the narratives and memories of those affected by the attacks. The Center for History and New Media at George Mason University and the American Social History Project/Center for Media and Learning at the City University of New York Graduate Center also began to collect personal testimonies, which are available on line in their September 11 Digital Archive. Like the local memorials, personal stories remind us of the human toll of September 11. In the testimony excerpted below, Tom Masiello reconstructs the confusion and terror that reigned in Manhattan that day.

On September 11th (February 7, 2002)

Tom Masiello

The morning starts as all mornings when I travel on business: Up, shower, iron the day's clothes, pack the briefcase and go. For some reason, as I'm leaving the room I linger longer, looking around to see if I am forgetting anything. I look at my keys sitting on the coffee table. I say, "You don't need those," then, for some reason, I grab them and put them in my briefcase. I leave many other things that I use daily, such as my laptop AC adapter, and for some reason, take more note of the fact that I am leaving these things than usual. I'm running a little later than I'd like: it's about 8:10 and I usually try to be on site an hour before the 9:00 AM start of the session I'm conducting.

I come out of the front of the Marriott and begin to cross West Street for the 75-or-so-yard-walk to 2 World Financial Center, which is directly across the street from the World Trade Center complex. The day is one of those in late summer that is an exquisite harbinger of a crisp clean fall and a holdover of the warmth of summer. The air is crisp, dry and clean, holding a hint that by noon it will be comfortably warm. There is not a cloud in the sky and it is bright blue.

Excerpted from Story #48, The September 11 Digital Archive at <http://911digitalarchive.org/stories/details/903>.

255

I go through a pretty typical routine to set up the room in which I will conduct the meeting. The meeting room has lots of windows that look out on West Street, the Marriott and the Trade Center. My main contact at the meeting site, Christine, who works for my client, Deloitte & Touche, has already done a lot to set up the room. This is great because I'm feeling a bit behind schedule. I chat with Christine for a few minutes. . . .

As I finish setting up for the meeting I dial Nancy, my fiancée, on the cell phone. We always try to speak just before I start teaching a seminar because we know it will be hard to connect during the day. I look at my watch and note that it is about 8:45. As the phone is ringing, I hear what sounds like a low flying airplane outside. I remark to myself, out loud, "that's strange for a plane to fly low enough to hear inside a building down here." Nancy answers the phone and I hear what sounds like a loud backfire of a truck outside the window. I look out the window. I think the first thing Nancy hears me say, almost at a scream is "Oh my God! The World Trade Center just blew up!" I am looking at the flash of fire and smoke from the south part of the building and see the west side blow out. "Oh my God! Oh my God!" Nancy hears me say again and again. . . .

I'm looking around out of the window and describing the scene to Nancy.

A man is running in circles in front of the Marriott where I had walked a few minutes before. He is on fire and flames cover his entire body. Another man is chasing him, hitting at him with his bare hands trying to put out the flames. I think, "I should run out there with something and help." But as more debris falls from the burning building I'm not sure I can do much good by the time I get out there. Somehow, it seems safer and more sensible to stay in the building. The man on fire falls to the ground. Someone else comes out of the Marriott with a blanket, or something, and the two men put out the flames. The burned man lays motionless, smoldering, his facial skin, burned black, clearly visible from across the street.

Almost two blocks away, south of the burning tower, there is a parking lot and I can see cars on fire there. Burning debris has been shooting from the building literally over the south tower and down onto the street hitting cars and other buildings. It is strangely quite. I look at my watch and note that it is getting close to 9:00 and the appointed time for my meeting. I think, "I wonder how long I should delay the start of the meeting?" Nothing is happening on the street. There is no sign of fire or rescue vehicles yet. The man lying on the ground still smolders. No one is emerging from the West Street exits of the tower. Then, I see people running around from behind the Marriott. It is a stream of people who have clearly been evacuated from the towers. They run around the Marriott, cross West Street and start gathering on the corner near 2 World Financial. . . .

Fire fighters and police pour out of the vehicles and charge into the burning tower. I'm looking up at the burning hole and it seems like a lot of debris is still falling. As I look closer at the debris I notice some of it seems to be moving as it falls. I realize that some of the "debris" is people falling, or maybe jumping, out of the building. I'm aware that I'm saying over and over, "Oh my God, these poor people, these poor people in that building." I feel myself start to cry. I'm still describing what I'm seeing to Nancy. I'm aware that my voice is very high-pitched, almost a scream.

I'm looking all around the scene and up at the burning hole. I scream into the phone, "Holy shit, oh my God, it's another plane, a big one a 757 or something! Oh my God, Oh my God, it just hit the other tower! It just flew right into the other tower!" Now, and for the first time, a slight feeling of panic comes over me. I'm trying to make sense of what I'm seeing. "How can this happen, how can two planes fly into both towers, one right after another?" I'm aware that I keep repeating these questions to myself and to Nancy. I feel desperate for an answer. I watch the huge explosion of the second plane. The fireball it makes as it explodes goes up to the top of the tower. It takes out a huge section of the building about 2/3rds up on the south side and the west side of the building blows out. A tremendous amount of debris is raining out of the building setting fire to many things around.

Nancy tells me that they are saying on the news that a second plane has hit. They start to evacuate the building I'm in. The cell phone cuts out. I lose Nancy. I can't get a signal and I'm trying to redial her. I feel confused about where it's safer, in the building or out on the street. I start to leave the building, purposely leaving my briefcase behind remembering that you are supposed to leave things behind when you evacuate a building. I'm thinking, "I'll come back for it later." I'm almost to the exit stairway and I realize, "Nobody's coming back here." All my money, identification and my computer are in the briefcase. I run back to the room, all the time feeling that this is not a very smart thing to do. I grab the briefcase. By now most of the floor is evacuated. I go down to the second level of the building into the atrium. People are running everywhere. No one is sure where to go. Someone asks me where he should go. I say, "I don't think the front exit is a good idea, that opens to West Street where debris is falling." I ask someone if there are any other exits. Several people seem unsure about which exits to use. I decide that the side exit seems a better choice. I feel a slight sense of panic because no one seems to know the right thing to do and it seems that everyone is on his or her own. . . .

As I come out onto the street, hundreds, maybe thousands of people are standing on the corners looking up at the burning buildings. I note that many people are trying to make cell phone calls in frustration and no one is able to get out. As I look up at the towers, I start thinking that it is probably not safe to stay so close to the towers. Debris is still falling. I am suddenly overcome with nausea. I keep thinking about the people who were in these buildings where the planes hit. I start to cry and gag. As I walk I'm trying not to vomit. Then, I begin to realize what's happening. Those planes didn't just fly into the towers. They must have been hijacked. "This is a terrorist attack! This is a terrorist attack!" I'm repeating to myself.

I manage to calm my stomach and force myself to try to think clearly. I decide that there are two things I need to do: call Nancy to let her know I'm OK and get off the island. I keep trying my cell phone as I make my way slowly south. I can't get through and I see that everyone on the streets who have now come out of all the buildings around are also not able to make calls. I decide that I have to make it to the Brooklyn Bridge where I know I can walk across to Brooklyn and find some of my family and I have to find a pay phone. I think, "Who knows how long it will be before I can come back here and get my car." As I'm walking south, people are standing everywhere looking up at the towers. I'm looking at the hole in the south tower thinking that it's not safe to be standing around; I need to put distance between me and that building in case it falls.

Some people are sitting on park benches trying their phones repeatedly. Others are buying big soft pretzels and sodas from street vendors. People are looking up, some are talking, most are not. Some people are crying. I keep crying, thinking about those people in the buildings where the planes hit, feeling what must have been the horror of their last moments. I realize that, amidst all of these people witnessing the same thing, I am totally alone. I'm making my way south, winding in and out of groups of people on the streets. I'm moving slowly, but purposefully, looking for a pay phone. The few I see have lines of 20–100 people at them. I keep moving, thinking about getting over the bridge. As I'm walking I am turning back and looking at the two buildings burning.

I pass a man who is holding onto a fence, his legs weak, unable to hold him up. I look at his face. It is so contorted it seems to have been painted by Picasso. I say, " Are you OK?" He starts to cry. "My friends are up there, my friends are up there," he repeats. He is sobbing. I'm crying uncontrollably and I grab him and hold onto him very tightly. Two other people come over to us and we are all holding on to each other crying. I'm not sure how long we stand there.

I keep moving south, looking for a pay phone, looking back at the buildings as I walk. I realize that if I am going to walk across to Brooklyn it might be a while. I stop and buy two bottles of water at a stand in Battery Park. I notice the Statue of Liberty across the harbor and I get a strange, surreal feeling about the contradiction in what I have been witnessing and that serene symbol of freedom. I'm looking for a pay phone and having no luck. I stand on a line of about 50 people for a phone, then realize it will be hours before I get to it. I keep moving. I look back and as I do, I see the top of the south tower start sinking. The building is sinking into itself! It's collapsing. I can hear a sound like a freight train coming and I can see this mounting mushroom cloud growing and growing and exploding down the narrow streets towards me. People around me are screaming. They start running everywhere. We are in a narrow area with many benches and fences and people are running and screaming. They are running to the edge of the island where there is no place to go but in the water.

This is the first moment in which I feel total panic. I start yelling to people not to run, that people will get trampled. My mind clicks off and my body seems to take over. I have always thought that I would face my last moments on this planet bravely and with dignity. But that's not what's happening to my body. My heart is racing. I can't breathe. My legs are heavy as in a dream when you run from danger. The only message my mind is playing is: "This is it for you. This is where it all ends. No it can't be. This is it. I have seen my kids for the last time. My God, no, no."

As the smoke and ash cover the area, there's no way to tell exactly what's coming at us. Will we be hit by parts of the building? Will we suffocate in the smoke? Will we be trampled by panic-stricken others? I'm moving south fast in the smoke and ash. It is almost totally black. I'm covered with smoke and ash. I'm coughing, trying to hold part of my shirt up to my mouth to filter the air. It is very ineffective. Some people are going up stairs into the ferry building. There seems like no other place to go to flee the smoke. I go in too, thinking that this might not be a good idea. I get up inside the glass-enclosed waiting room. It is totally black outside and people keep pouring into the terminal. While the smoke is not yet filling the terminal it is getting smoky. I am coughing, as are other people. I'm feeling tremendous fear that this place will fill with smoke and the crowds in here will panic and the same body feeling starts to take over. I try to get hold of myself. I talk to someone next to me. She is scared too. They announce that a ferry is leaving for Staten Island. I think that I should take it to get off Manhattan, but I'm not sure what I would do once I get over there. I think I would be stranded. Then, I look at the ferry and the people pouring onto it. I immediately feel that the ferry will not be safe. It looks overloaded and I say to the woman standing next me "That looks like another chapter of this disaster waiting to happen." She agrees and says that even though she lives in Staten Island, her better judgment tells her not to get on it.

The smoke seems to clear and I notice that there are many pay phones in the terminal. I wait a few moments for a phone and call Nancy. When I get through to her, she is crying, hysterical. It's only then that I realize that it's been over an hour since she heard from me. She's telling me about the collapse of the building and crying that she didn't know what happened to me. She is frantic. I'm telling her what I see and what's happening around me. I tell her that I saw the building collapse and what my plan is. "As soon as the smoke clears enough, I'm going to get over the Brooklyn Bridge."

The smoke seems to clear enough and I tell her I'm going to leave. Just then she screams, "Oh my God, the other building just collapsed!" Within minutes the air is filled with smoke again and it's totally black outside. I start to cry. I say to Nancy, "My God, My God, all those rescue workers who went into those buildings! They are probably gone! They are probably crushed! They were all right at the base of those buildings!" I'm sobbing uncontrollably. I can't stop thinking of those people who I saw go into those buildings. . . . Anticipating that it will be hard for me to find another pay phone once I leave, I give Nancy all the phone numbers for my kids and family and ask her to try to call them. . . .

I walk up the ramp to the Brooklyn Bridge. There are others around me, heading the same way. Police, rescue vehicles and fire trucks are flying by me in all directions. There is no other traffic. As I make my way up the ramp, I pass many burned papers. I stop to look at them and realize that here, blocks from the explosions, are burned office papers that a few hours before had sat on someone's desk. I keep starting to cry. I stop often and hold my face in my hands.

I get to the point at which I should be able to walk over the bridge. By now, I am shoulder to shoulder with many other people headed in the same direction. The police have closed the bridge to all traffic, even pedestrian. People are still walking in a long stream, 5 to 7 abreast, all filing down a street. I am very confused. I don't know where everyone is going although I following the flow. Now, I'm not sure where to go or what to do. . . .

I make my way towards the Manhattan Bridge and find that it is open. A 7-people wide stream is flowing over the walkway. I notice that my feet are sore and hurting. My briefcase has become an uncomfortable burden and I keep shifting it to different positions. Then, I start to cry because I feel so lucky to be alive, to be able to feel uncomfortable. As I walk over the bridge, I am looking back at the smoke coming from the trade center area and feel overcome by not seeing the towers there. I see the Statue of Liberty again in the harbor and the same contradictory feeling comes over me.

A loud roar overhead causes everyone around me to stop walking and look around urgently, some ducking. It takes a moment but I see an F18 fighter circling the tip of Manhattan. I think I should feel safer but I suddenly grasp a new way of life where Manhattan needs to be patrolled by fighter jets. Even though it is about 80 degrees, I feel myself shiver uncontrollably. As the huge stream of people slowly walks over the bridge, I hear a woman behind me yelling "get out of my way, get out of my way." She pushes past me and other people around start yelling at her. "Hey, where do you think you're gonna get, bitch." But I know as soon as she passes me, by the look on her face, what's going on. She affirms my belief when she screams back at them, "I have to get off this bridge before something else happens." I know she is scared. I think, "All of us on this bridge are." I feel uncomfortable about the reaction of those who taunted her and even more so at my own lack of response to them. "We are all just scared," I say to myself.

I make my way over to Brooklyn and there is this huge throng of people pouring into the streets around the bridge. Still, there is no clarity about where to go and this is a part of Brooklyn I don't know well. I start thinking that I've got a lot of walking to do and I need to buy some running shoes or something. But, all the stores around are closed. I walk looking for familiar names of streets. As I keep walking, I see one sporting goods store that is open. I go in and buy some running shoes. There are several other people in the store, who have been walking, doing the same thing.

I resume my walk and finally, I see a sign for 5th Avenue. I know that about 5 miles along that street I will make it to one of my relative's houses. I keep trying my cell phone and find out that I can make some calls. I get in touch with Nancy and update her on my progress. She tells me who she has contacted and that my brother will come to pick me up where ever I am. I tell her that there is no way he can get to where I am because all the streets have been closed off. I'll have to make it up 5th further. I get to about 15th Street and I call Nancy. She tells me to call my sister who tells me my brother is working just a few blocks away. She calls him and in ten minutes he is there. He gets out of his car to greet me and I sink into his arms sobbing, crying. He cries too. . . .

About the Contributors

R. Scott Appleby is Professor of History at the University of Notre Dame.

Mary Marshall Clark is Director of the Oral History Research Office, Columbia University.

Nur Bilge Criss is Assistant Professor in the Department of International Relations of Bilkent University, Ankara, Turkey.

Nick Cullather is Associate Professor of History at Indiana University.

Michael H. Hunt is Everett H. Emerson Professor of History at the University of North Carolina at Chapel Hill.

Bruce R. Kuniholm is Professor of Public Policy and History in the Terry Sanford Institute of Public Policy at Duke University.

Bruce B. Lawrence is Nancy and Jeffrey Marcus Humanities Professor, Professor of Islamic Studies, and Chair, Department of Religion, at Duke University. He specializes in premodern Islamic civilization and modern Islamic ideologies.

Ussama Makdisi is Associate Professor in the Department of History at Rice University. He is currently working on a history of early American involvement with the Arab world.

Melani McAlister is Associate Professor of American Studies at George Washington University.

Joanne Meyerowitz is Professor of History at Indiana University and editor of the *Journal of American History*.

John Prados is an experienced observer of intelligence activities. He holds a Ph.D. in political science from Columbia University and is a senior analyst with the National Security Archive in Washington, D.C.

263

Emily S. Rosenberg is DeWitt Wallace Professor of History at Macalester College.

Marilyn Blatt Young is Professor of History at New York University and Director of the International Center for Advanced Studies Project on the Cold War as Global Conflict.

Index

ABC (television), 97, 98
'Abdu, Muhammad, 145
Achille Lauro, 106
Adams, John, 133
"Address to a Joint Session of Congress and the American People" (Bush, excerpted), 241–43
Afghani, Jamal al-Din al-, 145
Afghanistan, 2, 18, 22–55, 121, 199, 204, 213; history of, 25–31, 193; post-September 11th U.S. relations with, 15, 17, 47, 73, 75, 77–78, 81–93, 96, 112, 197; pre-September 11th U.S. involvement in, 4, 17, 23, 25, 29–48, 73–80, 195; and Russian/Soviet relations, 23, 192, 195; and terrorism, 175, 182. *See also* Soviet Union, invasion of Afghanistan; Taliban
Afghan Women and Children Relief Act, 82, 83
Africa, 84, 139, 150, 179, 180, 184, 186; North, 16, 168
Aidid, Mohammed Farah, 110
AIDS, 86, 185
Albright, Madeleine, 152, 213
Algeria, 16, 133, 170, 171
Algerian Islamic Salvation Front (FIS), 148
Al-Jazeera (network), 22–23, 86, 150, 165
Allison, Robert J., 133
Al-Qaeda, 73, 170, 174n. 25, 175, 184, 192, 198. *See also* bin Laden, Osama
America. *See* U.S. foreign policy; U.S. government; U.S. military; U.S. nationalism
American Board of Commissioners for Foreign Missions, 134
American College (Persia), 132
American College (Turkey). *See* Robert College
American Council of Trustees and Alumni, 12
American Israel Public Affairs Committee, 151

American University (Cairo), 132
American University of Beirut, 132, 137. *See also* Syrian Protestant College
Amin, Qasim, 137
Anderson, Benedict, 96
Anglo-Iranian Oil Company, 143
Annan, Kofi, 199, 202
anti-Americanism, 4, 18, 213; in Arab world, 131–56; and Palestine, 148–53; in Turkey, 56–72. *See also* U.S. foreign policy, and anti-Americanism
Antiballistic Missile Treaty, 197
Antonius, George, 148–49
Appleby, R. Scott, 5
Arab-Israeli Wars: 1967 Six-Day War, 58–59, 146, 167
Arab world: Arab-American relations, 3, 106, 132; and English language, 137; and Europe, 139; immigration to U.S., 138; nationalism of, 143, 146; representation of, 12, 104–5, 107, 108, 141–42, 178; and Soviet Union, 194; and U.S. missionaries, 133–37. *See also* anti-Americanism; *individual countries;* Islam; Middle East
Arafat, Yasir, 151, 160
Armed Islamic Group (GIA), 170
Ashcroft, John, 112
Asia, 9, 150, 179, 180, 184, 186; Central, 17, 39, 69, 182, 192; East, 12, 18; South, 23, 177, 182; Southeast, 16, 61; Southwest, 191, 195, 197, 201, 203
Aspen, Les, 213
Atatürk, Mustafa Kemal, 57, 61, 65, 165
Atlantic, 41
"axis of evil," 18, 184, 201
Azerbaijan, 79

Baghdad Pact, 194
Balfour, Arthur James, 139
Balfour Declaration, 139, 141
Balkan Pact, 193

265